THE BOOK OF LIFE

WISDOM IS BETTER THAN RUBIES

From an oil painting by Edwin John Prittie, painted
expressly for The Book of Life

OUTSIDE the door of a house in an Oriental
village a father is reading from a manuscript
of the Old Testament to his two sons, in-
structing them possibly in the Law and the
Prophets, holding their rapt attention while
he reads to them one of the splendid stories
of heroism and devotion.

THE
BOOK OF LIFE

ARRANGED AND EDITED BY

NEWTON MARSHALL HALL, A.M., D.D.
PASTOR EMERITUS OF THE NORTH CHURCH, SPRINGFIELD, MASSACHUSETTS
AUTHOR OF CIVIC RIGHTEOUSNESS AND CIVIC PRIDE

AND

IRVING FRANCIS WOOD, Ph.D., D.D.
PROFESSOR OF RELIGION AND BIBLICAL LITERATURE
SMITH COLLEGE, NORTHAMPTON, MASSACHUSETTS
AUTHOR OF THE SPIRIT OF GOD IN BIBLICAL LITERATURE

JOINT AUTHORS OF THE BIBLE STORY,
EARLY DAYS OF ISRAEL, DAYS OF THE KINGS OF ISRAEL,
ADULT CLASSES AND HOW TO
TEACH THEM

VOLUME FIVE
BIBLE POETRY

JOHN RUDIN & COMPANY INC.
CHICAGO

INTERNATIONAL AND IMPERIAL COPYRIGHTS SECURED
ALL RIGHTS RESERVED IN ALL COUNTRIES

EIGHTH EDITION

PRINTED IN THE U. S. A.

VICTORY
EDITION

The Entrance of THY WORD Giveth Light

MCMXXXIX

Preface

THE Bible is full of poetry. Many Biblical poems will be found in other volumes of this series. Here, however, is assembled that great collection of marvellous poems and songs, the Psalms, the inspired music of the Old Testament, ranging from the lyric to the majestic organ music of the hymns of faith and contrition. Some of the personal experiences of men who have been in all the ages helped and comforted by these poems are given in the form of notes prefixed to the Psalms.

The Book of Job, one of the most sublime poems in all literature, is given in dramatic form.

The Book of Proverbs and selections from Ecclesiasticus and Ecclesiastes are grouped with the Psalms because they are in poetic form. Proverbs and Ecclesiasticus, a book of the Apocrypha, are not so much poetry as manuals for the conduct of society: wise precepts bearing upon human life as it is lived in the home and in the market-place, advice of the greatest value with respect to the relations of parents and children, principles of conduct for men in business and in public life. Full of profound practical wisdom, they deserve to be much better known by modern readers than they are.

Contents

VOLUME V

Poetry in the Bible

THE Bible being what it is,—a book of universal range, a mingling of divine thought with human experience, sweeping the vast scale of existence from the lowest depths of earth to the highest ramparts of heaven,— such a book must of necessity contain poetry. Prose is well enough for ordinary historical narrative. It will serve to tell the story of the struggle between Moses and Pharaoh; it will serve to describe the escape of Israel from bondage: but for the experience of that night of despair changing to awe-stricken hope, when the host marched in silence along the road which God had opened through the sea; for the emotions of the morning which followed, when they came, still half afraid, to gaze upon the faces of the Egyptians dead upon the seashore — for such experiences, prose is inadequate, and Moses must break out into that splendid, exultant strain of triumph:

> "I will sing unto the LORD; for he hath triumphed gloriously:
> The horse and his rider hath he thrown into the sea.
> The LORD is my strength and song,
> And he is become my salvation:
> He is my God, and I will prepare him an habitation;
> My father's God, and I will exalt him."

The exploits of David in camp and field may be told in prose, but no prose, however stately, can satisfy the soul of the young musician when he gazes into the star-sown spaces of the night, when his thought leaps up

to the consciousness that God is behind it all and through
it all, that the faintest atom of star-dust was made by
him, and, like Orion and the Pleiades, is obedient to
his will. At such moments must the poet sing:

"The heavens declare the glory of God
  And the firmament showeth his handiwork;
Day unto day uttereth speech
  And night unto night showeth knowledge."

The chief difference between Hebrew poetry and our
modern English rhymed verse is in the absence of
rhyme. The characteristic of Hebrew poetry is rhythm,
the musical flow of selected syllables, broken into lines
of appropriate length. Alliteration was frequently em-
ployed. Some of the Bible was intended to be sung
and was written for that purpose. "Music was a favorite element in Hebrew life. No festive occasion was
complete without it. It was part of every celebration,
of every gathering of the people, as well as of worship."

In our English translations, much of the characteristic
quality of the outward forms of Hebrew poetry is lost;
yet it is wonderful how much is really retained. Hebrew
poetry becomes in English blank verse, and the fact
that Hebrew form lends itself so perfectly to rhythm in
the English translation is one of the marvels of human
language. Some of the finest examples of blank verse in
English are found in the translation of the Scriptures.
It seems impossible not to believe that the translators
were actually inspired in their choice of words and
arrangement of phrases. In the following selection, how
majestic the cadence, how close to nature's own solemn
music!

"Or ever the silver cord be loosed
  Or the golden bowl be broken

Or the pitcher be broken at the fountain
Or the wheel broken at the cistern.
Then shall the dust return to the earth
  As it was:
And the spirit shall return unto God
  Who gave it."

"Parallelism," to use a technical word to express a very simple fact, is one of the most important elements in Hebrew poetry. Parallelism has been described as a logical rhythm in distinction from a verbal rhythm. There are three principal kinds of parallelism:

1. Synonymous parallelism — in which the second line reinforces and emphasizes the first.

"The heavens declare the glory of God
And the firmament showeth His handiwork."
                                    —Psalm 19:1.

2. Antithetic parallelism — in which the second member shows a contrast; like the obverse side of the same coin.

"Every prudent man dealeth with knowledge:
But a fool layeth open his folly."
                                    —Proverbs 13:16.

3. Synthetic parallelism — in which the second member continues the thought.

"Where no wood is there the fire goeth out;
So where there is no talebearer the strife ceaseth."
                                    —Proverbs 26:20.

Other forms of parallelism are noted by scholars, but these are the most simple and easily understood.

The acrostic is used not infrequently in Hebrew poetry. The most notable examples are Psalms 9, 119, 37, and the Book of Lamentations. An explanation of the Acrostic form will be found in the introduction of Lamentations.

While rhythm may be made a technical matter and its rules to some extent discovered, its real essence is in the beauty and sublimity of the thought. The thoughts of many English writers flow in such rhythmic numbers. Ruskin, Carlyle, Bunyan, express themselves in a sort of rhythmic blank verse. Much of Blackmore's "Lorna Doone" is blank verse. So, much of the Bible which is not printed in the form of poetry is really such in its beauty and its grandeur. In the New Testament, much of the teaching of Jesus is in poetic form. The parable of the Prodigal Son is an example.

> "A certain man had two sons.
>   And the younger of them said to his father,
>   'Father, give me the portion of goods that falleth
>   to me'
>   And he divided with them his living."
>
> —Luke 15:11, 12.

Again and again Paul breaks away from the petty contentions of the churches and soars to the heights of glorious poetry.

> "So also is the resurrection of the dead.
>   It is sown in corruption;
>   It is raised in incorruption:
>   It is sown in dishonour;
>   It is raised in glory:
>   It is sown in weakness;
>   It is raised in power."
>
> —I Cor. 15:42, 43.

The apostle's wonderful tribute to love in the thirteenth chapter of First Epistle to the Corinthians is all a poem.

The entire book of the Apocalypse of John is one glorious poem, like a great jewel, full of the most sublime imagery glowing with an unearthly beauty — sometimes red and menacing, again sweet and full of everlasting comfort.

> "And there shall be no night there;
> And they need no candle, neither light of the sun;
> For the Lord God giveth them light:
> And they shall reign forever and ever."
>
> —Revelation 22:5.

It is a fascinating and profitable exercise to write down in the form of blank verse those sublime passages in the Old and the New Testaments which by virtue of this lofty beauty of form and inspired thought are truly poetry, though not so distinguished in form. It is significant that the writers of the latest form of modern verse are depending more upon rhythm than upon rhyme for this effect.

The form of Hebrew poetry is, then, simple, majestic, and rich in its beauty. It depends for its effect upon no cheap ornamentation, upon no tricks, but upon principles of beauty and power, fundamental and profound. Its forms are based upon the principles of all high and pure art: they are the product of inspiration, from a perception of the mind of God himself, working out the idea of beauty as he works it out in nature, in wood and field, in mountain summit and wind-swept sky.

The chief characteristic of the thought of Hebrew poetry is the same as that of all great poetry, the truth visualized through the imagination. Poetry finds its material first in every-day life: its incidents, its experiences; over the life which to the ordinary mind may seem dull, unattractive, uneventful, the poet throws a charm, like the fire-light in a humble cottage room, which joins with leaping shadows to glorify the rudest objects. This power Wordsworth had, at his best, to a very high degree, making the answer of the child reveal a profound philosophy, and seeing in the most common flower a meaning "too deep for tears." The power of investing the actual facts of life with imaginative charm was a prominent quality in the mind of Christ. He was the true poet. He saw the beauty which lies beneath the clod and is dormant in the most sinful life, because he saw everything in its harmonious relationship to the mind and heart of God. Such poetry is not untrue. To use a paradox, it is really truer than truth itself. The ordinary mind is often deceived by appearances: that which lies upon the surface, which is perceived by the superficial sight, is often absolutely misleading. It is that which lies beneath the surface, that which is seen by the "inward eye," which is really true. The power of seeing the hidden truth, the deeper truth, was possessed by the poets of the Bible to a very high degree.

The Hebrew poet, no less than the poet of other races, to a greater extent, perhaps, than those of other races, adorns his poetry with figures of speech, symbols, similes, illustrations, likenesses, just as the builder adorns the severe and classic outlines of his temple with carvings and windows of rich glass. The poetry of the Bible is like the cathedral window through which the rainbow lights of heaven play upon the marbles of impressive and momentous truths. "Day unto day uttereth speech," sings the poet. Days do not actually speak, but it would be a sad and somber world if the poets did not show us that they really do. The Bible is, at times, a very somber and a very terrible book in its revelation of sin and the consequences of sin, but it is also a book of sunshine and of joy, of gladness and song, for these are the gifts of God to his people.

The Psalms

T HE collection of poetry which we call the Book of Psalms is, with the exception of the New Testament, the most precious book in the literature of the world. For sublimity of thought, lofty spiritual sentiment, breadth and range of vision, as well as for beauty of form and expression, these short poems stand at the very forefront of the literature of all time.

The Psalms were not, of course, all written by David, though the name of the "sweet singer of Israel" is appropriately given to the collection, which embodies the rich spiritual experience of the life of the people. "The Book of Psalms is a living book, the out-pouring of Israel's soul through the centuries, a growing well of the joys and sorrows, the praises and exaltations, the hopes and enthusiasms, of the Jewish people and its most gifted singers. As we read it, we seem to hear again those cries and sighs, those praises and prayers, that music and musing, issuing from the various parts of Israel's dispersion."

The appeal of the Psalms has been well nigh universal. All sorts of people, old and young, rich and poor, fortunate and unfortunate, find the Psalms helpful. About other parts of the Bible men differ and even quarrel violently. The Psalms are read in all churches of all creeds. They have been loved in all ages, by the saints of the early church, by the captains of the Puritan age, by the modern scholar. Quotations from the Psalms are found in inscriptions on public buildings, on sundials and coins, on the seals of governments, colleges, and public institutions of all kinds. They are interwoven in the very texture of our English speech. No part of the Bible has been so often translated and paraphrased. They have been read and sung as a part of church worship; they are used at the marriage service and at the burial of the dead. They have been used on occasions of great public rejoicing as well as at times of national sorrow. And yet the greatest use and value of the Psalms has been perhaps in the home, in the hearts of individuals. The splendid music of the Psalms, "Lift up your heads, O ye gates," rolls gloriously through the vaulted aisles of great cathedrals, but these poems are particularly suited to the spiritual needs of men and women at close range, for comfort, for consolation, for inspiration. This is because they came out of the hearts of men who had experienced all these emotions and, looking to God, found peace and rest.

Any age which neglects the Psalms does so at its own peril, the peril of finding its literature cheap and uninspired. Any individual who neglects the Psalms does so at his peril, the peril of spiritual degeneration and decay. For the witness to their power is universal and cannot be denied.

The Man Who Delights in God's Law

The 1st Psalm was a favorite of such diverse characters as Jerome and Byron. Byron learned it by heart when he was a boy.

BLESSED is the man that walketh not in the
counsel of the ungodly,
Nor standeth in the way of sinners,
Nor sitteth in the seat of the scornful.
But his delight is in the law of the LORD;
And in his law doth he meditate day and night.
And he shall be like a tree planted by the rivers of
water,
That bringeth forth his fruit in his season;
His leaf also shall not wither;
And whatsoever he doeth shall prosper.

The ungodly are not so:
But are like the chaff which the wind driveth away.
Therefore the ungodly shall not stand in the judgment,
Nor sinners in the congregation of the righteous.
For the LORD knoweth the way of the righteous:
But the way of the ungodly shall perish. — Psalm 1.

The Lord Is Above Kings

Luther said of the 2nd Psalm, "I love this Psalm with all my heart. It strikes and flashes valiantly among kings, princes, counsellors, judges."

WHY do the heathen rage,
        And the people imagine a vain thing?
        The kings of the earth set themselves,
And the rulers take counsel together,
Against the LORD, and against his anointed, saying,
"Let us break their bands asunder,
And cast away their cords from us."
He that sitteth in the heavens shall laugh:
The LORD shall have them in derision.
Then shall he speak unto them in his wrath,
And vex them in his sore displeasure.
Yet have I set my king
Upon my holy hill of Zion.

I will declare the decree:
The LORD hath said unto me,
"Thou art my Son;
This day have I begotten thee.
Ask of me, and I shall give thee the heathen for thine
        inheritance,
And the uttermost parts of the earth for thy pos-
        session.
Thou shalt break them with a rod of iron;
Thou shalt dash them in pieces like a potter's vessel."

Be wise now therefore, O ye kings:
Be instructed, ye judges of the earth.
Serve the LORD with fear,

And rejoice with trembling.

Kiss the Son, lest he be angry, and ye perish from the
way,

When his wrath is kindled but a little.

Blessed are all they that put their trust in him.

— Psalm 2.

WINNOWING

By Professor Elihu Grant

These women are winnowing the grain. They have cleared a place in the
field. The oxen have trodden out the grain, and now the women using wooden
shovels toss it up and the wind blows away the chaff. You can see the chaff in
the picture as the grain is tossed up. "The ungodly are not so, but are like
the chaff which the wind driveth away."—*Psalm 1:4.*

Thou Art My Shield

In the army of Marshal Prince de Condé, the Huguenot commander, known as "The Great Condé," the sentries were posted and relieved to the chanting of Psalms. The words from the 3rd Psalm, "LORD, how are they increased that trouble me," was the signal of danger.

LORD, how are they increased that trouble me!
Many are they that rise up against me.
Many there be which say of my soul,
"There is no help for him in God."
But thou, O LORD, art a shield for me;
My glory, and the lifter up of mine head.

I cried unto the LORD with my voice,
And he heard me out of his holy hill.
I laid me down and slept;
I awaked; for the LORD sustained me.
I will not be afraid of ten thousands of people,
That have set themselves against me round about.

Arise, O LORD; save me, O my God:
For thou hast smitten all mine enemies upon the cheek
bone;
Thou hast broken the teeth of the ungodly.
Salvation belongeth unto the LORD:
Thy blessing is upon thy people.   — Psalm 3.

An Evening Psalm

Bishop Nicolas Ridley was burned at the stake near Balliol College, Oxford University, in the year 1555. The night before his execution, his brother offered to remain with him until morning. He said, "No, I will go to bed and sleep as quietly as I ever did in my life, for it is Thou, Lord, only that makest me to dwell in safety."

The great Augustine was especially moved before his consecration, by the 4th Psalm. "When I called upon Thee, Thou didst hear me, O God of my righteousness: Thou hast set me at liberty when I was in trouble; have mercy upon me and hearken unto my prayer."

HEAR me when I call, O God of my righteousness:
Thou hast enlarged me when I was in distress;
Have mercy upon me, and hear my prayer.

O ye sons of men, how long will ye turn my glory into shame?
How long will ye love vanity, and seek after leasing?
But know that the LORD hath set apart him that is godly for himself:
The LORD will hear when I call unto him.

Stand in awe, and sin not:
Commune with your own heart upon your bed, and be still.
Offer the sacrifices of righteousness,
And put your trust in the LORD.

There be many that say, "Who will shew us any good?"
LORD, lift thou up the light of thy countenance upon us.
Thou hast put gladness in my heart,
More than in the time that their corn and their wine increased.
I will both lay me down in peace, and sleep:
For thou, LORD, only makest me dwell in safety.

— Psalm 4.

I Will Speak to the Lord in the Morning

Louis IX of France, called "Saint Louis," died on August 25, 1270, before the walls of Tunis, while he was on a crusade. He was laid by his own request on a bed of ashes, and his last words were the 7th verse of the 5th Psalm: "But as for me, I will come into Thy house, in the multitude of Thy mercy; and in Thy fear will I worship toward Thy holy temple."

GIVE ear to my words, O LORD, consider my meditation.
Hearken unto the voice of my cry, my King, and my God:
For unto thee will I pray.
My voice shalt thou hear in the morning, O LORD;
In the morning will I direct my prayer unto thee, and will look up.
For thou art not a God that hath pleasure in wickedness:
Neither shall evil dwell with thee.
The foolish shall not stand in thy sight:
Thou hatest all workers of iniquity.
Thou shalt destroy them that speak leasing:
The LORD will abhor the bloody and deceitful man.
But as for me, I will come into thy house in the multitude of thy mercy:
And in thy fear will I worship toward thy holy temple.

Lead me, O LORD, in thy righteousness because of mine enemies;
Make thy way straight before my face,
For there is no faithfulness in their mouth;
Their inward part is very wickedness;

Their throat is an open sepulcher;
They flatter with their tongue.
Destroy thou them, O God;
Let them fall by their own counsels;
Cast them out in the multitude of their transgressions;
For they have rebelled against thee.

But let all those that put their trust in thee rejoice:
Let them ever shout for joy, because thou defendest
    them:
Let them also that love thy name be joyful in thee.
For thou, LORD, wilt bless the righteous;
With favour wilt thou compass him as with a shield.

                                  — Psalm 5.

Rebuke Me Not in Thine Anger

Henry II was responsible for the death of Thomas a Becket in Canterbury Cathedral, December 29, 1170. The murder of the great champion of the church brought no satisfaction to Henry. The troubles of the kingdom increased, and in July four years later, the king entered Canterbury, naked except for a hair-shirt and a cloak, to do penance at Becket's tomb. He entered the cathedral and kissed the stone where Becket fell. Prostrate before the tomb, he repeated the 6th Psalm: "O Lord, rebuke me not in Thine anger." He was then scourged by the bishops, abbots, and the whole company of monks.

O LORD, rebuke me not in thine anger,
Neither chasten me in thy hot displeasure.
Have mercy upon me, O LORD; for I am weak:
O LORD, heal me; for my bones are vexed.
My soul is also sore vexed:
But thou, O LORD, how long?
Return, O LORD, deliver my soul:
Oh save me for thy mercies' sake.
For in death there is no remembrance of thee:
In the grave who shall give thee thanks?
I am weary with my groaning;
All the night make I my bed to swim;
I water my couch with my tears.
Mine eye is consumed because of grief;
It waxeth old because of all mine enemies.

Depart from me, all ye workers of iniquity;
For the LORD hath heard the voice of my weeping.
The LORD hath heard my supplication;
The LORD will receive my prayer.
Let all mine enemies be ashamed and sore vexed:
Let them return and be ashamed suddenly.   — Psalm 6.

Save Me from My Enemies

O LORD my God, in thee do I put my trust:
Save me from all them that persecute me, and
deliver me:
Lest he tear my soul like a lion,
Rending it in pieces, while there is none to deliver.

O LORD my God, if I have done this;
If there be iniquity in my hands;
If I have rewarded evil unto him that was at peace with
me;
(Yea, I have delivered him that without cause is mine
enemy:)
Let the enemy persecute my soul, and take it;
Yea, let him tread down my life upon the earth,
And lay mine honour in the dust.

Arise, O LORD, in thine anger,
Lift up thyself because of the rage of mine enemies:
And awake for me to the judgment that thou hast com-
manded.
So shall the congregation of the people compass thee
about:
For their sakes therefore return thou on high.

The LORD shall judge the people:
Judge me, O LORD, according to my righteousness,
And according to mine integrity that is in me.
Oh let the wickedness of the wicked come to an end;
but establish the just:
For the righteous God trieth the hearts and reins.
My defence is of God,
Which saveth the upright in heart.

God judgeth the righteous,
And God is angry with the wicked every day.
If he turn not, he will whet his sword;
He hath bent his bow, and made it ready.
He hath also prepared for him the instruments of death;
He ordaineth his arrows against the persecutors.
Behold, he travaileth with iniquity,
And hath conceived mischief, and brought forth false-
hood.
He made a pit, and digged it, and is fallen into the ditch
which he made.
His mischief shall return upon his own head,
And his violent dealing shall come down upon his
own pate.
I will praise the LORD according to his righteousness:
And will sing praise to the name of the LORD most high.

— Psalm 7.

What Is Man that Thou Art Mindful of Him?

Bernard Palissy, the famous Huguenot potter of France, was a very devout man. In his effort to find the glaze which afterward made the Palissy ware celebrated, he threw even his household furniture into his furnace, for he had been reduced to poverty by his experiments. Wandering in the fields, he found comfort in the Psalms, and especially in the 4th verse of the 8th Psalm: "What is man that Thou art mindful of him?"

O LORD our Lord,
    How excellent is thy name in all the earth!
    Who hast set thy glory above the heavens.
Out of the mouth of babes and sucklings hast thou
    ordained strength
Because of thine enemies,
That thou mightest still the enemy and the avenger.

When I consider thy heavens, the work of thy fingers,
The moon and the stars, which thou hast ordained;
What is man, that thou art mindful of him?
And the son of man, that thou visitest him?
For thou hast made him a little lower than the angels,
And hast crowned him with glory and honour.
Thou madest him to have dominion over the works of
    thy hands;
Thou hast put all things under his feet:
All sheep and oxen,
Yea, and the beasts of the field;
The fowl of the air, and the fish of the sea,
And whatsoever passeth through the paths of the seas.

O LORD our Lord,
How excellent is thy name in all the earth!   — Psalm 8.

He Forgetteth Not the Cry of the Humble

Archbishop Laud was executed on Tower Hill, on the 10th of January, 1645. He met death with great courage, and quoted on the scaffold verse 12 of the 9th Psalm: "When he maketh inquisition for blood, he remembereth them: he forgetteth not the cry of the humble."

I WILL praise thee, O Lord, with my whole heart;
 I will shew forth all thy marvellous works.
 I will be glad and rejoice in thee:
I will sing praise to thy name, O thou most High.

When mine enemies are turned back,
They shall fall and perish at thy presence.
For thou hast maintained my right and my cause;
Thou satest in the throne judging right.
Thou hast rebuked the heathen, thou hast destroyed
 the wicked,
Thou hast put out their name forever and ever.
O thou enemy, destructions are come to a perpetual end:
And thou hast destroyed cities;
Their memorial is perished with them.

But the Lord shall endure forever:
He hath prepared his throne for judgment.
And he shall judge the world in righteousness,
He shall minister judgment to the people in uprightness.
The Lord also will be a refuge for the oppressed,
A refuge in times of trouble.
And they that know thy name will put their trust in
 thee:
For thou, Lord, hast not forsaken them that seek thee.

Sing praises to the LORD, which dwelleth in Zion:
Declare among the people his doings.
When he maketh inquisition for blood, he remember-
eth them:
He forgetteth not the cry of the humble.

Have mercy upon me, O LORD; consider my trouble
which I suffer of them that hate me,
Thou that liftest me up from the gates of death:
That I may shew forth all thy praise
In the gates of the daughter of Zion:
I will rejoice in thy salvation.

The heathen are sunk down in the pit that they made:
In the net which they hid is their own foot taken.
The LORD is known by the judgment which he
executeth:
The wicked is snared in the work of his own hands.
The wicked shall be turned into hell,
And all the nations that forget God.
For the needy shall not alway be forgotten:
The expectation of the poor shall not perish forever.
Arise, O LORD; let not man prevail:
Let the heathen be judged in thy sight.
Put them in fear, O LORD:
That the nations may know themselves to be but men.

— Psalm 9.

The Lord Is King Forever and Ever

WHY standest thou afar off, O Lord?
Why hidest thou thyself in times of trouble?
The wicked in his pride doth persecute the poor:
Let them be taken in the devices that they have imag-
ined.
For the wicked boasteth of his heart's desire,
And blesseth the covetous, whom the Lord abhorreth.
The wicked, through the pride of his countenance, will
not seek after God:
God is not in all his thoughts.
His ways are always grievous;
Thy judgments are far above out of his sight:
As for all his enemies, he puffeth at them.
He hath said in his heart, "I shall not be moved:
For I shall never be in adversity."
His mouth is full of cursing and deceit and fraud:
Under his tongue is mischief and vanity.
He sitteth in the lurking places of the villages:
In the secret places doth he murder the innocent:
His eyes are privily set against the poor.
He lieth in wait secretly as a lion in his den:
He lieth in wait to catch the poor:
He doth catch the poor, when he draweth him into his
net.
He croucheth, and humbleth himself,
That the poor may fall by his strong ones.
He hath said in his heart, "God hath forgotten:
He hideth his face; he will never see it."

Arise, O Lord; O God, lift up thine hand:
Forget not the humble.

Wherefore doth the wicked contemn God?
He hath said in his heart, "Thou wilt not require it."
Thou hast seen it; for thou beholdest mischief and
    spite, to requite it with thy hand:
The poor committeth himself unto thee;
Thou art the helper of the fatherless.
Break thou the arm of the wicked and the evil man:
Seek out his wickedness till thou find none.
The LORD is King forever and ever:

The heathen are perished out of his land.
LORD, thou hast heard the desire of the humble:
Thou wilt prepare their heart, thou wilt cause thine ear
    to hear:
To judge the fatherless and the oppressed,
That the man of the earth may no more oppress.

                               —Psalm 10.

The Lord Loveth Righteousness

Mary, Queen of Scots, was executed at Fotheringay, February 8, 1587. A contemporary account says that the executioner dropped to his knees on the scaffold and begged her forgiveness. "I forgive all," she replied. Then with a handkerchief bound over her eyes she "kneeled down upon the cushion resolutely, and without any feare of deathe, sayde allowde in Latinn the Psalme, 'In Te, Domine.'" This is the 11th Psalm, beginning, "In the Lord put I my trust."

IN the LORD put I my trust:
How say ye to my soul,
"Flee as a bird to your mountain?"
For, lo, the wicked bend their bow,
They make ready their arrow upon the string,
That they may privily shoot at the upright in heart.
If the foundations be destroyed,
What can the righteous do?

The LORD is in his holy temple,
The LORD's throne is in heaven:
His eyes behold, his eyelids try, the children of men.
The LORD trieth the righteous:
But the wicked and him that loveth violence his soul
hateth.
Upon the wicked he shall rain snares,
Fire and brimstone, and an horrible tempest:
This shall be the portion of their cup.
For the righteous LORD loveth righteousness;
His countenance doth behold the upright. — Psalm 11.

Help in Time of Need

Those who are in danger upon the sea have often turned to the Psalms for comfort. An old account tells of the wreck of the ship *Tobie*, of London, in 1593. She was cast ashore on the Barbary coast, and broke up so fast that there was not time to make a raft. "Seeing nothing but present death approach, we committed ourselves unto the LORD, and beganne with doleful tune and heavy hearts to sing the 12th Psalme: 'Helpe, LORD, for good and godly men.' Howbeit before we had finished foure verses, the waves of the sea had stoped the breathes of most of our men, and only twelve, by God's providence, gote on shoare."

HELP, LORD; for the godly man ceaseth;
For the faithful fail from among the children of
men.
They speak vanity every one with his neighbour:
With flattering lips and with a double heart do they
speak.
The LORD shall cut off all flattering lips,
And the tongue that speaketh proud things:
Who have said, "With our tongue will we prevail;
Our lips are our own: who is lord over us?"
"For the oppression of the poor, for the sighing of the
needy,
Now will I arise," saith the LORD;
"I will set him in safety from him that puffeth at him."

The words of the LORD are pure words:
As silver tried in a furnace of earth,
Purified seven times.
Thou shalt keep them, O LORD,
Thou shalt preserve them from this generation forever.
The wicked walk on every side,
When the vilest men are exalted.   — Psalm 12.

The Lord Will Deal Bountifully

Gregory of Decapolis tells of a noble Saracen, converted by a vision of the Lamb of God, who sought a Christian teacher, learned the Psalms by heart and departed to convert his native land. He was stoned to death by those who refused to receive his message, and died repeating the 3rd verse of the 13th Psalm: "Lighten mine eyes, lest I sleep the sleep of death."

HOW long wilt thou forget me, O LORD? forever?
How long wilt thou hide thy face from me?
How long shall I take counsel in my soul,
Having sorrow in my heart daily?
How long shall mine enemy be exalted over me?
Consider and hear me, O LORD my God:
Lighten mine eyes, lest I sleep the sleep of death;
Lest mine enemy say, "I have prevailed against him":
And those that trouble me rejoice when I am moved.

But I have trusted in thy mercy;
My heart shall rejoice in thy salvation.
I will sing unto the LORD,
Because he hath dealt bountifully with me. — Psalm 13.

The Fool Said, "There Is no God"

Bacon in his essay, "On Atheism," comments on the 1st verse of the 14th Psalm: "The fool who saith in his heart 'There is no God,' saith it rather by rote to himself, as that he would have than that he can thoroughly believe it or be persuaded of it."

Henry Martyn (1781–1812), the great English missionary to India, wrote in his diary of a dangerous journey, "I beguiled the hours of the night by thinking of the 14th Psalm."

THE fool hath said in his heart, "There is no God."
They are corrupt, they have done abominable works.
There is none that doeth good.
The LORD looked down from heaven upon the children of men,
To see if there were any that did understand, and seek God.
They are all gone aside, they are all together become filthy:
There is none that doeth good, no, not one.

Have all the workers of iniquity no knowledge?
Who eat up my people as they eat bread,
And call not upon the LORD.
There were they in great fear:
For God is in the generation of the righteous.
Ye have shamed the counsel of the poor,
Because the LORD is his refuge.

O that the salvation of Israel were come out of Zion!
When the LORD bringeth back the captivity of his people,
Jacob shall rejoice, and Israel shall be glad.

— Psalm 14.

Who Shall Dwell in God's Tabernacle?

An entry in the journal of Henry Martyn reads, "10 September, 1812. All day in the village writing down notes on the 15th and 16th Psalms."

L ORD, who shall abide in thy tabernacle?
 Who shall dwell in thy holy hill?
  He that walketh uprightly, and worketh right-
   eousness,
And speaketh the truth in his heart.
He that backbiteth not with his tongue,
Nor doeth evil to his neighbour,
Nor taketh up a reproach against his neighbour.
In whose eyes a vile person is contemned;
But he honoureth them that fear the LORD.
He that sweareth to his own hurt, and changeth not.
He that putteth not out his money to usury,
Nor taketh reward against the innocent.
He that doeth these things shall never be moved.

         — Psalm 15.

A Goodly Heritage

PRESERVE me, O God: for in thee do I put my
trust.
O my soul, thou hast said unto the LORD,
"Thou art my Lord:"
"My goodness extendeth not to thee;
But to the saints that are in the earth,
And to the excellent, in whom is all my delight.
Their sorrows shall be multiplied that hasten after
another god:
Their drink offerings of blood will I not offer,
Nor take up their names into my lips."
The LORD is the portion of mine inheritance and of my
cup:
Thou maintainest my lot.

The lines are fallen unto me in pleasant places;
Yea, I have a goodly heritage.
I will bless the LORD, who hath given me counsel:
My reins also instruct me in the night seasons.
I have set the LORD always before me:
Because he is at my right hand, I shall not be moved.
Therefore my heart is glad, and my glory rejoiceth:
My flesh also shall rest in hope.
For thou wilt not leave my soul in hell;
Neither wilt thou suffer thine Holy One to see corrup-
tion.
Thou wilt shew me the path of life:
In thy presence is fulness of joy;
At thy right hand there are pleasures forevermore.

— Psalm 16.

Under the Shadow of Thy Wings

John Howard (1726–90) was the pioneer in English prison re-
form. In his visits to the prisons of England and the Continent, which
were filthy and terrible beyond description, full of prison fever, small-
pox and all sorts of loathsome diseases, he was in constant peril of his
life. He was sustained constantly by the thought of the 5th verse of
the 17th Psalm, "Hold up my goings in Thy paths."

HEAR the right, O LORD, attend unto my cry,
　　Give ear unto my prayer, that goeth not out
　　　　of feigned lips.
Let my sentence come forth from thy presence;
Let thine eyes behold the things that are equal.
Thou hast proved mine heart; thou hast visited me
　　in the night;
Thou hast tried me, and shalt find nothing;
I am purposed that my mouth shall not transgress.
Concerning the works of men, by the word of thy lips
I have kept me from the paths of the destroyer.
Hold up my goings in thy paths,
That my footsteps slip not.

I have called upon thee, for thou wilt hear me, O God:
Incline thine ear unto me, and hear my speech.
Shew thy marvellous lovingkindness,
O thou that savest by thy right hand them which put
　　their trust in thee
From those that rise up against them.
Keep me as the apple of the eye,
Hide me under the shadow of thy wings,
From the wicked that oppress me,
From my deadly enemies, who compass me about.

They are inclosed in their own fat:
With their mouth they speak proudly.
They have now compassed us in our steps:
They have set their eyes bowing down to the earth;
Like as a lion that is greedy of his prey,
And as it were a young lion lurking in secret places.

Arise, O Lord,
Disappoint him, cast him down:
Deliver my soul from the wicked, which is thy sword:
From men which are thy hand, O Lord,
From men of the world, which have their portion in this
    life,
And whose belly thou fillest with thy hid treasure:
They are full of children,
And leave the rest of their substance to their babes.
As for me, I will behold thy face in righteousness:
I shall be satisfied, when I awake, with thy likeness.

— Psalm 17.

A Song of Deliverance

Clovis, emperor of the Franks, won a great victory over Alaric
and the Visigoths at Vouglé in the year 507. He encamped near
Tours and sent his messengers to the church in which Saint Martin
was buried to inquire if any omen of victory might be given him. As
his soldiers entered the church, the choir was chanting the words of
the 18th Psalm: "Thou hast girded me with strength unto the battle:
Thou hast subdued under me those that rose up against me." Clovis
pressed on. Alaric fell by his hand and all southern Gaul was con-
quered by the Franks.

I WILL love thee, O LORD, my strength.
  The LORD is my rock, and my fortress, and my
      deliverer;
My God, my strength, in whom I will trust;
My buckler, and the horn of my salvation, and my high
    tower.
I will call upon the LORD, who is worthy to be praised:
So shall I be saved from mine enemies.

The sorrows of death compassed me,
And the floods of ungodly men made me afraid.
The sorrows of hell compassed me about:
The snares of death prevented me.
In my distress I called upon the LORD,
And cried unto my God:
He heard my voice out of his temple,
And my cry came before him, even into his ears.

Then the earth shook and trembled;
The foundations also of the hills moved
And were shaken, because he was wroth.
There went up a smoke out of his nostrils,
And fire out of his mouth devoured:

Coals were kindled by it.
He bowed the heavens also, and came down:
And darkness was under his feet.
And he rode upon a cherub, and did fly:
Yea, he did fly upon the wings of the wind.
He made darkness his secret place;
His pavilion round about him were dark waters and
    thick clouds of the skies.
At the brightness that was before him his thick clouds
    passed,
Hail stones and coals of fire.
The Lord also thundered in the heavens,
And the Highest gave his voice;
Hail stones and coals of fire.
Yea, he sent out his arrows, and scattered them;
And he shot out lightnings, and discomfited them.
Then the channels of waters were seen,
And the foundations of the world were discovered
At thy rebuke, O Lord,
At the blast of the breath of thy nostrils.
He sent from above, he took me,
He drew me out of many waters.
He delivered me from my strong enemy,
And from them which hated me: for they were too
    strong for me.
They prevented me in the day of my calamity:
But the Lord was my stay.
He brought me forth also into a large place;
He delivered me, because he delighted in me.
The Lord rewarded me according to my righteousness;
According to the cleanness of my hands hath he recom-
    pensed me.
For I have kept the ways of the Lord,
And have not wickedly departed from my God.

For all his judgments were before me,
And I did not put away his statutes from me.
I was also upright before him,
And I kept myself from mine iniquity.
Therefore hath the LORD recompensed me according
    to my righteousness,
According to the cleanness of my hands in his eyesight.
With the merciful thou wilt shew thyself merciful;
With an upright man thou wilt shew thyself upright;
With the pure thou wilt shew thyself pure;
And with the froward thou wilt shew thyself froward.
For thou wilt save the afflicted people;
But wilt bring down high looks.

For thou wilt light my candle:
The LORD my God will enlighten my darkness.
For by thee I have run through a troop;
And by my God have I leaped over a wall.
As for God, his way is perfect:
The word of the LORD is tried:
He is a buckler to all those that trust in him.

For who is God save the LORD?
Or who is a rock save our God?
It is God that girdeth me with strength,
And maketh my way perfect.
He maketh my feet like hinds' feet,
And setteth me upon my high places.
He teacheth my hands to war,
So that a bow of steel is broken by mine arms.
Thou hast also given me the shield of thy salvation:
And thy right hand hath holden me up,
And thy gentleness hath made me great.
Thou hast enlarged my steps under me,
That my feet did not slip.

I have pursued mine enemies, and overtaken them:
Neither did I turn again till they were consumed.
I have wounded them that they were not able to rise:
They are fallen under my feet.
For thou hast girded me with strength unto the battle:
Thou hast subdued under me those that rose up against
    me.
Thou hast also given me the necks of mine enemies;
That I might destroy them that hate me.
They cried, but there was none to save them:
Even unto the LORD, but he answered them not.
Then did I beat them small as the dust before the wind:
I did cast them out as the dirt in the streets.
Thou hast delivered me from the strivings of the people;
And thou hast made me the head of the heathen:
A people whom I have not known shall serve me.
As soon as they hear of me, they shall obey me:
The strangers shall submit themselves unto me.
The strangers shall fade away,
And be afraid out of their close places.

The LORD liveth; and blessed be my rock;
And let the God of my salvation be exalted.
It is God that avengeth me,
And subdueth the people under me.
He delivereth me from mine enemies:
Yea, thou liftest me up above those that rise up against me:
Thou hast delivered me from the violent man.
Therefore will I give thanks unto thee, O LORD, among
    the heathen,
And sing praises unto thy name.
Great deliverance giveth he to his king;
And sheweth mercy to his anointed,
To David, and to his seed forevermore.   — Psalm 18.

The Spacious Firmament on High

A student is said to have disparaged the beauty of the Psalms in the presence of his teacher, who told him to "go home and write one." Not only is it an impossible task to write one which shall equal the original in beauty and power, but it is difficult to make a paraphrase even, which shall be adequate. Joseph Addison, however, wrote paraphrases of the 23rd Psalm and of the 19th Psalm, which preserve in a remarkable way the very spirit of these two great Psalms. The version of the 19th Psalm, "The Spacious Firmament on High," appeared in the "Spectator" for August 23, 1712 (No. 465). It has also been set to splendid music by Haydn.

> The spacious firmament on high,
> With all the blue ethereal sky,
> And spangled heavens, a shining frame,
> Their great Original proclaim.
>
> The unwearied sun, from day to day,
> Does his Creator's power display,
> And publishes to every land
> The work of an Almighty Hand.
>
> Soon as the evening shades prevail,
> The moon takes up the wondrous tale,
> And nightly to the listening earth
> Repeats the story of her birth;
>
> While all the stars that round her burn,
> And all the planets in their turn,
> Confirm the tidings as they roll,
> And spread the truth from pole to pole.
>
> What though in solemn silence all
> Move round the dark terrestrial ball?
> What though no real voice nor sound
> Amid their radiant orbs be found?
>
> In reason's ear they all rejoice,
> And utter forth a glorious voice;
> Forever singing, as they shine,
> "The Hand that made us is divine."

T̲HE heavens declare the glory of God;
    And the firmament sheweth his handywork.
    Day unto day uttereth speech,
And night unto night sheweth knowledge.
There is no speech nor language,
Where their voice is not heard.
Their line is gone out through all the earth,
And their words to the end of the world.
In them hath he set a tabernacle for the sun,
Which is as a bridegroom coming out of his chamber,
And rejoiceth as a strong man to run a race.
His going forth is from the end of the heaven,
And his circuit unto the ends of it:
And there is nothing hid from the heat thereof.

The law of the LORD is perfect, converting the soul:
The testimony of the LORD is sure, making wise the
    simple.
The statutes of the LORD are right, rejoicing the heart:
The commandment of the LORD is pure, enlightening
    the eyes.
The fear of the LORD is clean, enduring forever:
The judgments of the LORD are true and righteous alto-
    gether.
More to be desired are they than gold, yea, than much
    fine gold:
Sweeter also than honey and the honeycomb.
Moreover by them is thy servant warned:
And in keeping of them there is great reward.

Who can understand his errors?
Cleanse thou me from secret faults.
Keep back thy servant also from presumptuous sins;
Let them not have dominion over me: then shall I be
    upright,

And I shall be innocent from the great transgression.
Let the words of my mouth, and the meditation of my
　　heart, be acceptable in thy sight,
O LORD, my strength, and my redeemer.　　— Psalm 19.

MOUNT CARMEL

　　This picture shows the long ridge of Mount Carmel rising above the waters
of the Mediterranean.

A Song for the Day of Trouble

Some of the paraphrases of the Psalms were very dear to the users of them. This is especially true of the Scottish version. Sir James Simpson (1811–70), the famous physician, discoverer of chloroform, was brought up at Bathgate by his mother. Mrs. Simpson used often to repeat the 20th Psalm in the Scottish paraphrase:

'Jehovah hear thee in the day when trouble he doth send
And let the name of Jacob's God thee from all ill defend:
O let Him help send from above, out of His sanctuary;
From Zion, His own holy hill, let Him give strength to thee.'

This was known and loved by the distinguished scientist throughout his life as his "Mother's Psalm."

THE LORD hear thee in the day of trouble;
The name of the God of Jacob defend thee;
Send thee help from the sanctuary,
And strengthen thee out of Zion;
Remember all thy offerings,
And accept thy burnt sacrifice;
Grant thee according to thine own heart,
And fulfil all thy counsel.
We will rejoice in thy salvation,
And in the name of our God we will set up our banners:
The LORD fulfil all thy petitions.

Now know I that the LORD saveth his anointed;
He will hear him from his holy heaven
With the saving strength of his right hand.
Some trust in chariots, and some in horses:
But we will remember the name of the LORD our God.
They are brought down and fallen:
But we are risen, and stand upright.
Save, LORD:
Let the king hear us when we call.
— Psalm 20.

Thou Hast Given Him His Heart's Desire

THE king shall joy in thy strength, O LORD;
  And in thy salvation how greatly shall he rejoice!
    Thou hast given him his heart's desire,
And hast not withholden the request of his lips.
For thou preventest him with the blessings of goodness:
Thou settest a crown of pure gold on his head.
He asked life of thee, and thou gavest it him,
Even length of days forever and ever.
His glory is great in thy salvation:
Honour and majesty hast thou laid upon him.
For thou hast made him most blessed forever:
Thou hast made him exceeding glad with thy countenance.
For the king trusteth in the LORD,
And through the mercy of the most High he shall not be moved.
Thine hand shall find out all thine enemies:
Thy right hand shall find out those that hate thee.
Thou shalt make them as a fiery oven in the time of thine anger:
The LORD shall swallow them up in his wrath,
And the fire shall devour them.
Their fruit shalt thou destroy from the earth,
And their seed from among the children of men.
For they intended evil against thee:
They imagined a mischievous device,
Which they are not able to perform.
Therefore shalt thou make them turn their back,
When thou shalt make ready thine arrows upon thy strings against the face of them.
Be thou exalted, LORD, in thine own strength:
  So will we sing and praise thy power.   — Psalm 21.

Why Hast Thou Forsaken Me?

The first verse of the Psalm contains the pathetic words spoken by Jesus on the cross, "My God, my God, why hast Thou forsaken me?"

MY God, my God, why hast thou forsaken me?
Why art thou so far from helping me, and from
the words of my roaring?
O my God, I cry in the daytime, but thou hearest not;
And in the night season, and am not silent.
But thou art holy,
O thou that inhabitest the praises of Israel.
Our fathers trusted in thee:
They trusted, and thou didst deliver them.
They cried unto thee, and were delivered:
They trusted in thee, and were not confounded.

But I am a worm, and no man;
A reproach of men, and despised of the people.
All they that see me laugh me to scorn:
They shoot out the lip, they shake the head, saying,
"He trusted on the LORD that he would deliver him:
Let him deliver him, seeing he delighted in him."

But thou art he that took me out of the womb:
Thou didst make me hope when I was upon my mother's
breasts.
I was cast upon thee from the womb:
Thou art my God from my mother's belly.
Be not far from me; for trouble is near;
For there is none to help.
Many bulls have compassed me:
Strong bulls of Bashan have beset me round.

They gaped upon me with their mouths,
As a ravening and a roaring lion.
I am poured out like water,
And all my bones are out of joint:
My heart is like wax;
It is melted in the midst of my bowels.
My strength is dried up like a potsherd;
And my tongue cleaveth to my jaws;
And thou hast brought me into the dust of death
For dogs have compassed me:
The assembly of the wicked have inclosed me:
They pierced my hands and my feet.
I may tell all my bones:
They look and stare upon me.
They part my garments among them,
And cast lots upon my vesture.
But be not thou far from me, O Lord:
O my strength, haste thee to help me.
Deliver my soul from the sword;
My darling from the power of the dog.
Save me from the lion's mouth:
For thou hast heard me from the horns of the unicorns.

I will declare thy name unto my brethren:
In the midst of the congregation will I praise thee.
Ye that fear the Lord, praise him;
All ye the seed of Jacob, glorify him;
And fear him, all ye the seed of Israel.
For he hath not despised nor abhorred the affliction
    of the afflicted;
Neither hath he hid his face from him;
But when he cried unto him, he heard.
My praise shall be of thee in the great congregation:
I will pay my vows before them that fear him.

THE PASTURE LANDS OF PALESTINE

Photograph by W. A. Pottenger
expressly for The Book of Life

"HE leadeth me in green pastures." —
Psalm 23.

In such pasture lands as these, Saul,
David, Amos, and the Patriarchs kept their
flocks and herds.

The meek shall eat and be satisfied:
They shall praise the LORD that seek him:
Your heart shall live forever.
All the ends of the world shall remember and turn unto
    the LORD:
And all the kindreds of the nations shall worship before
    thee.
For the kingdom is the LORD's:
And he is the governor among the nations.
All they that be fat upon earth shall eat and worship:
All they that go down to the dust shall bow before him:
And none can keep alive his own soul.
A seed shall serve him;
It shall be accounted to the Lord for a generation.
They shall come, and shall declare his righteousness
Unto a people that shall be born, that he hath done this.

— Psalm 22.

The Shepherd Psalm

Addison made a paraphrase of this Psalm only less beautiful than that of the 19th. It appeared in the "Spectator" for July 26, 1712 (No. 441). "David," he wrote, "has very beautifully expressed the steady reliance on God Almighty in his 23rd Psalm, which is a kind of pastoral hymn, and filled with those allusions which are usually found in that kind of writing."

The 23rd Psalm and the Lord's Prayer are, perhaps, the best, the most widely known, the most greatly loved pieces of literature in the world. They appeal to every heart; they are above the divisions of the church, the differences of creed, in the serene atmosphere of universal faith and worship.

The 23rd Psalm was chosen by Augustine to be the hymn of the martyrs.

THE LORD is my shepherd; I shall not want.
　　He maketh me to lie down in green pastures:
　　He leadeth me beside the still waters.
He restoreth my soul:
He leadeth me in the paths of righteousness for his
　　name's sake.
Yea, though I walk through the valley of the shadow
　　of death,
I will fear no evil: for thou art with me;
Thy rod and thy staff they comfort me.
Thou preparest a table before me in the presence of
　　mine enemies:
Thou anointest my head with oil; my cup runneth over.
Surely goodness and mercy shall follow me all the
　　days of my life:
And I will dwell in the house of the LORD forever.

—Psalm 23.

Lift Up Your Heads, O Ye Gates

THE earth is the LORD's, and the fulness thereof;
The world, and they that dwell therein.
For he hath founded it upon the seas,
And established it upon the floods.
Who shall ascend into the hill of the LORD?
Or who shall stand in his holy place?
He that hath clean hands, and a pure heart;
Who hath not lifted up his soul unto vanity,
Nor sworn deceitfully.
He shall receive the blessing from the LORD,
And righteousness from the God of his salvation.
This is the generation of them that seek him,
That seek thy face, O Jacob.

Lift up your heads, O ye gates;
And be ye lift up, ye everlasting doors;
And the King of glory shall come in.
Who is this King of glory?
The LORD strong and mighty,
The LORD mighty in battle.
Lift up your heads, O ye gates;
Even lift them up, ye everlasting doors;
And the King of glory shall come in.
Who is this King of glory?
The LORD of hosts,
He is the King of glory.

— Psalm 24.

The Secret of the Lord Is Among Them that Fear Him

One of the most saintly and beloved characters of church history was St. François de Sales (1567–1622), bishop of Geneva. He possessed a brilliant intellect and rare personal charm. His mind was so steeped in the Psalter that he used the language of the Psalms constantly. During his last illness, he was asked if he feared death. "Mine eyes are ever toward the Lord; for He shall pluck my feet out of the net," he replied.— Psalm 25:15.

The Psalms were a great comfort to those who passed through the terrible scenes of the Indian Mutiny. One fugitive from the mutineers, William Edwards, an English magistrate, wrote in his diary, "It is at such times I feel the real blessing the Psalms are. They never fail to give peace and refreshment when all is dark and gloomy within and without. This morning, for instance, I derived unspeakable comfort from the 14th and 17th verses of the 25th Psalm.

UNTO thee, O Lord, do I lift up my soul.
O my God, I trust in thee:
Let me not be ashamed,
Let not mine enemies triumph over me.
Yea, let none that wait on thee be ashamed:
Let them be ashamed which transgress without cause.
Shew me thy ways, O Lord;
Teach me thy paths.
Lead me in thy truth, and teach me:
For thou art the God of my salvation;
On thee do I wait all the day.
Remember, O Lord, thy tender mercies and thy loving-
    kindnesses;
For they have been ever of old.
Remember not the sins of my youth, nor my trans-
    gressions:

THE DAMASCUS GATE OF JERUSALEM

Photograph by W. A. Pottenger
expressly for The Book of Life

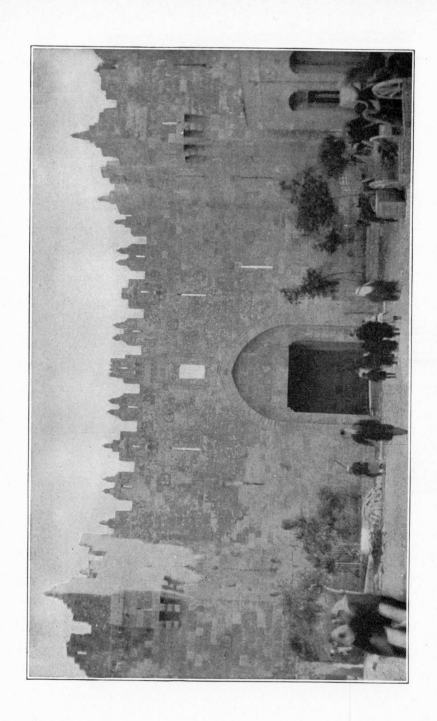

According to thy mercy remember thou me
For thy goodness' sake, O LORD.

Good and upright is the LORD:
Therefore will he teach sinners in the way.
The meek will he guide in judgment:
And the meek will he teach his way.
All the paths of the LORD are mercy and truth
Unto such as keep his covenant and his testimonies.
For thy name's sake, O LORD,
Pardon mine iniquity; for it is great.

What man is he that feareth the LORD?
Him shall he teach in the way that he shall choose.
His soul shall dwell at ease;
And his seed shall inherit the earth.
The secret of the LORD is with them that fear him;
And he will shew them his covenant.

Mine eyes are ever toward the LORD;
For he shall pluck my feet out of the net.
Turn thee unto me, and have mercy upon me;
For I am desolate and afflicted.
The troubles of my heart are enlarged:
O bring thou me out of my distresses.
Look upon mine affliction and my pain;
And forgive all my sins.
Consider mine enemies; for they are many;
And they hate me with cruel hatred.
O keep my soul, and deliver me:
Let me not be ashamed; for I put my trust in thee.
Let integrity and uprightness preserve me;
For I wait on thee.
Redeem Israel, O God,
Out of all his troubles.   — Psalm 25.

I Have Loved Thy House

JUDGE me, O Lord; for I have walked in mine
   integrity:
      I have trusted also in the Lord; therefore I shall
         not slide.
Examine me, O Lord, and prove me;
Try my reins and my heart.
For thy lovingkindness is before mine eyes:
And I have walked in thy truth.
I have not sat with vain persons,
Neither will I go in with dissemblers.
I have hated the congregation of evil doers;
And will not sit with the wicked.
I will wash mine hands in innocency:
So will I compass thine altar, O Lord:
That I may publish with the voice of thanksgiving,
And tell of all thy wondrous works.

Lord, I have loved the habitation of thy house,
And the place where thine honour dwelleth.
Gather not my soul with sinners,
Nor my life with bloody men:
In whose hands is mischief,
And their right hand is full of bribes.
But as for me, I will walk in mine integrity:
Redeem me, and be merciful unto me.
My foot standeth in an even place:
In the congregations will I bless the Lord.　　— Psalm 26.

The Lord Is My Light and My Salvation

The motto of Oxford University is "Dominus illuminatio mea," "Lord, my light," from the 1st verse of the 27th Psalm.

One of the heroes and martyrs of missions was Commander Allen Gardiner (1794–1851) of the Royal Navy of England, who, leaving the service, conducted a mission for some years in Africa, then went to Tierra del Fuego with six others, to establish mission work there. They landed on the barren Falkland Islands in December. When a relief ship arrived, the following September, not one of the party was living. The diary of the commander, which was found with his body, contains many references to the Psalms, the 27th Psalm, verse 14, among them.

THE LORD is my light and my salvation; whom shall I fear?
> The LORD is the strength of my life; of whom shall I be afraid?

When the wicked, even mine enemies and my foes,
Came upon me to eat up my flesh, they stumbled and fell.
Though an host should encamp against me,
My heart shall not fear:
Though war should rise against me,
In this will I be confident.

One thing have I desired of the LORD, that will I seek after;
That I may dwell in the house of the LORD all the days of my life,
To behold the beauty of the LORD, and to enquire in his temple.
For in the time of trouble he shall hide me in his pavilion:

In the secret of his tabernacle shall he hide me;
He shall set me up upon a rock.
And now shall mine head be lifted up above mine ene-
mies round about me:
Therefore will I offer in his tabernacle sacrifices of joy;
I will sing, yea, I will sing praises unto the LORD.

Hear, O LORD, when I cry with my voice:
Have mercy also upon me, and answer me.
When thou saidst, "Seek ye my face"; my heart said
unto thee,
"Thy face, LORD, will I seek."
Hide not thy face far from me;
Put not thy servant away in anger:
Thou hast been my help;
Leave me not, neither forsake me, O God of my salva-
tion.
When my father and my mother forsake me,
Then the LORD will take me up.

Teach me thy way, O LORD,
And lead me in a plain path,
Because of mine enemies.
Deliver me not over unto the will of mine enemies:
For false witnesses are risen up against me, and such as
breathe out cruelty.
I had fainted, unless I had believed to see the good-
ness of the LORD
In the land of the living.
Wait on the LORD:
Be of good courage, and he shall strengthen thine heart:
Wait, I say, on the LORD.   — Psalm 27.

Unto Thee Will I Cry

UNTO thee will I cry, O LORD my rock;
    Be not silent to me:
    Lest, if thou be silent to me,
I become like them that go down into the pit.
Hear the voice of my supplications, when I cry unto
    thee,
When I lift up my hands toward thy holy oracle.

Draw me not away with the wicked,
And with the workers of iniquity,
Which speak peace to their neighbours,
But mischief is in their hearts.
Give them according to their deeds, and according to
    the wickedness of their endeavours:
Give them after the work of their hands;
Render to them their desert.
Because they regard not the works of the LORD,
Nor the operation of his hands,
He shall destroy them, and not build them up.

Blessed be the LORD,
Because he hath heard the voice of my supplications.
The LORD is my strength and my shield;
My heart trusted in him, and I am helped:
Therefore my heart greatly rejoiceth;
And with my song will I praise him.
The LORD is their strength,
And he is the saving strength of his anointed.
Save thy people, and bless thine inheritance:
Feed them also, and lift them up forever.   —Psalm 28.

The God of the Thunders

George Herbert (1593–1632), poet and clergyman of the village of Bemerton, near Salisbury, England, used for the motto of his book, "Sacred Poems and Private Ejaculations," "In his temple doth every man speak of his glory," from the 29th Psalm, verse 9.

GIVE unto the LORD, O ye mighty,
    Give unto the LORD glory and strength,
    Give unto the LORD the glory due unto his name;
Worship the LORD in the beauty of holiness.

The voice of the LORD is upon the waters:
The God of glory thundereth:
The LORD is upon many waters.
The voice of the LORD is powerful;
The voice of the LORD is full of majesty.
The voice of the LORD breaketh the cedars;
Yea, the LORD breaketh the cedars of Lebanon.
He maketh them also to skip like a calf;
Lebanon and Sirion like a young unicorn.
The voice of the LORD divideth the flames of fire.
The voice of the LORD shaketh the wilderness;
The LORD shaketh the wilderness of Kadesh.
The voice of the LORD maketh the hinds to calve,
And discovereth the forests:
And in his temple doth every one speak of his glory.

The LORD sitteth upon the flood;
Yea, the LORD sitteth King forever.
The LORD will give strength unto his people;
The LORD will bless his people with peace.   — Psalm 29.

ON THE HIGH SLOPES OF THE LEBANONS

Photograph by Professor Lewis Bayles Paton

"THE VOICE of the LORD is powerful:
The voice of the LORD is full of majesty.
The voice of the LORD breaketh the
cedars;
Yea, the LORD breaketh the cedars of
Lebanon."—*Psalm 29:4-5.*

Joy Cometh With the Morning

I WILL extol thee, O LORD; for thou hast lifted me
     up,
     And hast not made my foes to rejoice over me.
O LORD my God,
I cried unto thee, and thou hast healed me.
O LORD, thou hast brought up my soul from the grave:
Thou hast kept me alive, that I should not go down to
     the pit.
Sing unto the LORD, O ye saints of his,
And give thanks at the remembrance of his holiness.
For his anger endureth but a moment;
In his favour is life:
Weeping may endure for a night, but joy cometh in
     the morning.
And in my prosperity I said, "I shall never be moved."
LORD, by thy favour thou hast made my mountain to
     stand strong:
Thou didst hide thy face, and I was troubled.
I cried to thee, O LORD;
And unto the LORD I made supplication.
What profit is there in my blood, when I go down to
     the pit?
Shall the dust praise thee? Shall it declare thy truth?
Hear, O LORD, and have mercy upon me:
LORD, be thou my helper.
Thou hast turned for me my mourning into dancing:
Thou hast put off my sackcloth, and girded me with
     gladness;
To the end that my glory may sing praise to thee, and
     not be silent.
O LORD my God, I will give thanks unto thee forever.

— Psalm 30.

Into Thy Hand

"Into thy hand I commit my spirit." These words from the 5th verse of the 31st Psalm have been more often upon the lips of the dying than any others. They are the last recorded words of Jesus. Stephen, the martyr of the early church; Basil the Great, Bishop of Cæsarea; Charlemagne; Thomas a Becket; John Hus; Luther; Melanchthon; Tasso; Columbus; Emperor Charles V; Thomas Cromwell; Bishop Hooper; Bishop Ridley; Lady Jane Grey; The Duke of Suffolk; Mary, Queen of Scots; George Herbert; John Knox; Cardinal Newman,— these are a few only of the names of those who have found the Psalm a consolation in the final moments of life.

IN thee, O LORD, do I put my trust; let me never be ashamed: deliver me in thy righteousness.
Bow down thine ear to me; deliver me speedily:
Be thou my strong rock, for an house of defence to save me.
For thou art my rock and my fortress;
Therefore for thy name's sake lead me, and guide me.
Pull me out of the net that they have laid privily for me:
For thou art my strength.
Into thine hand I commit my spirit:
Thou hast redeemed me, O LORD God of truth.
I have hated them that regard lying vanities:
But I trust in the LORD.
I will be glad and rejoice in thy mercy:
For thou hast considered my trouble;
Thou hast known my soul in adversities;
And hast not shut me up into the hand of the enemy:
Thou hast set my feet in a large room.

Have mercy upon me, O LORD,
For I am in trouble:

Mine eye is consumed with grief, yea, my soul and my
   belly.
For my life is spent with grief, and my years with sigh-
   ing:
My strength faileth
Because of mine iniquity, and my bones are consumed.
I was a reproach among all mine enemies,
But especially among my neighbours, and a fear to
   mine acquaintance:
They that did see me without fled from me.
I am forgotten as a dead man out of mind:
I am like a broken vessel.
For I have heard the slander of many:
Fear was on every side:
While they took counsel together against me,
They devised to take away my life.

But I trusted in thee, O LORD:
I said, "Thou art my God."
My times are in thy hand:
Deliver me from the hand of mine enemies, and from
   them that persecute me.
Make thy face to shine upon thy servant:
Save me for thy mercies' sake.
Let me not be ashamed, O LORD; for I have called
   upon thee:
Let the wicked be ashamed, and let them be silent in
   the grave.
Let the lying lips be put to silence;
Which speak grievous things proudly and contemptu-
   ously against the righteous.

O how great is thy goodness, which thou hast laid up
   for them that fear thee;

Which thou hast wrought for them that trust in thee
   before the sons of men!
Thou shalt hide them in the secret of thy presence from
   the pride of man:
Thou shalt keep them secretly in a pavilion from the
   strife of tongues.
Blessed be the LORD:
For he hath shewed me his marvellous kindness in a
   strong city.
For I said in my haste,
"I am cut off from before thine eyes:"
Nevertheless thou heardest the voice of my supplica-
   tions when I cried unto thee.

O love the LORD, all ye his saints:
For the LORD preserveth the faithful,
And plentifully rewardeth the proud doer.
Be of good courage, and he shall strengthen your heart,
All ye that hope in the LORD.   — Psalm 31.

I Will Guide Thee with Mine Eye

Augustine had inscribed upon the walls of his room the 32d Psalm
so that its words might be the first thing which he saw in the morning.

BLESSED is he whose transgression is forgiven,
whose sin is covered.
Blessed is the man unto whom the LORD im-
puteth not iniquity,
And in whose spirit there is no guile.

When I kept silence, my bones waxed old
Through my roaring all the day long.
For day and night thy hand was heavy upon me:
My moisture is turned into the drought of summer.
I acknowledged my sin unto thee, and mine iniquity
have I not hid.
I said, "I will confess my transgressions unto the
LORD";
And thou forgavest the iniquity of my sin.
For this shall every one that is godly pray unto thee in
a time when thou mayest be found:
Surely in the floods of great waters they shall not come
nigh unto him.
Thou art my hiding place: thou shalt preserve me
from trouble;
Thou shalt compass me about with songs of deliver-
ance.
I will instruct thee and teach thee in the way which
thou shalt go:
I will guide thee with mine eye.
Be ye not as the horse, or as the mule, which have no
understanding:

Whose mouth must be held in with bit and bridle,
Lest they come near unto thee.

Many sorrows shall be to the wicked:
But he that trusteth in the LORD, mercy shall compass
    him about.
Be glad in the LORD, and rejoice, ye righteous:
And shout for joy, all ye that are upright in heart.

                                    —Psalm 32.

THE MOUNT HERMON COUNTRY

Photograph by Underwood & Underwood

This picture shows the beautiful scenery of Northern Palestine in the vicinity
of Mount Hermon. The river is the Litany, crossed by the graceful arch of an
old Roman bridge. There are many references to "the Hermons" in the poetry
of the Bible. The snowy summit of Mount Hermon is visible from elevations in
nearly all parts of Palestine.

Blessed Is the Nation Whose God Is the Lord

This story is told of the siege of Rochelle in France (1627–28). During the siege a certain widow generously helped her poorer neighbors with her surplus of food. Her sister-in-law remonstrated. The reply was "The Lord will provide. Behold, the eye of the Lord is upon them that fear him, upon them that hope in his mercy; to deliver their soul from death, and to keep them alive in famine." Psalm 33:18, 19.

REJOICE in the LORD, O ye righteous:
For praise is comely for the upright.
Praise the LORD with harp:
Sing unto him with the psaltery and an instrument of
ten strings.
Sing unto him a new song;
Play skilfully with a loud noise.

For the word of the LORD is right;
And all his works are done in truth.
He loveth righteousness and judgment:
The earth is full of the goodness of the LORD.
By the word of the LORD were the heavens made;
And all the host of them by the breath of his mouth.
He gathereth the waters of the sea together as an heap:
He layeth up the depth in storehouses.

Let all the earth fear the LORD:
Let all the inhabitants of the world stand in awe of him.
For he spake, and it was done;
He commanded, and it stood fast.
The LORD bringeth the counsel of the heathen to
naught:

He maketh the devices of the people of none effect.
The counsel of the LORD standeth forever,
The thoughts of his heart to all generations.

Blessed is the nation whose God is the LORD;
And the people whom he hath chosen for his own in-
    heritance.
The LORD looketh from heaven;
He beholdeth all the sons of men.
From the place of his habitation he looketh
Upon all the inhabitants of the earth.
He fashioneth their hearts alike;
He considereth all their works.
There is no king saved by the multitude of an host:
A mighty man is not delivered by much strength.
An horse is a vain thing for safety:
Neither shall he deliver any by his great strength.
Behold, the eye of the LORD is upon them that fear him,
Upon them that hope in his mercy;
To deliver their soul from death,

And to keep them alive in famine.
Our soul waiteth for the LORD:
He is our help and our shield.
For our heart shall rejoice in him,
Because we have trusted in his holy name.
Let thy mercy, O LORD, be upon us,
According as we hope in thee.   — Psalm 33

Comfort for the Broken Heart

Theodore, the Martyr, a young soldier, who was burned in 306, chanted the 1st verse of the 34th Psalm, "I will bless the Lord at all times: his praise shall continually be in my mouth."

A century before Augustine brought Christianity from Rome to southern Britain, Saint Columba (521–597) was laboring in northern Britain. His headquarters were at the sacred isle of Iona. It is said that he could repeat the Psalms by heart before he could read the alphabet. On the last day of his life, he was copying the Psalter when he came to the 10th verse of the 34th Psalm: "The young lions do lack and suffer hunger: but they that seek the Lord shall not want any good thing;" He laid down his pen and said, "Here I make an end, what follows Baithen shall write." The old chronicler who tells the story adds that the last verse was fit for Columba, who should lack none of the treasures of eternity; and for Baithen, who succeeded him both as a teacher and as a writer, it was fitting that he should write the words that followed: "Come, ye children, hearken unto me: I will teach you the fear of the Lord."

I WILL bless the Lord at all times:
His praise shall continually be in my mouth.
My soul shall make her boast in the Lord:
The humble shall hear thereof, and be glad.
O magnify the Lord with me,
And let us exalt his name together.
I sought the Lord, and he heard me,
And delivered me from all my fears.
They looked unto him, and were lightened:
And their faces were not ashamed.
This poor man cried, and the Lord heard him,
And saved him out of all his troubles.
The angel of the Lord encampeth round about them
    that fear him,
And delivereth them.

O taste and see that the LORD is good:
Blessed is the man that trusteth in him.
O fear the LORD, ye his saints:
For there is no want to them that fear him.
The young lions do lack, and suffer hunger:
But they that seek the LORD shall not want any good
    thing.

Come, ye children, hearken unto me:
I will teach you the fear of the LORD.
What man is he that desireth life,
And loveth many days, that he may see good?
Keep thy tongue from evil,
And thy lips from speaking guile.
Depart from evil, and do good;
Seek peace, and pursue it.
The eyes of the LORD are upon the righteous,
And his ears are open unto their cry.
The face of the LORD is against them that do evil,
To cut off the remembrance of them from the earth.
The righteous cry, and the LORD heareth,
And delivereth them out of all their troubles.
The LORD is nigh unto them that are of a broken heart;
And saveth such as be of a contrite spirit.
Many are the afflictions of the righteous:
But the LORD delivereth him out of them all.
He keepeth all his bones:
Not one of them is broken.
Evil shall slay the wicked:
And they that hate the righteous shall be desolate.

The LORD redeemeth the soul of his servants:
And none of them that trust in him shall be desolate.

                                     — Psalm 34.

Plead My Cause, O Lord

The Spanish flagship of the Great Armada, which was sent from Spain to conquer England in 1588, bore as a motto the 23rd verse of the 35th Psalm: "Stir up thyself, and awake to my judgment, even unto my cause, my God and my Lord."

PLEAD my cause, O LORD, with them that strive
    with me:
    Fight against them that fight against me.
Take hold of shield and buckler,
And stand up for mine help.
Draw out also the spear, and stop the way against them
    that persecute me:
Say unto my soul, "I am thy salvation."
Let them be confounded and put to shame that seek
    after my soul:
Let them be turned back and brought to confusion
    that devise my hurt.
Let them be as chaff before the wind:
And let the angel of the LORD chase them.
Let their way be dark and slippery:
And let the angel of the LORD persecute them.
For without cause have they hid for me their net in a
    pit,
Which without cause they have digged for my soul.
Let destruction come upon him at unawares;
And let his net that he hath hid catch himself:
Into that very destruction let him fall.
And my soul shall be joyful in the LORD:
It shall rejoice in his salvation.
All my bones shall say, "LORD, who is like unto thee,
Which deliverest the poor from him that is too strong
    for him,

Yea, the poor and the needy from him that spoileth
    him?"

False witnesses did rise up;
They laid to my charge things that I knew not.
They rewarded me evil for good
To the spoiling of my soul.
But as for me, when they were sick, my clothing was
    sackcloth:
I humbled my soul with fasting;
And my prayer returned into mine own bosom.
I behaved myself as though he had been my friend or
    brother:
I bowed down heavily, as one that mourneth for his
    mother.
But in mine adversity they rejoiced, and gathered
    themselves together:
Yea, the abjects gathered themselves together against
    me, and I knew it not;
They did tear me, and ceased not:
With hypocritical mockers in feasts,
They gnashed upon me with their teeth.

LORD, how long wilt thou look on?
Rescue my soul from their destructions,
My darling from the lions.
I will give thee thanks in the great congregation:
I will praise thee among much people.
Let not them that are mine enemies wrongfully rejoice
    over me:
Neither let them wink with the eye that hate me with-
    out a cause.
For they speak not peace:
But they devise deceitful matters against them that are
    quiet in the land.

Yea, they opened their mouth wide against me,
And said, "Aha, aha, our eye hath seen it."
This thou hast seen, O LORD: keep not silence:
O LORD, be not far from me.
Stir up thyself, and awake to my judgment,
Even unto my cause, my God and my LORD.
Judge me, O LORD my God, according to thy righteous-
    ness;
And let them not rejoice over me.
Let them not say in their hearts, "Ah, so would we have
    it":
Let them not say, "We have swallowed him up."
Let them be ashamed and brought to confusion to-
    gether that rejoice at mine hurt:
Let them be clothed with shame and dishonour that
    magnify themselves against me.
Let them shout for joy, and be glad, that favour my
    righteous cause:
Yea, let them say continually, "Let the LORD be mag-
    nified,
Which hath pleasure in the prosperity of his servant."
And my tongue shall speak of thy righteousness
And of thy praise all the day long.   — Psalm 35.

In Thy Light Shall We See Light

THE transgression of the wicked saith within my
　　heart
　　That there is no fear of God before his eyes.
For he flattereth himself in his own eyes,
Until his iniquity be found to be hateful.
The words of his mouth are iniquity and deceit:
He hath left off to be wise, and to do good.
He deviseth mischief upon his bed;
He setteth himself in a way that is not good;
He abhorreth not evil.
Thy mercy, O LORD, is in the heavens;
And thy faithfulness reacheth unto the clouds.
Thy righteousness is like the great mountains;
Thy judgments are a great deep:
O LORD, thou preservest man and beast.
How excellent is thy lovingkindness, O God!
Therefore the children of men put their trust under the
　　shadow of thy wings.
They shall be abundantly satisfied with the fatness of
　　thy house;
And thou shalt make them drink of the river of thy
　　pleasures.
For with thee is the fountain of life:
In thy light shall we see light.
O continue thy lovingkindness unto them that know
　　thee;
And thy righteousness to the upright in heart.
Let not the foot of pride come against me,
And let not the hand of the wicked remove me.
There are the workers of iniquity fallen:
They are cast down, and shall not be able to rise.

— Psalm 36.

𝕴𝖆𝖎𝖙 𝕻𝖆𝖙𝖎𝖊𝖓𝖙𝖑𝖞 𝖋𝖔𝖗 𝖙𝖍𝖊 𝕷𝖔𝖗𝖉

There is no more romantic story in the annals of the church than that of David Livingstone (1813–1873), who began life as a poor Scotch boy working in a cotton factory and who became the great missionary-explorer of Africa. When he was nine years old, he won a New Testament in Sunday school for learning by heart the 119th Psalm. When he was ten years old, he went to work, and at the age of twenty-seven he sailed for Africa to begin his wonderful career. His favorite text, one which comforted him in all the deadly perils which menaced him, was the 5th verse of the 37th Psalm: "Commit thy way unto the LORD; trust also in him; and he shall bring it to pass."

FRET not thyself because of evildoers,
  Neither be thou envious against the workers
    of iniquity.
For they shall soon be cut down like the grass,
And wither as the green herb.

Trust in the LORD, and do good;
So shalt thou dwell in the land, and verily thou shalt be
    fed.
Delight thyself also in the LORD;
And he shall give thee the desires of thine heart.

Commit thy way unto the LORD; trust also in him;
And he shall bring it to pass.
And he shall bring forth thy righteousness as the light,
And thy judgment as the noonday.

Rest in the LORD, and wait patiently for him:
Fret not thyself because of him who prospereth in his
    way,
Because of the man who bringeth wicked devices to
    pass,

Cease from anger, and forsake wrath:

Fret not thyself in any wise to do evil.
For evildoers shall be cut off:
But those that wait upon the LORD, they shall inherit
the earth.

For yet a little while, and the wicked shall not be:
Yea, thou shalt diligently consider his place, and it
shall not be.
But the meek shall inherit the earth;
And shall delight themselves in the abundance of peace.

The wicked plotteth against the just,
And gnasheth upon him with his teeth.
The LORD shall laugh at him:
For he seeth that his day is coming.

The wicked have drawn out the sword, and have bent
their bow,
To cast down the poor and needy,
And to slay such as be of upright conversation.
Their sword shall enter into their own heart,
And their bows shall be broken.

A little that a righteous man hath
Is better than the riches of many wicked.
For the arms of the wicked shall be broken:
But the LORD upholdeth the righteous.

The LORD knoweth the days of the upright:
And their inheritance shall be forever.
They shall not be ashamed in the evil time:
And in the days of famine they shall be satisfied.

But the wicked shall perish,
And the enemies of the LORD shall be as the fat of
    lambs:
They shall consume; into smoke shall they consume
    away.

The wicked borroweth, and payeth not again:
But the righteous sheweth mercy, and giveth.
For such as be blessed of him shall inherit the earth;
And they that be cursed of him shall be cut off.

The steps of a good man are ordered by the LORD:
And he delighteth in his way.
Though he fall, he shall not be utterly cast down:
For the LORD upholdeth him with his hand.

I have been young, and now am old;
Yet have I not seen the righteous forsaken,
Nor his seed begging bread.
He is ever merciful, and lendeth;
And his seed is blessed.

Depart from evil, and do good;
And dwell forevermore.
For the LORD loveth judgment,
And forsaketh not his saints;
They are preserved forever:

But the seed of the wicked shall be cut off.
The righteous shall inherit the land,
And dwell therein forever.

The mouth of the righteous speaketh wisdom,
And his tongue talketh of judgment.
The law of his God is in his heart;
None of his steps shall slide.

The wicked watcheth the righteous,
And seeketh to slay him.
The LORD will not leave him in his hand,
Nor condemn him when he is judged.

Wait on the LORD, and keep his way,
And he shall exalt thee to inherit the land:
When the wicked are cut off, thou shalt see it.

I have seen the wicked in great power,
And spreading himself like a green bay-tree.
Yet he passed away, and, lo, he was not:
Yea, I sought him, but he could not be found.

Mark the perfect man, and behold the upright:
For the end of that man is peace.
But the transgressors shall be destroyed together:
The end of the wicked shall be cut off.

But the salvation of the righteous is of the LORD:
He is their strength in the time of trouble.
And the LORD shall help them, and deliver them:
He shall deliver them from the wicked,
And save them, because they trust in him.

— Psalm 37.

The Burdened Soul

Bishop John Hooper (?–1555), burned at the stake at Gloucester, was a lover of the Psalms. He especially recommended Psalms 6, 30, 31, 38, and 69, for their lessons of "patience and consolation at times when the mind can take no understanding, nor the heart any joy of God's promises."

O LORD, rebuke me not in thy wrath:
Neither chasten me in thy hot displeasure.
For thine arrows stick fast in me.
And thy hand presseth me sore.
There is no soundness in my flesh because of thine
anger;
Neither is there any rest in my bones because of my sin.
For mine iniquities are gone over mine head:
As an heavy burden they are too heavy for me.
My wounds stink and are corrupt
Because of my foolishness.
I am troubled; I am bowed down greatly;
I go mourning all the day long.
For my loins are filled with a loathsome disease:
And there is no soundness in my flesh.
I am feeble and sore broken:
I have roared by reason of the disquietness of my heart.

LORD, all my desire is before thee;
And my groaning is not hid from thee.
My heart panteth, my strength faileth me:
As for the light of mine eyes, it also is gone from me.
My lovers and my friends stand aloof from my sore;
And my kinsmen stand afar off.
They also that seek after my life lay snares for me:
And they that seek my hurt speak mischievous things,

And imagine deceits all the day long.
But I, as a deaf man, heard not;
And I was as a dumb man that openeth not his mouth.
Thus I was as a man that heareth not,
And in whose mouth are no reproofs.

For in thee, O LORD, do I hope:
Thou wilt hear, O LORD my God.
For I said, "Hear me,"
Lest otherwise they should rejoice over me:
When my foot slippeth, they magnify themselves
    against me.
For I am ready to halt,
And my sorrow is continually before me.
For I will declare mine iniquity;
I will be sorry for my sin.
But mine enemies are lively, and they are strong:
And they that hate me wrongfully are multiplied.
They also that render evil for good are mine adver-
    saries;
Because I follow the thing that good is.
Forsake me not, O LORD:
O my God, be not far from me.
Make haste to help me,
O LORD my salvation.   — Psalm 38.

While I Was Musing the Fire Burned

The first printed metrical version of the Psalms for church worship was made by a French author named Marot, and John Calvin, the famous theologian of Geneva. This version contained seventeen Psalms, twelve by Marot and five by Calvin. It was printed at Strassburg in 1539. One of Calvin's favorite Psalms was the 39th.

I SAID, "I will take heed to my ways,
    That I sin not with my tongue:
    I will keep my mouth with a bridle,
While the wicked is before me."
I was dumb with silence, I held my peace, even from
    good;
And my sorrow was stirred.
My heart was hot within me,
While I was musing the fire burned:
Then spake I with my tongue,
"LORD, make me to know mine end,
And the measure of my days, what it is;
That I may know how frail I am.
Behold, thou hast made my days as an handbreadth;
And mine age is as nothing before thee:
Verily every man at his best state is altogether vanity.
Surely every man walketh in a vain shew:
Surely they are disquieted in vain:
He heapeth up riches, and knoweth not who shall
    gather them."
And now, LORD, what wait I for?
My hope is in thee.
Deliver me from all my transgressions:
Make me not the reproach of the foolish.
I was dumb, I opened not my mouth;

Because thou didst it.
Remove thy stroke away from me:
I am consumed by the blow of thine hand.
When thou with rebukes dost correct man for iniquity,
Thou makest his beauty to consume away like a moth:
Surely every man is vanity.
Hear my prayer, O LORD, and give ear unto my cry;
Hold not thy peace at my tears:
For I am a stranger with thee,
And a sojourner, as all my fathers were.
O spare me, that I may recover strength,
Before I go hence, and be no more.   — Psalm 39.

He Hath Put a New Song in My Mouth

The language of the Psalms was constantly on the lips of Oliver Cromwell, farmer, soldier, Lord Protector of England; in his private devotions, in battle, in his public addresses, he constantly quoted the words of the Psalter.

I WAITED patiently for the LORD;
 And he inclined unto me, and heard my cry.
 He brought me up also out of an horrible pit,
  out of the miry clay,
And set my feet upon a rock, and established my goings.
And he hath put a new song in my mouth, even praise
 unto our God:
Many shall see it, and fear,
And shall trust in the LORD.

Blessed is that man that maketh the LORD his trust,
And respecteth not the proud, nor such as turn aside
 to lies.
Many, O LORD my God, are thy wonderful works which
 thou hast done,
And thy thoughts which are to us-ward:
They cannot be reckoned up in order unto thee:
If I would declare and speak of them,
They are more than can be numbered.
Sacrifice and offering thou didst not desire;
Mine ears hast thou opened:
Burnt offering and sin offering hast thou not required.
Then said I, "Lo, I come":
In the volume of the book it is written of me,
"I delight to do thy will, O my God":

Yea, thy law is within my heart.
I have preached righteousness in the great congrega-
tion:
Lo, I have not refrained my lips,
O LORD, thou knowest.
I have not hid thy righteousness within my heart;
I have declared thy faithfulness and thy salvation:
I have not concealed thy lovingkindness and thy truth
from the great congregation.
Withhold not thou thy tender mercies from me, O
LORD:
Let thy lovingkindness and thy truth continually pre-
serve me.

For innumerable evils have compassed me about:
Mine iniquities have taken hold upon me, so that I am
not able to look up;
They are more than the hairs of mine head: therefore
my heart faileth me.
Be pleased, O LORD, to deliver me:
O LORD, make haste to help me.
Let them be ashamed and confounded together
That seek after my soul to destroy it;
Let them be driven backward and put to shame
That wish me evil.
Let them be desolate for a reward of their shame
That say unto me, "Aha, aha."
Let all those that seek thee rejoice and be glad in thee:
Let such as love thy salvation say continually,
"The LORD be magnified."
But I am poor and needy;
Yet the LORD thinketh upon me:
Thou art my help and my deliverer;
Make no tarrying, O my God.   —Psalm 40.

When All Else Fails

BLESSED is he that considereth the poor:
The Lord will deliver him in time of trouble.
The Lord will preserve him, and keep him alive;
And he shall be blessed upon the earth:
And thou wilt not deliver him unto the will of his
enemies.
The Lord will strengthen him upon the bed of lan-
guishing:
Thou wilt make all his bed in his sickness.
I said, "Lord, be merciful unto me:
Heal my soul; for I have sinned against thee.
Mine enemies speak evil of me,
'When shall he die, and his name perish?'
And if he come to see me, he speaketh vanity:
His heart gathereth iniquity to itself;
When he goeth abroad, he telleth it.
All that hate me whisper together against me:
Against me do they devise my hurt.
'An evil disease,' say they, 'cleaveth fast unto him:
And now that he lieth he shall rise up no more.'
Yea, mine own familiar friend, in whom I trusted, which
did eat of my bread,
Hath lifted up his heel against me.
But thou, O Lord, be merciful unto me, and raise me up.
That I may requite them.
By this I know that thou favourest me,
Because mine enemy doth not triumph over me.
And as for me, thou upholdest me in mine integrity,
And settest me before thy face forever.
Blessed be the Lord God of Israel
From everlasting, and to everlasting.
Amen, and Amen."

— Psalm 41.

Why Art Thou Cast Down?

AS the hart panteth after the water brooks,
So panteth my soul after thee, O God.
My soul thirsteth for God, for the living God:
When shall I come and appear before God?
My tears have been my meat day and night,
While they continually say unto me,
"Where is thy God?"
When I remember these things, I pour out my soul in me:
For I had gone with the multitude, I went with them
to the house of God,
With the voice of joy and praise, with a multitude that
kept holyday.
Why art thou cast down, O my soul?
And why art thou disquieted in me?
Hope thou in God: for I shall yet praise him
For the help of his countenance.

O my God, my soul is cast down within me:
Therefore will I remember thee from the land of
Jordan,
And of the Hermonites, from the hill Mizar.
Deep calleth unto deep at the noise of thy waterspouts:
All thy waves and thy billows are gone over me.
Yet the LORD will command his lovingkindness in the
daytime,
And in the night his song shall be with me,
And my prayer unto the God of my life.
I will say unto God my rock, "Why hast thou for-
gotten me?
Why go I mourning because of the oppression of the
enemy?"

As with a sword in my bones, mine enemies reproach
    me;
While they say daily unto me, "Where is thy God?"
Why art thou cast down, O my soul?
And why art thou disquieted within me?
Hope thou in God: for I shall yet praise him,
Who is the health of my countenance, and my God.
                                        — Psalm 42.

Send Out Thy Light and Truth

JUDGE me, O God, and plead my cause against an
    ungodly nation:
        O deliver me from the deceitful and unjust man.
For thou art the God of my strength: why dost thou
    cast me off?
Why go I mourning because of the oppression of the
    enemy?
O send out thy light and thy truth: let them lead me;
Let them bring me unto thy holy hill,
And to thy tabernacles.
Then will I go unto the altar of God,
Unto God my exceeding joy:
Yea, upon the harp will I praise thee, O God my God.
Why art thou cast down, O my soul?
And why art thou disquieted within me?
Hope in God: for I shall yet praise him,
Who is the health of my countenance, and my God.
                                        — Psalm 43.

Our Fathers Have Told Us

WE have heard with our ears, O God, our fathers
　　have told us,
　　　　What work thou didst in their days, in the
　　　　times of old.
How thou didst drive out the heathen with thy hand,
　　and plantedst them;
How thou didst afflict the people, and cast them out.
For they got not the land in possession by their own
　　sword,
Neither did their own arm save them:
But thy right hand, and thine arm, and the light of thy
　　countenance,
Because thou hadst a favour unto them.

Thou art my King, O God:
Command deliverances for Jacob.
Through thee will we push down our enemies:
Through thy name will we tread them under that rise
　　up against us.
For I will not trust in my bow,
Neither shall my sword save me.
But thou hast saved us from our enemies,
And hast put them to shame that hated us.
In God we boast all the day long,
And praise thy name forever.

But thou hast cast off, and put us to shame;
And goest not forth with our armies.
Thou makest us to turn back from the enemy:
And they which hate us spoil for themselves.
Thou hast given us like sheep appointed for meat;

And hast scattered us among the heathen.
Thou sellest thy people for naught,
And dost not increase thy wealth by their price.
Thou makest us a reproach to our neighbours,
A scorn and a derision to them that are round about us.
Thou makest us a byword among the heathen,
A shaking of the head among the people.
My confusion is continually before me,
And the shame of my face hath covered me,
For the voice of him that reproacheth and blasphemeth;
By reason of the enemy and avenger.

All this is come upon us; yet have we not forgotten
    thee,
Neither have we dealt falsely in thy covenant.
Our heart is not turned back,
Neither have our steps declined from thy way;
Though thou hast sore broken us in the place of
    dragons,
And covered us with the shadow of death.
If we have forgotten the name of our God,
Or stretched out our hands to a strange god;
Shall not God search this out?
For he knoweth the secrets of the heart.
Yea, for thy sake are we killed all the day long;
We are counted as sheep for the slaughter.

Awake, why sleepest thou, O LORD?
Arise, cast us not off forever.
Wherefore hidest thou thy face,
And forgettest our affliction and our oppression?
For our soul is bowed down to the dust:
Our belly cleaveth unto the earth.
Arise for our help,
And redeem us for thy mercies' sake.   — Psalm 44.

A Marriage Song

Hildebrand, the son of a carpenter, afterward Pope Gregory VII, subjected the government of the State to that of the Church. But he also reformed many abuses which had crept into the Church in the 11th century. In 1077 the Emperor Henry IV, of Germany, in the garments of a penitent, waited for three days outside the gate of the castle of Canossa to do penance before Gregory. He himself, however, was defeated and died, broken-hearted, in the castle of Salerno. His last words were taken from the 7th verse of the 45th Psalm: "I have loved righteousness, and hated iniquity: —and therefore I die in exile."

MY heart is inditing a good matter:
I speak of the things which I have made
touching the king:
My tongue is the pen of a ready writer.

Thou art fairer than the children of men:
Grace is poured into thy lips:
Therefore God hath blessed thee forever.
Gird thy sword upon thy thigh, O most mighty,
With thy glory and thy majesty.
And in thy majesty ride prosperously
Because of truth and meekness and righteousness;
And thy right hand shall teach thee terrible things.
Thine arrows are sharp
In the heart of the king's enemies;
Whereby the people fall under thee.

Thy throne, O God, is forever and ever:
The sceptre of thy kingdom is a right sceptre.
Thou lovest righteousness, and hatest wickedness:
Therefore God, thy God, hath anointed thee
With the oil of gladness above thy fellows.

All thy garments smell of myrrh, and aloes, and cassia,
Out of the ivory palaces, whereby they have made thee
 glad.
Kings' daughters were among thy honourable women:
Upon thy right hand did stand the queen in gold of
 Ophir.

Hearken, O daughter, and consider, and incline thine
 ear;
Forget also thine own people, and thy father's house;
So shall the king greatly desire thy beauty:
For he is thy LORD; and worship thou him.
And the daughter of Tyre shall be there with a gift,
Even the rich among the people shall intreat thy
 favour.

The king's daughter is all glorious within:
Her clothing is of wrought gold.
She shall be brought unto the king in raiment of needle-
 work:
The virgins her companions that follow her shall be
 brought unto thee.
With gladness and rejoicing shall they be brought:
They shall enter into the king's palace.
Instead of thy fathers shall be thy children,
Whom thou mayest make princes in all the earth.
I will make thy name to be remembered in all genera-
 tions:
Therefore shall the people praise thee forever and ever.

— Psalm 45.

𝔄 𝔐𝔦𝔤𝔥𝔱𝔶 𝔉𝔬𝔯𝔱𝔯𝔢𝔰𝔰 𝔍𝔰 𝔒𝔲𝔯 𝔊𝔬𝔡

One of the great hymns of the church is Luther's "Ein feste Burg ist unser Gott," "A mighty fortress is our God," adapted from the 46th Psalm. It voices the magnificent courage of the great reformer, the courage which spoke in his words before the Council at Worms,—"I cannot and will not retract anything. It is neither wise nor right to do aught against conscience. Here I stand. God help me, I cannot otherwise. Amen." Yet sometimes even Luther's stout courage almost failed him, and then he would turn to his friend, Melanchthon, and say, "Come, Philip, let us sing the 46th Psalm."

Thomas Carlyle greatly loved Luther's hymn, and made a translation of it:

"A safe stronghold our God is still,
A trusty shield and weapon;
He'll help us clear from all the ill
That hath us now o'ertaken.
The Ancient Prince of Hell
Hath risen with purpose fell;
Strong mail of Craft and Power
He weareth in this hour;
On earth is not his fellow."

GOD is our refuge and strength, a very present help in trouble.
Therefore will not we fear, though the earth be removed,
And though the mountains be carried into the midst of the sea;
Though the waters thereof roar and be troubled,
Though the mountains shake with the swelling thereof.

There is a river, the streams whereof shall make glad the city of God,
The holy place of the tabernacles of the most High.

God is in the midst of her; she shall not be moved:
God shall help her, and that right early.
The heathen raged, the kingdoms were moved:
He uttered his voice, the earth melted.
The LORD of hosts is with us;
The God of Jacob is our refuge.

Come, behold the works of the LORD,
What desolations he hath made in the earth.
He maketh wars to cease unto the end of the earth;
He breaketh the bow, and cutteth the spear in sunder;
He burneth the chariot in the fire.
Be still, and know that I am God:
I will be exalted among the heathen, I will be exalted
    in the earth.
The LORD of hosts is with us;
The God of Jacob is our refuge.   — Psalm 46.

A Song of Triumph

O CLAP your hands, all ye people;
Shout unto God with the voice of triumph.
For the LORD most high is terrible;
He is a great King over all the earth.
He shall subdue the people under us,
And the nations under our feet.
He shall choose our inheritance for us,
The excellency of Jacob whom he loved.

God is gone up with a shout,
The LORD with the sound of a trumpet.
Sing praises to God, sing praises:
Sing praises unto our King, sing praises.
For God is the King of all the earth:
Sing ye praises with understanding.

God reigneth over the heathen:
God sitteth upon the throne of his holiness.
The princes of the people are gathered together,
Even the people of the God of Abraham:
For the shields of the earth belong unto God:
He is greatly exalted.   — Psalm 47.

A Song of the Glory of Zion

GREAT is the LORD, and greatly to be praised
   In the city of our God, in the mountain of his
      holiness.
Beautiful for situation, the joy of the whole earth,
Is Mount Zion, on the sides of the north,
The city of the great King.
God is known in her palaces for a refuge.
For, lo, the kings were assembled, they passed by to-
   gether.
They saw it, and so they marveled;
They were troubled, and hasted away.
Fear took hold upon them there,
And pain, as of a woman in travail.
Thou breakest the ships of Tarshish with an east wind.
As we have heard, so have we seen
In the city of the LORD of hosts, in the city of our God:
God will establish it forever.
We have thought of thy lovingkindness, O God,
In the midst of thy temple.
According to thy name, O God,
So is thy praise unto the ends of the earth:
Thy right hand is full of righteousness.
Let Mount Zion rejoice,
Let the daughters of Judah be glad,
Because of thy judgments.
Walk about Zion, and go round about her:
Tell the towers thereof.
Mark ye well her bulwarks,
Consider her palaces;
That ye may tell it to the generation following.
For this God is our God forever and ever:
He will be our guide even unto death.   — Psalm 48.

A Song for All Conditions of Men

Matthew Arnold, in his "Obermann once more," quotes Psalm 49:7 —

> "From David's lips this word did roll
> 'Tis true and living yet;
> No man can save his brother's soul
> Nor pay his brother's debt."

HEAR this, all ye people;
Give ear, all ye inhabitants of the world:
Both low and high, rich and poor, together.
My mouth shall speak of wisdom;
And the meditation of my heart shall be of under-
standing.
I will incline mine ear to a parable:
I will open my dark saying upon the harp.

Wherefore should I fear in the days of evil,
When the iniquity of my heels shall compass me about?
They that trust in their wealth,
And boast themselves in the multitude of their riches;
None of them can by any means redeem his brother,
Nor give to God a ransom for him:
For the redemption of their soul is precious,
And it ceaseth forever:
That he should still live forever, and not see corruption.
For he seeth that wise men die,
Likewise the fool and the brutish person perish,
And leave their wealth to others.
Their inward thought is, that their houses shall con-
tinue forever.
And their dwelling places to all generations;
They call their lands after their own names.

Nevertheless man being in honour abideth not:
He is like the beasts that perish.

This their way is their folly:
Yet their posterity approve their sayings.
Like sheep they are laid in the grave;
Death shall feed on them;
And the upright shall have dominion over them in the
    morning;
And their beauty shall consume in the grave from their
    dwelling.
But God will redeem my soul from the power of the
    grave:
For he shall receive me.

Be not thou afraid when one is made rich,
When the glory of his house is increased;
For when he dieth he shall carry nothing away:
His glory shall not descend after him.
Though while he lived he blessed his soul:
And men will praise thee, when thou doest well to thy-
    self.
He shall go to the generation of his fathers;
They shall never see light.
Man that is in honour, and understandeth not,
Is like the beasts that perish.   — Psalm 49.

The Cattle Upon a Thousand Hills Are the Lord's

Origen (185–253), was one of the greatest figures in the early church. He had suffered many tortures for his faith, but once under the stress of pain, he recanted and sacrificed to Caesar. This momentary weakness brought great sorrow to his sensitive soul. At Jerusalem he was asked to preach. He opened the Psalter at the 16th verse of the 50th Psalm.

THE mighty God, even the LORD, hath spoken,
And called the earth from the rising of the sun
unto the going down thereof.
Out of Zion, the perfection of beauty,
God hath shined.
Our God shall come, and shall not keep silence:
A fire shall devour before him,
And it shall be very tempestuous round about him.
He shall call to the heavens from above,
And to the earth, that he may judge his people.
"Gather my saints together unto me;
Those that have made a covenant with me by sacrifice.
And the heavens shall declare his righteousness:
For God is judge himself.

Hear, O my people, and I will speak;
O Israel, and I will testify against thee:
I am God, even thy God.
I will not reprove thee for thy sacrifices or thy burnt
offerings,
To have been continually before me.
I will take no bullock out of thy house,
Nor he goats out of thy folds.
For every beast of the forest is mine,

The High Summits of the Lebanons

Photograph by Professor Lewis Bayles Paton

This is a fine picture of the great mountain wall which rises in northern Palestine. The cliffs are almost above the tree line, only a few shrubs growing here and there in the crevices of the rocks. Palestine is a land of magnificent scenery.

"I will lift up mine eyes unto the hills, from whence cometh my help."

And the cattle upon a thousand hills.
I know all the fowls of the mountains:
And the wild beasts of the field are mine.
If I were hungry, I would not tell thee
For the world is mine, and the fulness thereof.
Will I eat the flesh of bulls,
Or drink the blood of goats?
Offer unto God thanksgiving;
And pay thy vows unto the most High:
And call upon me in the day of trouble;
I will deliver thee, and thou shalt glorify me."

But unto the wicked God saith,
"What hast thou to do to declare my statutes,
Or that thou shouldest take my covenant in thy mouth?
Seeing thou hatest instruction,
And castest my words behind thee.
When thou sawest a thief, then thou consentedst with
    him,
And hast been partaker with adulterers.
Thou givest thy mouth to evil,
And thy tongue frameth deceit.
Thou sittest and speakest against thy brother;
Thou slanderest thine own mother's son.
These things hast thou done, and I kept silence;
Thou thoughtest that I was altogether such an one as
    thyself:
But I will reprove thee, and set them in order before
    thine eyes.

Now consider this, ye that forget God,
Lest I tear you in pieces, and there be none to deliver."
Whoso offereth praise glorifieth me:
And to him that ordereth his conversation aright
Will I shew the salvation of God.   — Psalm 50.

A Clean Heart and a Right Spirit

Savonarola (1452–1498), the great reformer of Florence, was writing a commentary on the 31st and the 51st Psalms during his last days. He was executed in the Square of the Signoria. Michael Angelo's famous portrait of Savonarola has for a motto the 13th verse of the 51st Psalm: "Then will I teach transgressors thy ways; and sinners shall be converted unto thee."

On his way to the scaffold in the Grande Place in Brussels, Count Egmont repeated portions of the 51st Psalm. The execution of Count Egmont and Count Horn by the decree of Philip of Spain marked the beginning of the revolt of the Netherlands against Spain.

The great headmaster of Rugby, Thomas Arnold, on his death-bed, repeated verse 12 of the 51st Psalm, "Restore unto me the joy of thy salvation; and uphold me with thy free spirit."

HAVE mercy upon me, O God, according to thy lovingkindness:
According unto the multitude of thy tender mercies blot out my transgressions.
Wash me throughly from mine iniquity,
And cleanse me from my sin.
For I acknowledge my transgressions:
And my sin is ever before me.
Against thee, thee only, have I sinned,
And done this evil in thy sight:
That thou mightest be justified when thou speakest,
And be clear when thou judgest.

Behold, I was shapen in iniquity;
And in sin did my mother conceive me.
Behold, thou desirest truth in the inward parts:
And in the hidden part thou shalt make me to know wisdom.

Purge me with hyssop, and I shall be clean:
Wash me, and I shall be whiter than snow.
Make me to hear joy and gladness;
That the bones which thou hast broken may rejoice.
Hide thy face from my sins,
And blot out all mine iniquities.
Create in me a clean heart, O God;
And renew a right spirit within me.
Cast me not away from thy presence;
And take not thy holy spirit from me.
Restore unto me the joy of thy salvation;
And uphold me with thy free spirit.
Then will I teach transgressors thy ways;
And sinners shall be converted unto thee.
Deliver me from bloodguiltiness, O God, thou God of
    my salvation:
And my tongue shall sing aloud of thy righteousness.

O Lord, open thou my lips;
And my mouth shall shew forth thy praise.
For thou desirest not sacrifice; else would I give it:
Thou delightest not in burnt offering.
The sacrifices of God are a broken spirit:
A broken and a contrite heart, O God, thou wilt not
    despise.

Do good in thy good pleasure unto Zion:
Build thou the walls of Jerusalem.
Then shalt thou be pleased with the sacrifices of right-
    eousness, with burnt offering and whole burnt
    offering:
Then shall they offer bullocks upon thine altar.

— Psalm 51.

The Evil Man

WHY boastest thou thyself in mischief, O mighty man?
>　　The goodness of God endureth continually.
Thy tongue deviseth mischiefs;
Like a sharp razor, working deceitfully.
Thou lovest evil more than good;
And lying rather than to speak righteousness.
Thou lovest all devouring words, O thou deceitful
>　　tongue.
God shall likewise destroy thee forever,
He shall take thee away, and pluck thee out of thy
>　　dwelling place,
And root thee out of the land of the living.

The righteous also shall see, and fear,
And shall laugh at him:
"Lo, this is the man that made not God his strength;
But trusted in the abundance of his riches,
And strengthened himself in his wickedness."
But I am like a green olive-tree in the house of God:
I trust in the mercy of God forever and ever.
I will praise thee forever, because thou hast done it:
And I will wait on thy name; for it is good before thy
>　　saints.　　　　　　　　　　— Psalm 52.

The Workers of Iniquity

THE fool hath said in his heart, "There is no God."
Corrupt are they, and have done abominable
iniquity:
There is none that doeth good.
God looked down from heaven upon the children of
men,
To see if there were any that did understand,
That did seek God.
Every one of them is gone back: they are altogether
become filthy;
There is none that doeth good, no, not one.

Have the workers of iniquity no knowledge
Who eat up my people as they eat bread?
They have not called upon God.
There were they in great fear, where no fear was:
For God hath scattered the bones of him that en-
campeth against thee:
Thou hast put them to shame, because God hath
despised them.

Oh that the salvation of Israel were come out of Zion!
When God bringeth back the captivity of his people,
Jacob shall rejoice, and Israel shall be glad.

— Psalm 53.

Strangers Are Risen Against Me

SAVE me, O God, by thy name,
And judge me by thy strength.
Hear my prayer, O God;
Give ear to the words of my mouth.
For strangers are risen up against me,
And oppressors seek after my soul:
They have not set God before them.

Behold, God is mine helper:
The LORD is with them that uphold my soul.
He shall reward evil unto mine enemies:
Cut them off in thy truth.
I will freely sacrifice unto thee:
I will praise thy name, O LORD; for it is good.
For he hath delivered me out of all trouble:
And mine eye hath seen his desire upon mine enemies.

— Psalm 54.

Cast Thy Burden on the Lord

GIVE ear to my prayer, O God;
  And hide not thyself from my supplication.
  Attend unto me, and hear me:
I mourn in my complaint, and make a noise;
Because of the voice of the enemy,
Because of the oppression of the wicked:
For they cast iniquity upon me, and in wrath they hate
  me.
My heart is sore pained within me:
And the terrors of death are fallen upon me.
Fearfulness and trembling are come upon me,
And horror hath overwhelmed me.
And I said, "Oh that I had wings like a dove!
For then would I fly away, and be at rest.
Lo, then would I wander far off,
And remain in the wilderness.
I would hasten my escape
From the windy storm and tempest."

Destroy, O LORD, and divide their tongues:
For I have seen violence and strife in the city.
Day and night they go about it upon the walls thereof:
Mischief also and sorrow are in the midst of it.
Wickedness is in the midst thereof:
Deceit and guile depart not from her streets.
For it was not an enemy that reproached me;
Then I could have borne it:
Neither was it he that hated me that did magnify him-
  self against me;
Then I would have hid myself from him:
But it was thou, a man mine equal,

My guide, and mine acquaintance.
We took sweet counsel together,
And walked unto the house of God in company.
Let death seize upon them,
And let them go down quick into hell:
For wickedness is in their dwellings, and among them.

As for me, I will call upon God; and the LORD shall
save me.
Evening, and morning, and at noon, will I pray, and
cry aloud:
And he shall hear my voice.
He hath delivered my soul in peace from the battle
that was against me:
For there were many with me.
God shall hear, and afflict them,
Even he that abideth of old.
Because they have no changes,
Therefore they fear not God.

He hath put forth his hands against such as be at peace
with him:
He hath broken his covenant.
The words of his mouth were smoother than butter,
But war was in his heart:
His words were softer than oil,
Yet were they drawn swords.

Cast thy burden upon the LORD, and he shall sustain
thee:
He shall never suffer the righteous to be moved.
But thou, O God, shalt bring them down into the pit
of destruction:
Bloody and deceitful men shall not live out half their
days;
But I will trust in thee.   — Psalm 55.

Thou Hast Delivered My Soul

BE merciful unto me, O God: for man would
        swallow me up;
    He fighting daily oppresseth me.
Mine enemies would daily swallow me up:
For they be many that fight against me, O thou most High.
What time I am afraid,
I will trust in thee.
In God I will praise his word,
In God I have put my trust:
I will not fear what flesh can do unto me.
Every day they wrest my words:
All their thoughts are against me for evil.
They gather themselves together, they hide themselves,
They mark my steps,
When they wait for my soul.
Shall they escape by iniquity?
In thine anger cast down the people, O God.
Thou tellest my wanderings:
Put thou my tears into thy bottle:
Are they not in thy book?
When I cry unto thee, then shall mine enemies turn back:
This I know; for God is for me.
In God will I praise his word:
In the LORD will I praise his word.
In God have I put my trust:
I will not be afraid what man can do unto me.
Thy vows are upon me, O God:
I will render praises unto thee.
For thou hast delivered my soul from death:
Wilt not thou deliver my feet from falling,
That I may walk before God
In the light of the living?   — Psalm 56.

My Heart Is Fixed Upon Thee

BE merciful unto me, O God, be merciful unto me:
    For my soul trusteth in thee:
       Yea, in the shadow of thy wings will I make my
          refuge,
Until these calamities be overpast.
I will cry unto God most high;
Unto God that performeth all things for me.
He shall send from heaven, and save me
From the reproach of him that would swallow me up.
God shall send forth his mercy and his truth.
My soul is among lions:
And I lie even among them that are set on fire,
Even the sons of men, whose teeth are spears and
    arrows,
And their tongue a sharp sword.
Be thou exalted, O God, above the heavens;
Let thy glory be above all the earth.
They have prepared a net for my steps;
My soul is bowed down:
They have digged a pit before me,
Into the midst whereof they are fallen themselves.
My heart is fixed, O God, my heart is fixed:
I will sing and give praise.
Awake up, my glory; awake, psaltery and harp:
I myself will awake early.
I will praise thee, O Lord, among the people:
I will sing unto thee among the nations.
For thy mercy is great unto the heavens,
And thy truth unto the clouds.
Be thou exalted, O God, above the heavens:
Let thy glory be above all the earth.   — Psalm 57.

Like the Deaf Adder

DO ye indeed speak righteousness, O congregation?
    Do ye judge uprightly, O ye sons of men?
    Yea, in heart ye work wickedness;
Ye weigh the violence of your hands in the earth.
The wicked are estranged from the womb:
They go astray as soon as they be born, speaking lies.
Their poison is like the poison of a serpent:
They are like the deaf adder that stoppeth her ear;
Which will not hearken to the voice of charmers,
Charming never so wisely.

Break their teeth, O God, in their mouth:
Break out the great teeth of the young lions, O LORD.
Let them melt away as waters which run continually:
When he bendeth his bow to shoot his arrows, let them
    be as cut in pieces.
As a snail which melteth, let every one of them pass
    away:
Like the untimely birth of a woman, that they may not
    see the sun.
Before your pots can feel the thorns,
He shall take them away as with a whirlwind, both
    living, and in his wrath.

The righteous shall rejoice when he seeth the vengeance:
He shall wash his feet in the blood of the wicked.
So that a man shall say, "Verily there is a reward for
    the righteous:
Verily he is a God that judgeth in the earth."

               — Psalm 58.

Deliver Me from Mine Enemies

DELIVER me from mine enemies, O my God:
Defend me from them that rise up against me.
Deliver me from the workers of iniquity,
And save me from bloody men.
For, lo, they lie in wait for my soul:
The mighty are gathered against me;
Not for my transgression, nor for my sin, O Lord.
They run and prepare themselves without my fault:
Awake to help me, and behold.
Thou therefore, O Lord God of hosts, the God of Israel,
Awake to visit all the heathen:
Be not merciful to any wicked transgressors.

They return at evening:
They make a noise like a dog, and go round about the
     city.
Behold, they belch out with their mouth:
Swords are in their lips:
"For who," say they, "doth hear?"
But thou, O Lord, shalt laugh at them;
Thou shalt have all the heathen in derision.
Because of his strength will I wait upon thee:
For God is my defence.

The God of my mercy shall prevent me:
God shall let me see my desire upon mine enemies.
Slay them not, lest my people forget:
Scatter them by thy power; and bring them down,
O Lord our shield.
For the sin of their mouth and the words of their lips
Let them even be taken in their pride:

And for cursing and lying which they speak.
Consume them in wrath, consume them, that they may
    not be:
And let them know that God ruleth in Jacob
Unto the ends of the earth.

And at evening let them return;
And let them make a noise like a dog,
And go round about the city.
Let them wander up and down for meat,
And grudge if they be not satisfied.
But I will sing of thy power;
Yea, I will sing aloud of thy mercy in the morning:
For thou hast been my defence
And refuge in the day of my trouble.
Unto thee, O my strength, will I sing:
For God is my defence, and the God of my mercy.

                            — Psalm 59.

We Shall Do Valiantly

O GOD, thou hast cast us off, thou hast scattered us,
Thou hast been displeased; O turn thyself to us
again.
Thou hast made the earth to tremble;
Thou hast broken it: heal the breaches thereof; for it
shaketh.
Thou hast shewed thy people hard things:
Thou hast made us to drink the wine of astonishment.
Thou hast given a banner to them that fear thee,
That it may be displayed because of the truth.
That thy beloved may be delivered;
Save with thy right hand, and hear me.
God hath spoken in his holiness; I will rejoice;
I will divide Shechem, and mete out the valley of
Succoth.
Gilead is mine, and Manasseh is mine;
Ephraim also is the strength of mine head;
Judah is my lawgiver:
Moab is my washpot;
Over Edom will I cast out my shoe:
Philistia, triumph thou because of me.
Who will bring me into the strong city?
Who will lead me into Edom?
Wilt not thou, O God, which hadst cast us off?
And thou, O God, which didst not go out with our
armies?
Give us help from trouble:
For vain is the help of man.
Through God we shall do valiantly:
For he it is that shall tread down our enemies.

— Psalm 60.

The Rock that Is Higher than I

HEAR my cry, O God;
 Attend unto my prayer.
  From the end of the earth will I cry unto thee,
When my heart is overwhelmed:
Lead me to the rock that is higher than I.
For thou hast been a shelter for me,
And a strong tower from the enemy.

I will abide in thy tabernacle forever:
I will trust in the covert of thy wings.
For thou, O God, hast heard my vows:
Thou hast given me the heritage of those that fear thy
 name.

Thou wilt prolong the king's life:
And his years as many generations.
He shall abide before God forever:
O prepare mercy and truth, which may preserve him.
So will I sing praise unto thy name forever,
That I may daily perform my vows.   — Psalm 61.

From Him Cometh My Salvation

TRULY my soul waiteth upon God:
   From him cometh my salvation.
   He only is my rock and my salvation;
He is my defence; I shall not be greatly moved.
How long will ye imagine mischief against a man?
Ye shall be slain all of you:
As a bowing wall shall ye be, and as a tottering fence.
They only consult to cast him down from his excellency:
They delight in lies:
They bless with their mouth, but they curse inwardly.
My soul, wait thou only upon God;
For my expectation is from him.
He only is my rock and my salvation:
He is my defence; I shall not be moved.
In God is my salvation and my glory:
The rock of my strength, and my refuge, is in God.
Trust in him at all times;
Ye people, pour out your heart before him:
God is a refuge for us.
Surely men of low degree are vanity, and men of high
   degree are a lie:
To be laid in the balance, they are altogether lighter
   than vanity.
Trust not in oppression, and become not vain in robbery:
If riches increase, set not your heart upon them.
God hath spoken once;
Twice have I heard this;
That power belongeth unto God.
Also unto thee, O Lord, belongeth mercy:
For thou renderest to every man according to his work.

— Psalm 62.

"When I Meditate on Thee in the Night Watches"

By W. L. Taylor

Copyright by The Curtis Publishing Company

From a Copley Print; copyright by Curtis and
Cameron, Inc., Boston, Massachusetts

In this picture we may suppose that the
youthful David has soothed the mind of
Saul and has fallen asleep himself, while
the king, his mind now untroubled, thinks
of the Creator and his works.

Early Will I Seek Thee

The morning hymn of the Eastern Christians, the favorite of Saint Chrysostom, and of Beza, the French reformer, was the 63rd Psalm.

O GOD, thou art my God; early will I seek thee:
My soul thirsteth for thee, my flesh longeth
for thee
In a dry and thirsty land, where no water is;
To see thy power and thy glory,
So as I have seen thee in the sanctuary.

Because thy lovingkindness is better than life,
My lips shall praise thee.
Thus will I bless thee while I live:
I will lift up my hands in thy name.
My soul shall be satisfied as with marrow and fatness;
And my mouth shall praise thee with joyful lips:
When I remember thee upon my bed,
And meditate on thee in the night watches.

Because thou hast been my help,
Therefore in the shadow of thy wings will I rejoice.
My soul followeth hard after thee:
Thy right hand upholdeth me.
But those that seek my soul, to destroy it,
Shall go into the lower parts of the earth.
They shall fall by the sword:
They shall be a portion for foxes.
But the king shall rejoice in God;
Every one that sweareth by him shall glory:
But the mouth of them that speak lies shall be stopped.

— Psalm 63.

The Secret Counsel of the Wicked

HEAR my voice, O God, in my prayer:
Preserve my life from fear of the enemy.
Hide me from the secret counsel of the wicked;
From the insurrection of the workers of iniquity:
Who whet their tongue like a sword,
And bend their bows to shoot their arrows, even bitter
    words:
That they may shoot in secret at the perfect:
Suddenly do they shoot at him, and fear not.
They encourage themselves in an evil matter:
They commune of laying snares privily;
They say, "Who shall see them?"
They search out iniquities; they accomplish a diligent
    search:
Both the inward thought of every one of them, and the
    heart, is deep.

But God shall shoot at them with an arrow;
Suddenly shall they be wounded.
So they shall make their own tongue to fall upon them-
    selves:
All that see them shall flee away.
And all men shall fear, and shall declare the work of
    God;
For they shall wisely consider of his doing.
The righteous shall be glad in the LORD, and shall trust
    in him;
And all the upright in heart shall glory.   —Psalm 64.

A Song of Thanksgiving for Abundant Harvests

PRAISE waiteth for thee, O God, in Zion:
    And unto thee shall the vow be performed.
    O thou that hearest prayer,
Unto thee shall all flesh come.
Iniquities prevail against me:
As for our transgressions, thou shalt purge them away.
Blessed is the man whom thou choosest, and causest to
    approach unto thee,
That he may dwell in thy courts:
We shall be satisfied with the goodness of thy house,
Even of thy holy temple.

By terrible things in righteousness wilt thou answer
    us,
O God of our salvation;
Who art the confidence of all the ends of the earth,
And of them that are afar off upon the sea:
Which by his strength setteth fast the mountains;
Being girded with power:
Which stilleth the noise of the seas, the noise of their
    waves,
And the tumult of the people.
They also that dwell in the uttermost parts are afraid
    at thy tokens:
Thou makest the outgoings of the morning and evening
    to rejoice.

Thou visitest the earth, and waterest it:
Thou greatly enrichest it with the river of God,
Which is full of water:

Thou preparest them corn, when thou hast so provided
    for it.
Thou waterest the ridges thereof abundantly:
Thou settlest the furrows thereof:
Thou makest it soft with showers:
Thou blessest the springing thereof.
Thou crownest the year with thy goodness;
And thy paths drop fatness.
They drop upon the pastures of the wilderness:
And the little hills rejoice on every side.
The pastures are clothed with flocks;
The valleys also are covered over with corn;
They shout for joy, they also sing.   — Psalm 65.

THE HILL COUNTRY OF PALESTINE
Photograph by Professor Lewis Bayles Paton

"Thou crownest the year with thy goodness; and thy paths drop fatness.
They drop upon the pastures of the wilderness: and the hills rejoice on every side.
The pastures are clothed with flocks; the valleys also are covered over with corn; they shout for joy, they also sing."

I Will Declare What He Hath Done for My Soul

"Pilgrim's Progress" is saturated with the language of Scripture and especially the phraseology of the Psalms. The motto of Bunyan's "Grace abounding to the chief of sinners" is the 16th verse of the 66th Psalm, "Come and hear, all ye that fear God, and I will declare what he hath done for my soul."

MAKE a joyful noise unto God, all ye lands:
    Sing forth the honour of his name:
    Make his praise glorious.
Say unto God, "How terrible art thou in thy works!
Through the greatness of thy power shall thine ene-
    mies submit themselves unto thee.
All the earth shall worship thee,
And shall sing unto thee;
They shall sing to thy name."

Come and see the works of God:
He is terrible in his doing toward the children of men.
He turned the sea into dry land:
They went through the flood on foot:
There did we rejoice in him.
He ruleth by his power forever;
His eyes behold the nations:
Let not the rebellious exalt themselves.

O bless our God, ye people,
And make the voice of his praise to be heard:
Which holdeth our soul in life,
And suffereth not our feet to be moved.
For thou, O God, hast proved us:
Thou hast tried us, as silver is tried.

Thou broughtest us into the net;
Thou laidst affliction upon our loins.
Thou hast caused men to ride over our heads;
We went through fire and through water;
But thou broughtest us out into a wealthy place.

I will go into thy house with burnt offerings:
I will pay thee my vows,
Which my lips have uttered,
And my mouth hath spoken, when I was in trouble.
I will offer unto thee burnt sacrifices of fatlings,
With the incense of rams;
I will offer bullocks with goats.

Come and hear, all ye that fear God,
And I will declare what he hath done for my soul.
I cried unto him with my mouth,
And he was extolled with my tongue.
If I regard iniquity in my heart,
The LORD will not hear me:
But verily God hath heard me;
He hath attended to the voice of my prayer.
Blessed be God,
Which hath not turned away my prayer,
Nor his mercy from me.   — Psalm 66.

All the Ends of the Earth Shall Fear Him

GOD be merciful unto us, and bless us;
And cause his face to shine upon us;
That thy way may be known upon earth,
Thy saving health among all nations.

Let the people praise thee, O God;
Let all the people praise thee.
O let the nations be glad and sing for joy:
For thou shalt judge the people righteously,
And govern the nations upon earth.

Let the people praise thee, O God;
Let all the people praise thee.
Then shall the earth yield her increase;
And God, even our own God, shall bless us.
God shall bless us;
And all the ends of the earth shall fear him.

— Psalm 67.

Let God Arise

The favorite Psalm of the great emperor, Charlemagne, was the 68th.

At the battle of Dunbar, where the Scotch forces were defeated by Cromwell's Ironsides, when the sun arose and Cromwell saw the enemy in his power, he cried in the words of the 68th Psalm, "Let God arise, let his enemies be scattered."

LET God arise, let his enemies be scattered:
   Let them also that hate him flee before him.
      As smoke is driven away, so drive them away:
As wax melteth before the fire,
So let the wicked perish at the presence of God.
But let the righteous be glad; let them rejoice before
      God:
Yea, let them exceedingly rejoice.

Sing unto God, sing praises to his name:
Extol him that rideth upon the heavens
By his name JAH, and rejoice before him.
A father of the fatherless, and a judge of the widows,
Is God in his holy habitation.
God setteth the solitary in families:
He bringeth out those which are bound with chains:
But the rebellious dwell in a dry land.
O God, when thou wentest forth before thy people,
When thou didst march through the wilderness;
The earth shook,
The heavens also dropped at the presence of God:
Even Sinai itself was moved at the presence of God, the
      God of Israel.
Thou, O God, didst send a plentiful rain,

Whereby thou didst confirm thine inheritance, when
    it was weary.
Thy congregation hath dwelt therein:
Thou, O God, hast prepared of thy goodness for the
    poor.

The LORD gave the word:
Great was the company of those that published it.
Kings of armies did flee apace:
And she that tarried at home divided the spoil.
Though ye have lien among the pots,
Yet shall ye be as the wings of a dove covered with
    silver,
And her feathers with yellow gold.
When the Almighty scattered kings in it,
It was white as snow in Salmon.

The hill of God is as the hill of Bashan;
An high hill as the hill of Bashan.
Why leap ye, ye high hills?
This is the hill which God desireth to dwell in;
Yea, the LORD will dwell in it forever.
The chariots of God are twenty thousand,
Even thousands of angels:
The Lord is among them, as in Sinai, in the holy place.
Thou hast ascended on high, thou hast led captivity
    captive:
Thou hast received gifts for men;
Yea, for the rebellious also, that the LORD God might
    dwell among them.
Blessed be the LORD, who daily loadeth us with benefits,
Even the God of our salvation.
He that is our God is the God of salvation;
And unto GOD the LORD belong the issues from death.

But God shall wound the head of his enemies,
And the hairy scalp of such an one as goeth on still in
　　his trespasses.
The LORD said, "I will bring again from Bashan,
I will bring my people again from the depths of the sea:
That thy foot may be dipped in the blood of thine
　　enemies,
And the tongue of thy dogs in the same."

They have seen thy goings, O God;
Even the goings of my God, my King, in the sanctuary.
The singers went before, the players on instruments
　　followed after;
Among them were the damsels playing with timbrels.
Bless ye God in the congregations,
Even the LORD, from the fountain of Israel.
There is little Benjamin with their ruler,
The princes of Judah and their council,
The princes of Zebulun, and the princes of Naphtali.
Thy God hath commanded thy strength:
Strengthen, O God, that which thou hast wrought for
　　us.
Because of thy temple at Jerusalem
Shall kings bring presents unto thee.
Rebuke the company of spearmen,
The multitude of the bulls, with the calves of the
　　people,
Till every one submit himself with pieces of silver:
Scatter thou the people that delight in war.
Princes shall come out of Egypt;
Ethiopia shall soon stretch out her hands unto God.

Sing unto God, ye kingdoms of the earth;
O sing praises unto the Lord;

To him that rideth upon the heavens of heavens, which
     were of old;
Lo, he doth send out his voice, and that a mighty voice.
Ascribe ye strength unto God:
His excellency is over Israel,
And his strength is in the clouds.
O God, thou art terrible out of thy holy places:
The God of Israel is he that giveth strength and power
     unto his people.
Blessed be God.   — Psalm 68.

The Waters Are Come in Unto My Soul

SAVE me, O God;
For the waters are come in unto my soul.
I sink in deep mire, where there is no standing:
I am come into deep waters, where the floods over-
flow me.
I am weary of my crying:
My throat is dried:
Mine eyes fail while I wait for my God.
They that hate me without a cause are more than the
hairs of mine head:
They that would destroy me, being mine enemies
wrongfully, are mighty:
Then I restored that which I took not away.
O God, thou knowest my foolishness;
And my sins are not hid from thee.
Let not them that wait on thee, O LORD God of hosts,
Be ashamed for my sake:
Let not those that seek thee be confounded for my
sake, O God of Israel.

Because for thy sake I have borne reproach;
Shame hath covered my face.
I am become a stranger unto my brethren,
And an alien unto my mother's children.
For the zeal of thine house hath eaten me up;
And the reproaches of them that reproached thee are
fallen upon me.
When I wept, and chastened my soul with fasting,
That was to my reproach.
I made sackcloth also my garment;
And I became a proverb to them.

They that sit in the gate speak against me;
And I was the song of the drunkards.

But as for me, my prayer is unto thee, O Lord, in an
    acceptable time:
O God, in the multitude of thy mercy hear me,
In the truth of thy salvation.
Deliver me out of the mire, and let me not sink:
Let me be delivered from them that hate me, and out of
    the deep waters.
Let not the waterflood overflow me,
Neither let the deep swallow me up,
And let not the pit shut her mouth upon me.
Hear me, O Lord; for thy lovingkindness is good:
Turn unto me according to the multitude of thy tender
    mercies.
And hide not thy face from thy servant;
For I am in trouble: hear me speedily.
Draw nigh unto my soul, and redeem it:
Deliver me because of mine enemies.

Thou hast known my reproach, and my shame, and my
    dishonour:
Mine adversaries are all before thee.
Reproach hath broken my heart; and I am full of
    heaviness:
And I looked for some to take pity, but there was none;
And for comforters, but I found none.
They gave me also gall for my meat;
And in my thirst they gave me vinegar to drink.

Let their table become a snare before them:
And that which should have been for their welfare, let
    it become a trap.

Let their eyes be darkened, that they see not;
And make their loins continually to shake.
Pour out thine indignation upon them,
And let thy wrathful anger take hold of them.
Let their habitation be desolate;
And let none dwell in their tents.
For they persecute him whom thou hast smitten;
And they talk to the grief of those whom thou hast
  wounded.
Add iniquity unto their iniquity:
And let them not come into thy righteousness.
Let them be blotted out of the book of the living,
And not be written with the righteous.

But I am poor and sorrowful:
Let thy salvation, O God, set me up on high.
I will praise the name of God with a song,
And will magnify him with thanksgiving.
This also shall please the LORD better than an ox
Or bullock that hath horns and hoofs.
The humble shall see this, and be glad:
And your heart shall live that seek God.
For the LORD heareth the poor,
And despiseth not his prisoners.
Let the heaven and earth praise him,
The seas, and everything that moveth therein.
For God will save Zion, and will build the cities of
  Judah:
That they may dwell there, and have it in possession.
The seed also of his servants shall inherit it:
And they that love his name shall dwell therein.

— Psalm 69.

Make No Tarrying, O Lord

MAKE haste, O God, to deliver me;
    Make haste to help me, O LORD.
        Let them be ashamed and confounded that
           seek after my soul:
Let them be turned backward, and put to confusion,
That desire my hurt.
Let them be turned back for a reward of their shame
That say, "Aha, aha."
Let all those that seek thee rejoice and be glad in thee:
And let such as love thy salvation say continually,
"Let God be magnified."
But I am poor and needy:
Make haste unto me, O God:
Thou art my help and my deliverer;
O LORD, make no tarrying.   — Psalm 70.

Forsake Me Not When My Strength Faileth

William Wilberforce (1759–1833), the great reformer who moved and carried the bill in Parliament abolishing the slave-trade wrote of the Psalms, "What wonderful compositions! What a decisive proof of the divine origin of the religion to which they belong! There is in the world nothing else like them." When he was violently attacked in the House of Commons, he wrote to his wife that he had been learning the 71st Psalm, which had been a real comfort to him.

George Herbert repeated, in his last sickness, the 9th verse of the 71st Psalm, "Forsake me not when my strength faileth."

IN thee, O LORD, do I put my trust:
    Let me never be put to confusion.
    Deliver me in thy righteousness, and cause me
        to escape:
Incline thine ear unto me, and save me.
Be thou my strong habitation, whereunto I may con-
    tinually resort:
Thou hast given commandment to save me;
For thou art my rock and my fortress.

Deliver me, O my God, out of the hand of the wicked,
Out of the hand of the unrighteous and cruel man.
For thou art my hope, O Lord GOD:
Thou art my trust from my youth.
By thee have I been holden up from the womb:
Thou art he that took me out of my mother's bowels:
My praise shall be continually of thee.
I am as a wonder unto many;
But thou art my strong refuge.

Let my mouth be filled with thy praise
And with thy honour all the day.
Cast me not off in the time of old age;
Forsake me not when my strength faileth.
For mine enemies speak against me;
And they that lay wait for my soul take counsel to-
    gether,
Saying, "God hath forsaken him:
Persecute and take him; for there is none to deliver
    him."
O God, be not far from me:
O my God, make haste for my help.
Let them be confounded and consumed that are ad-
    versaries to my soul;
Let them be covered with reproach and dishonour that
    seek my hurt.

But I will hope continually,
And will yet praise thee more and more.
My mouth shall shew forth thy righteousness
And thy salvation all the day;
For I know not the numbers thereof.
I will go in the strength of the Lord God:
I will make mention of thy righteousness, even of
    thine only.
O God, thou hast taught me from my youth:
And hitherto have I declared thy wondrous works.
Now also when I am old and greyheaded, O God, for-
    sake me not;
Until I have shewed thy strength unto this generation,
And thy power to every one that is to come.
Thy righteousness also, O God, is very high,
Who hast done great things:
O God, who is like unto thee!

Thou, which hast shewed me great and sore troubles,
Shalt quicken me again,
And shalt bring me up again from the depths of the
earth.
Thou shalt increase my greatness,
And comfort me on every side.
I will also praise thee with the psaltery,
Even thy truth, O my God: unto thee will I sing with
the harp,
O thou Holy One of Israel.
My lips shall greatly rejoice when I sing unto thee;
And my soul, which thou hast redeemed.
My tongue also shall talk of thy righteousness all the
day long:
For they are confounded, for they are brought unto
shame, that seek my hurt. — Psalm 71.

Let the Whole Earth Be Filled with His Glory

Athanasius, for whom the "Athanasian creed" is called, wrote an "Exposition of the Psalms." His favorite Psalm was the 72nd.

GIVE the king thy judgments, O God,
    And thy righteousness unto the king's son.
    He shall judge thy people with righteousness,
        and thy poor with judgment.
The mountains shall bring peace to the people,
And the little hills, by righteousness.
He shall judge the poor of the people,
He shall save the children of the needy,
And shall break in pieces the oppressor.
They shall fear thee as long as the sun and moon en-
    dure,
Throughout all generations.
He shall come down like rain upon the mown grass:
As showers that water the earth.
In his days shall the righteous flourish;
And abundance of peace so long as the moon endureth.

He shall have dominion also from sea to sea,
And from the river unto the ends of the earth.
They that dwell in the wilderness shall bow before him;
And his enemies shall lick the dust.
The kings of Tarshish and of the isles shall bring pres-
    ents:
The kings of Sheba and Seba shall offer gifts.
Yea, all kings shall fall down before him:
All nations shall serve him.

For he shall deliver the needy when he crieth;
The poor also, and him that hath no helper.
He shall spare the poor and needy,
And shall save the souls of the needy.
He shall redeem their soul from deceit and violence:
And precious shall their blood be in his sight.
And he shall live, and to him shall be given of the gold
    of Sheba:
Prayer also shall be made for him continually;
And daily shall he be praised.
There shall be an handful of corn in the earth upon the
    top of the mountains;
The fruit thereof shall shake like Lebanon:
And they of the city shall flourish like grass of the
    earth.
His name shall endure forever:
His name shall be continued as long as the sun:
And men shall be blessed in him:
All nations shall call him blessed.

Blessed be the LORD God, the God of Israel,
Who only doeth wondrous things.
And blessed be his glorious name forever:
And let the whole earth be filled with his glory; Amen,
    and Amen.
The prayers of David the son of Jesse are ended.

                                            — Psalm 72.

The Clean of Heart

Admiral Coligny was severely wounded at Jarnac, while commanding the Huguenot forces. As he was being carried from the field, a wounded soldier saluted him, and whispered, "Truly God is loving unto Israel, even unto such as are of a clean heart," the 1st verse of the 73rd Psalm. This, he said afterward, restored his courage and gave him the faith to go on with the struggle. Coligny was afterward a victim of the Massacre of St. Bartholomew, August 24, 1572.

Bishop Hooper, the martyr, confined in the terrible Fleet Street prison, in a "vile and stinking chamber," wrote these words: "All men and women have this life and this world appointed to them for their winter and season of storms. The summer draweth near and then shall we be fresh, orient, sweet, amiable, pleasant, acceptable, immortal and blessed, forever and ever: and no man shall take us from it. We must, therefore, in the meantime, learn out of this verse to say unto God whether it be winter or summer, pleasure or pain, liberty or imprisonment, life or death, 'Truly God is good to Israel, even to such as are of a clean heart.'"

TRULY God is good to Israel,
　　Even to such as are of a clean heart.
　　But as for me, my feet were almost gone;
My steps had well nigh slipped.
For I was envious at the foolish,
When I saw the prosperity of the wicked.
For there are no bands in their death:
But their strength is firm.
They are not in trouble as other men;
Neither are they plagued like other men.
Therefore pride compasseth them about as a chain;
Violence covereth them as a garment.
Their eyes stand out with fatness:
They have more than heart could wish.

They are corrupt, and speak wickedly concerning op-
pression:
They speak loftily.
They set their mouth against the heavens,
And their tongue walketh through the earth.
Therefore his people return hither:
And waters of a full cup are wrung out to them.
And they say, "How doth God know?
And is there knowledge in the most High?"
Behold, these are the ungodly, who prosper in the
world;
They increase in riches.
Verily I have cleansed my heart in vain,
And washed my hands in innocency.
For all the day long have I been plagued,
And chastened every morning.

If I say, "I will speak thus";
Behold, I should offend against the generation of thy
children.
When I thought to know this,
It was too painful for me;
Until I went into the sanctuary of God;
Then understood I their end.
Surely thou didst set them in slippery places:
Thou castedst them down into destruction.
How are they brought into desolation, as in a mo-
ment!
They are utterly consumed with terrors.
As a dream when one awaketh;
So, O Lord, when thou awakest,
Thou shalt despise their image.
Thus my heart was grieved,
And I was pricked in my reins,

So foolish was I, and ignorant:
I was as a beast before thee.

Nevertheless I am continually with thee:
Thou hast holden me by my right hand.
Thou shalt guide me with thy counsel,
And afterward receive me to glory.
Whom have I in heaven but thee?
And there is none upon earth that I desire beside thee.
My flesh and my heart faileth:
But God is the strength of my heart, and my portion
    forever.
For, lo, they that are far from thee shall perish:
Thou hast destroyed all them that go a whoring from
    thee.
But it is good for me to draw near to God:
I have put my trust in the LORD God,
That I may declare all thy works.   — Psalm 73.

The Day Is Thine; the Night also Is Thine

O GOD, why hast thou cast us off forever?
Why doth thine anger smoke against the sheep
of thy pasture?
Remember thy congregation, which thou hast pur-
chased of old;
The rod of thine inheritance, which thou hast redeemed;
This Mount Zion, wherein thou hast dwelt.
Lift up thy feet unto the perpetual desolations;
Even all that the enemy hath done wickedly in the
sanctuary.
Thine enemies roar in the midst of thy congregations;
They set up their ensigns for signs.
A man was famous according as he had lifted up axes
upon the thick trees.
But now they break down the carved work thereof
At once with axes and hammers.
They have cast fire into thy sanctuary,
They have defiled by casting down the dwelling place
of thy name to the ground.
They said in their hearts, "Let us destroy them to-
gether":
They have burned up all the synagogues of God in the
land.
We see not our signs:
There is no more any prophet:
Neither is there among us any that knoweth how
long.
O God, how long shall the adversary reproach?
Shall the enemy blaspheme thy name forever?

Why withdrawest thou thy hand, even thy right hand?
Pluck it out of thy bosom.

For God is my King of old,
Working salvation in the midst of the earth.
Thou didst divide the sea by thy strength:
Thou brakest the heads of the dragons in the waters.
Thou brakest the heads of leviathan in pieces,
And gavest him to be meat to the people inhabiting the
    wilderness.
Thou didst cleave the fountain and the flood:
Thou driedst up mighty rivers.
The day is thine, the night also is thine:
Thou hast prepared the light and the sun.
Thou hast set all the borders of the earth:
Thou hast made summer and winter.

Remember this, that the enemy hath reproached, O
    LORD,
And that the foolish people have blasphemed thy name.
O deliver not the soul of thy turtledove unto the multi-
    tude of the wicked:
Forget not the congregation of thy poor forever.
Have respect unto the covenant:
For the dark places of the earth are full of the habita-
    tions of cruelty.
O let not the oppressed return ashamed:
Let the poor and needy praise thy name.
Arise, O God, plead thine own cause:
Remember how the foolish man reproacheth thee daily.
Forget not the voice of thine enemies:
The tumult of those that rise up against thee increaseth
    continually.   — Psalm 74.

God Is the Judge

UNTO thee, O God, do we give thanks,
 Unto thee do we give thanks:
  For that thy name is near thy wondrous works
   declare.
When I shall receive the congregation I will judge up-
 rightly.
The earth and all the inhabitants thereof are dissolved:
I bear up the pillars of it.

I said unto the fools, "Deal not foolishly":
And to the wicked, "Lift not up the horn:
Lift not up your horn on high:
Speak not with a stiff neck.
For promotion cometh neither from the east,
Nor from the west, nor from the south.

But God is the judge:
He putteth down one, and setteth up another.
For in the hand of the LORD there is a cup, and the wine
  is red;
It is full of mixture; and he poureth out of the same:
But the dregs thereof, all the wicked of the earth shall
  wring them out, and drink them."

But I will declare forever;
I will sing praises to the God of Jacob.
All the horns of the wicked also will I cut off;
But the horns of the righteous shall be exalted.

          — Psalm 75.

SHORES OF THE MEDITERRANEAN

Photograph by W. A. Pottenger
expressly for The Book of Life

THIS PICTURE shows the shore line of the
Great Sea at Haifa. Taken from half way
up Mount Carmel.
"Thy way is in the sea, and thy path in
the great waters, and thy footsteps are
not known."

The Wrath of Man Shall Praise Thee

IN Judah is God known:
His name is great in Israel.
In Salem also is his tabernacle,
And his dwelling place in Zion.
There brake he the arrows of the bow,
The shield, and the sword, and the battle.

Thou art more glorious and excellent than the moun-
tains of prey.
The stouthearted are spoiled, they have slept their
sleep:
And none of the men of might have found their hands.
At thy rebuke, O God of Jacob,
Both the chariot and horse are cast into a dead sleep.

Thou, even thou, art to be feared:
And who may stand in thy sight when once thou art
angry?
Thou didst cause judgment to be heard from heaven;
The earth feared, and was still,
When God arose to judgment,
To save all the meek of the earth.

Surely the wrath of man shall praise thee:
The remainder of wrath shalt thou restrain.
Vow, and pay unto the LORD your God:
Let all that be round about him bring presents unto
him that ought to be feared.
He shall cut off the spirit of princes:
He is terrible to the kings of the earth.   — Psalm 76.

Thy Way Is in the Sea

John Bunyan, after his years of spiritual struggle, found the beginning of his peace of soul in the 77th Psalm, the verses beginning "I call to remembrance my song of the night," the 6th, 7th and 8th verses.

I CRIED unto God with my voice,
Even unto God with my voice; and he gave ear
unto me.
In the day of my trouble I sought the LORD:
My sore ran in the night, and ceased not:
My soul refused to be comforted.
I remembered God, and was troubled:
I complained, and my spirit was overwhelmed.
Thou holdest mine eyes waking:
I am so troubled that I cannot speak.
I have considered the days of old,
The years of ancient times.
I call to remembrance my song in the night:
I commune with mine own heart:
And my spirit made diligent search.
Will the LORD cast off forever?
And will he be favourable no more?
Is his mercy clean gone forever?
Doth his promise fail forevermore?
Hath God forgotten to be gracious?
Hath he in anger shut up his tender mercies?

And I said, "This is my infirmity:
But I will remember the years of the right hand of the
most High.
I will remember the works of the LORD:

Surely I will remember thy wonders of old.
I will meditate also of all thy work,
And talk of thy doings."

Thy way, O God, is in the sanctuary:
Who is so great a God as our God?
Thou art the God that doest wonders:
Thou hast declared thy strength among the people.
Thou hast with thine arm redeemed thy people,
The sons of Jacob and Joseph.
The waters saw thee, O God,
The waters saw thee; they were afraid:
The depths also were troubled.
The clouds poured out water:
The skies sent out a sound:
Thine arrows also went abroad.
The voice of thy thunder was in the heaven:
The lightnings lightened the world:
The earth trembled and shook.
Thy way is in the sea,
And thy path in the great waters,
And thy footsteps are not known.
Thou leddest thy people like a flock
By the hand of Moses and Aaron. — Psalm 77.

The Dealings of God with Israel

GIVE ear, O my people, to my law:
  Incline your ears to the words of my mouth.
  I will open my mouth in a parable:
I will utter dark sayings of old:
Which we have heard and known,
And our fathers have told us.
We will not hide them from their children,
Shewing to the generation to come the praises of the
    LORD,
And his strength, and his wonderful works that he hath
    done.

For he established a testimony in Jacob,
And appointed a law in Israel,
Which he commanded our fathers,
That they should make them known to their children:
That the generation to come might know them, even
    the children which should be born;
Who should arise and declare them to their children:
That they might set their hope in God,
And not forget the works of God,
But keep his commandments:
And might not be as their fathers,
A stubborn and rebellious generation;
A generation that set not their heart aright,
And whose spirit was not stedfast with God.

The children of Ephraim, being armed, and carrying
    bows,
Turned back in the day of battle.
They kept not the covenant of God,

And refused to walk in his law;
And forgat his works,
And his wonders that he had shewed them.
Marvellous things did he in the sight of their fathers,
In the land of Egypt, in the field of Zoan.
He divided the sea, and caused them to pass through;
And he made the waters to stand as an heap.
In the daytime also he led them with a cloud,
And all the night with a light of fire.
He clave the rocks in the wilderness,
And gave them drink as out of the great depths.
He brought streams also out of the rock,
And caused waters to run down like rivers.

And they sinned yet more against him
By provoking the most High in the wilderness.
And they tempted God in their heart
By asking meat for their lust.
Yea, they spake against God;
They said, "Can God furnish a table in the wilderness?
Behold, he smote the rock,
That the waters gushed out, and the streams over-
    flowed;
Can he give bread also?
Can he provide flesh for his people?"
Therefore the LORD heard this, and was wroth:
So a fire was kindled against Jacob,
And anger also came up against Israel;
Because they believed not in God,
And trusted not in his salvation:
Though he had commanded the clouds from above,
And opened the doors of heaven,
And had rained down manna upon them to eat,
And had given them of the corn of heaven.

Man did eat angels' food:
He sent them meat to the full.
He caused an east wind to blow in the heaven:
And by his power he brought in the south wind.
He rained flesh also upon them as dust,
And feathered fowls like as the sand of the sea:
And he let it fall in the midst of their camp,
Round about their habitations.
So they did eat, and were well filled:
For he gave them their own desire;
They were not estranged from their lust.
But while their meat was yet in their mouths,
The wrath of God came upon them,
And slew the fattest of them,
And smote down the chosen men of Israel.

For all this they sinned still,
And believed not for his wondrous works.
Therefore their days did he consume in vanity,
And their years in trouble.
When he slew them,
Then they sought him:
And they returned and enquired early after God.
And they remembered that God was their rock,
And the high God their redeemer.
Nevertheless they did flatter him with their mouth,
And they lied unto him with their tongues.
For their heart was not right with him,
Neither were they stedfast in his covenant.
But he, being full of compassion,
Forgave their iniquity, and destroyed them not:
Yea, many a time turned he his anger away,
And did not stir up all his wrath.
For he remembered that they were but flesh;

A wind that passeth away, and cometh not again.

How oft did they provoke him in the wilderness,
And grieve him in the desert!
Yea, they turned back and tempted God,
And limited the Holy One of Israel.
They remembered not his hand,
Nor the day when he delivered them from the enemy.
How he had wrought his signs in Egypt,
And his wonders in the field of Zoan:
And had turned their rivers into blood;
And their floods, that they could not drink.
He sent divers sorts of flies among them, which de-
voured them;
And frogs, which destroyed them.
He gave also their increase unto the caterpiller,
And their labour unto the locust.
He destroyed their vines with hail,
And their sycamore trees with frost.
He gave up their cattle also to the hail,
And their flocks to hot thunderbolts.
He cast upon them the fierceness of his anger,
Wrath, and indignation, and trouble,
By sending evil angels among them.
He made a way to his anger;
He spared not their soul from death,
But gave their life over to the pestilence;
And smote all the firstborn in Egypt;
The chief of their strength in the tabernacles of Ham:
But made his own people to go forth like sheep,
And guided them in the wilderness like a flock.
And he led them on safely, so that they feared not:
But the sea overwhelmed their enemies.
And he brought them to the border of his sanctuary,

Even to this mountain, which his right hand had pur-
chased.
He cast out the heathen also before them,
And divided them an inheritance by line,
And made the tribes of Israel to dwell in their tents.

Yet they tempted and provoked the most high God,
And kept not his testimonies:
But turned back, and dealt unfaithfully like their
fathers:
They were turned aside like a deceitful bow.
For they provoked him to anger with their high places,
And moved him to jealousy with their graven images.
When God heard this, he was wroth,
And greatly abhorred Israel:
So that he forsook the tabernacle of Shiloh,
The tent which he placed among men;
And delivered his strength into captivity,
And his glory into the enemy's hand.
He gave his people over also unto the sword;
And was wroth with his inheritance.
The fire consumed their young men;
And their maidens were not given to marriage.
Their priests fell by the sword;
And their widows made no lamentation.

Then the LORD awaked as one out of sleep,
And like a mighty man that shouteth by reason of wine.
And he smote his enemies in the hinder parts:
He put them to a perpetual reproach.
Moreover he refused the tabernacle of Joseph,
And chose not the tribe of Ephraim:
But chose the tribe of Judah,
The Mount Zion which he loved.

And he built his sanctuary like high palaces,
Like the earth which he hath established forever.
He chose David also his servant,
And took him from the sheepfolds:
From following the ewes great with young he brought
  him
To feed Jacob his people, and Israel his inheritance.
So he fed them according to the integrity of his heart;
And guided them by the skilfulness of his hands.

—Psalm 78.

A SHEPHERD AND HIS SHEEP
Photograph by the Reverend Frederick J. Moore

A shepherd leading his flock near David's Gate, Jerusalem. This is the
typical Palestinian way of leading the sheep, by the shepherd going before them.
—*John 10:4*—The Book of Life: Volume 6, Page 296.

A Lamentation for the Nation

This Psalm was used by the Jews at their service to lament the loss of Jerusalem. It was a favorite Psalm of the Huguenots, the Puritans, and others in the stress of persecution.

O GOD, the heathen are come into thine inheritance;
    Thy holy temple have they defiled;
They have laid Jerusalem on heaps.
The dead bodies of thy servants have they given to
    be meat unto the fowls of the heaven,
The flesh of thy saints unto the beasts of the earth.
Their blood have they shed like water round about
    Jerusalem;
And there was none to bury them.
We are become a reproach to our neighbours,
A scorn and derision to them that are round about us.

How long, LORD? Wilt thou be angry forever?
Shall thy jealousy burn like fire?
Pour out thy wrath upon the heathen that have not
    known thee,
And upon the kingdoms that have not called upon
    thy name.
For they have devoured Jacob,
And laid waste his dwelling place.
O remember not against us former iniquities:
Let thy tender mercies speedily prevent us:
For we are brought very low.

Help us, O God of our salvation, for the glory of
    thy name:

The Cedars on the Slopes of Lebanon

Photograph by Professor Lewis Bayles Paton

Lebanon was always in the mind of the poets of Israel as the source of glory and beauty and strength.

Solomon's Temple was built of the lumber cut from these trees.

"It shall blossom abundantly, and rejoice even with joy and singing; the glory of Lebanon shall be given unto it, the excellency of Carmel and Sharon, they shall see the glory of the Lord, and the excellency of our God." —Isaiah 35:2.

"The hills were covered with the shadow of it, and the boughs thereof were like the goodly cedars." —Psalm 80:10.

And deliver us, and purge away our sins, for thy
name's sake.

Wherefore should the heathen say, "Where is their
God?"

Let him be known among the heathen in our sight

By the revenging of the blood of thy servants which
is shed.

Let the sighing of the prisoner come before thee;

According to the greatness of thy power preserve
thou those that are appointed to die;

And render unto our neighbours sevenfold into their
bosom

Their reproach, wherewith they have reproached thee,
O Lord.

So we thy people and sheep of thy pasture

Will give thee thanks forever:

We will shew forth thy praise to all generations.

— Psalm 79.

STREET AT JERUSALEM
Photograph by W. A. Pottenger
expressly for The Book of Life

Cause Thy Face to Shine

GIVE ear, O Shepherd of Israel,
    Thou that leadest Joseph like a flock;
    Thou that dwellest between the cherubim,
        shine forth.
Before Ephraim and Benjamin and Manasseh stir
    up thy strength,
And come and save us.
Turn us again, O God, and cause thy face to shine;
And we shall be saved.

O Lord God of hosts,
How long wilt thou be angry against the prayer of
    thy people?
Thou feedest them with the bread of tears;
And givest them tears to drink in great measure.
Thou makest us a strife unto our neighbours:
And our enemies laugh among themselves.
Turn us again, O God of hosts,
And cause thy face to shine;
And we shall be saved.

Thou hast brought a vine out of Egypt:
Thou hast cast out the heathen, and planted it.
Thou preparedst room before it,
And didst cause it to take deep root, and it filled
    the land.
The hills were covered with the shadow of it,
And the boughs thereof were like the goodly cedars.
She sent out her boughs unto the sea,
And her branches unto the river.
Why hast thou then broken down her hedges,

So that all they which pass by the way do pluck her?
The boar out of the wood doth waste it,
And the wild beast of the field doth devour it.
Return, we beseech thee, O God of hosts:
Look down from heaven, and behold, and visit this
vine;
And the vineyard which thy right hand hath planted,
And the branch that thou madest strong for thyself.
It is burned with fire, it is cut down:
They perish at the rebuke of thy countenance.
Let thy hand be upon the man of thy right hand,
Upon the son of man whom thou madest strong for
thyself.
So will not we go back from thee:
Quicken us, and we will call upon thy name.
Turn us again, O LORD God of hosts,
Cause thy face to shine; and we shall be saved.

— Psalm 80.

CEDAR OF LEBANON
Photograph by the Reverend Frederick J. Moore
This cedar from Lebanon was the gift of the Palestine Government and is
in the grounds of the new Palace of Peace, Geneva, Switzerland. The Peace
Palace on the left was opened February 17, 1936.

Give Ear, O Shepherd of Israel

SING aloud unto God our strength:
Make a joyful noise unto the God of Jacob.
Take a psalm, and bring hither the timbrel,
The pleasant harp with the psaltery.
Blow up the trumpet in the new moon,
In the time appointed, on our solemn feast day.
For this was a statute for Israel,
And a law of the God of Jacob.
This he ordained in Joseph for a testimony,
When he went out through the land of Egypt:
Where I heard a language that I understood not.

I removed his shoulder from the burden:
His hands were delivered from the pots.
Thou calledst in trouble, and I delivered thee;
I answered thee in the secret place of thunder:
I proved thee at the waters of Meribah.
Hear, O my people, and I will testify unto thee:
O Israel, if thou wilt hearken unto me;
There shall no strange god be in thee;
Neither shalt thou worship any strange god.
I am the LORD thy God,
Which brought thee out of the land of Egypt:
Open thy mouth wide, and I will fill it.

But my people would not hearken to my voice;
And Israel would none of me.
So I gave them up unto their own hearts' lust:
And they walked in their own counsels.
O that my people had hearkened unto me,
And Israel had walked in my ways!

I should soon have subdued their enemies,
And turned my hand against their adversaries.
The haters of the LORD should have submitted them-
 selves unto him:
But their time should have endured forever.
He should have fed them also with the finest of the
 wheat:
And with honey out of the rock should I have satis-
 fied thee. — Psalm 81.

Deliver the Poor and Needy

GOD standeth in the congregation of the mighty;
 He judgeth among the gods.
 How long will ye judge unjustly,
And accept the persons of the wicked?
Defend the poor and fatherless:
Do justice to the afflicted and needy.
Deliver the poor and needy:
Rid them out of the hand of the wicked.
They know not, neither will they understand;
They walk on in darkness:
All the foundations of the earth are out of course.
I have said, "Ye are gods;
And all of you are children of the most High."
But ye shall die like men,
And fall like one of the princes.

Arise, O God, judge the earth:
For thou shalt inherit all nations. — Psalm 82.

A Prayer for Help Against the Enemies of Israel

KEEP not thou silence, O God:
   Hold not thy peace, and be not still, O God.
   For, lo, thine enemies make a tumult:
And they that hate thee have lifted up the head.
They have taken crafty counsel against thy people,
And consulted against thy hidden ones.
They have said, "Come, and let us cut them off from
     being a nation;
That the name of Israel may be no more in remem-
     brance."
For they have consulted together with one consent:
They are confederate against thee:
The tabernacles of Edom, and the Ishmaelites;
Of Moab, and the Hagarenes;
Gebal, and Ammon, and Amalek;
The Philistines with the inhabitants of Tyre;
Assur also is joined with them:
They have holpen the children of Lot.

Do unto them as unto the Midianites;
As to Sisera, as to Jabin, at the brook of Kison:
Which perished at En-dor:
They became as dung for the earth.
Make their nobles like Oreb, and like Zeeb:
Yea, all their princes as Zebah, and as Zalmunna:
Who said, "Let us take to ourselves
The houses of God in possession."
O my God, make them like a wheel;
As the stubble before the wind.

As the fire burneth a wood,
And as the flame setteth the mountains on fire;
So persecute them with thy tempest,
And make them afraid with thy storm.
Fill their faces with shame;
That they may seek thy name, O LORD.
Let them be confounded and troubled forever;
Yea, let them be put to shame, and perish:
That men may know that thou, whose name alone is
    JEHOVAH,
Art the most high over all the earth.   — Psalm 83.

Blessed Is the Man Whose Strength Is in Thee

Carlyle wrote, "Courage, my brave brothers all! Let us be found faithful and we shall not fail. Surely as the blue dome of heaven encircles us all, so does the Providence of the Lord of heaven. 'He will withhold no good thing from those that love him': Psalm 84:11. Then as it is the ancient Psalmist's faith, let it likewise be ours. It is the Alpha and Omega, I reckon, of all possessions that can belong to man."

HOW amiable are thy tabernacles, O LORD of hosts!
My soul longeth, yea, even fainteth for the courts of the LORD:
My heart and my flesh crieth out for the living God.
Yea, the sparrow hath found an house,
And the swallow a nest for herself,
Where she may lay her young,
Even thine altars, O LORD of hosts,
My King, and my God.
Blessed are they that dwell in thy house:
They will be still praising thee.

Blessed is the man whose strength is in thee;
In whose heart are the ways of them.
Who passing through the valley of Baca make it a well;
The rain also filleth the pools.
They go from strength to strength,
Every one of them in Zion appeareth before God.

O LORD God of hosts, hear my prayer:
Give ear, O God of Jacob.

Behold, O God our shield,
And look upon the face of thine anointed.
For a day in thy courts is better than a thousand.
I had rather be a doorkeeper in the house of my God,
Than to dwell in the tents of wickedness.
For the LORD God is a sun and shield:
The LORD will give grace and glory:
No good thing will he withhold from them that walk
    uprightly.
O LORD of hosts,
Blessed is the man that trusteth in thee.   — Psalm 84

Revive Us Again

LORD, thou hast been favourable unto thy land:
Thou hast brought back the captivity of Jacob.
Thou hast forgiven the iniquity of thy people,
Thou hast covered all their sin.
Thou hast taken away all thy wrath:
Thou hast turned thyself from the fierceness of thine
anger.
Turn us, O God of our salvation,
And cause thine anger toward us to cease.
Wilt thou be angry with us forever?
Wilt thou draw out thine anger to all generations?
Wilt thou not revive us again:
That thy people may rejoice in thee?
Shew us thy mercy, O LORD,
And grant us thy salvation.

I will hear what God the LORD will speak:
For he will speak peace unto his people, and to his
saints:
But let them not turn again to folly.
Surely his salvation is nigh them that fear him;
That glory may dwell in our land.
Mercy and truth are met together;
Righteousness and peace have kissed each other.
Truth shall spring out of the earth;
And righteousness shall look down from heaven.
Yea, the LORD shall give that which is good;
And our land shall yield her increase.
Righteousness shall go before him;
And shall set us in the way of his steps.　— Psalm 85.

A Street in Tyre

Photograph by Professor Lewis Bayles Paton

Full of Compassion and Mercy

In "Rizpah," Tennyson makes use of the 86th Psalm, the 15th verse.

"Sin? O yes—we are sinners, I know—let all that be,
        And read me a Bible verse of the Lord's goodness
            towards men—
'Full of compassion and mercy, the Lord', let me hear it
        again;
    'Full of compassion and mercy—long suffering!' Yes,
        O, Yes!"

BOW down thine ear, O LORD, hear me:
        For I am poor and needy.
            Preserve my soul; for I am holy:
O thou my God, save thy servant that trusteth in thee.
Be merciful unto me, O LORD:
For I cry unto thee daily.
Rejoice the soul of thy servant:
For unto thee, O LORD, do I lift up my soul.
For thou, LORD, art good, and ready to forgive;
And plenteous in mercy unto all them that call upon
        thee.

Give ear, O LORD, unto my prayer;
And attend to the voice of my supplications.
In the day of my trouble I will call upon thee:
For thou wilt answer me.
Among the gods there is none like unto thee, O LORD;
Neither are there any works like unto thy works.
All nations whom thou hast made shall come and
        worship before thee, O LORD;
And shall glorify thy name.

For thou art great, and doest wondrous things:
Thou art God alone.

Teach me thy way, O Lord; I will walk in thy truth:
Unite my heart to fear thy name.
I will praise thee, O Lord my God, with all my heart:
And I will glorify thy name forevermore.
For great is thy mercy toward me:
And thou hast delivered my soul from the lowest hell.

O God, the proud are risen against me,
And the assemblies of violent men have sought after
    my soul;
And have not set thee before them.
But thou, O Lord, art a God full of compassion, and
    gracious,
Long-suffering, and plenteous in mercy and truth.
O turn unto me, and have mercy upon me;
Give thy strength unto thy servant,
And save the son of thine handmaid.
Shew me a token for good;
That they which hate me may see it, and be ashamed:
Because thou, Lord, hast holpen me, and comforted
    me.   — Psalm 86.

Glorious Things Are Spoken of Thee, O City of God

Augustine used the 3rd verse of the 87th Psalm, "Glorious things are spoken of thee, O city of God," for the motto of his great religious work, "The City of God."

HIS foundation is in the holy mountains.
  The LORD loveth the gates of Zion
  More than all the dwellings of Jacob.
Glorious things are spoken of thee,
O city of God.
I will make mention of Rahab and Babylon to them
  that know me:
Behold Philistia, and Tyre, with Ethiopia; this man
  was born there.
And of Zion it shall be said, "This and that man was
  born in her:
And the highest himself shall establish her."
The LORD shall count, when he writeth up the people,
That this man was born there.
As well the singers as the players on instruments
  shall be there:
All my springs are in thee.   — Psalm 87.

A Song of Deep Distress

O LORD God of my salvation,
    I have cried day and night before thee:
    Let my prayer come before thee:
Incline thine ear unto my cry;
For my soul is full of troubles:
And my life draweth nigh unto the grave.
I am counted with them that go down into the pit:
I am as a man that hath no strength:
Free among the dead,
Like the slain that lie in the grave,
Whom thou rememberest no more:
And they are cut off from thy hand.

Thou hast laid me in the lowest pit,
In darkness, in the deeps.
Thy wrath lieth hard upon me,
And thou hast afflicted me with all thy waves.
Thou hast put away mine acquaintance far from me;
Thou hast made me an abomination unto them:
I am shut up, and I cannot come forth.

Mine eye mourneth by reason of affliction:
LORD, I have called daily upon thee,
I have stretched out my hands unto thee.
Wilt thou shew wonders to the dead?
Shall the dead arise and praise thee?
Shall thy lovingkindness be declared in the grave?
Or thy faithfulness in destruction?
Shall thy wonders be known in the dark?
And thy righteousness in the land of forgetfulness?

But unto thee have I cried, O LORD;
And in the morning shall my prayer prevent thee.
LORD, why castest thou off my soul?
Why hidest thou thy face from me?
I am afflicted and ready to die from my youth up:
While I suffer thy terrors I am distracted.
Thy fierce wrath goeth over me;
Thy terrors have cut me off.
They came round about me daily like water;
They compassed me about together.
Lover and friend hast thou put far from me,
And mine acquaintance into darkness.　　— Psalm 88.

Mercy Shall Be Built up Forever

I WILL sing of the mercies of the LORD forever:
  With my mouth will I make known thy faith-
    fulness to all generations.
For I have said, "Mercy shall be built up forever:
Thy faithfulness shalt thou establish in the very
    heavens."
I have made a covenant with my chosen,
I have sworn unto David, my servant,
Thy seed will I establish forever,
And build up thy throne to all generations.

And the heavens shall praise thy wonders, O LORD:
Thy faithfulness also in the congregation of the
    saints.
For who in the heaven can be compared unto the
    LORD?
Who among the sons of the mighty can be likened
    unto the LORD?
God is greatly to be feared in the assembly of the
    saints,
And to be had in reverence of all them that are about
    him.

O LORD God of hosts,
Who is a strong LORD like unto thee?
Or to thy faithfulness round about thee?
Thou rulest the raging of the sea:
When the waves thereof arise, thou stillest them.
Thou hast broken Rahab in pieces, as one that is
    slain;

Thou hast scattered thine enemies with the strong
    arm.
The heavens are thine, the earth also is thine:
As for the world and the fulness thereof, thou hast
    founded them.
The north and the south thou hast created them:
Tabor and Hermon shall rejoice in thy name.
Thou hast a mighty arm:
Strong is thy hand, and high is thy right hand.
Justice and judgment are the habitation of thy throne:
Mercy and truth shall go before thy face.
Blessed is the people that know the joyful sound:
They shall walk, O LORD, in the light of thy coun-
    tenance.
In thy name shall they rejoice all the day:
And in thy righteousness shall they be exalted.
For thou art the glory of their strength:
And in thy favour our horn shall be exalted.
For the LORD is our defence;
And the Holy One of Israel is our king.

Then thou spakest in vision to thy holy one,
And saidst, "I have laid help upon one that is mighty;
I have exalted one chosen out of the people.
I have found David, my servant;
With my holy oil have I anointed him:
With whom my hand shall be established:
Mine arm also shall strengthen him.
The enemy shall not exact upon him;
Nor the son of wickedness afflict him.
And I will beat down his foes before his face,
And plague them that hate him.
But my faithfulness and my mercy shall be with
    him:

And in my name shall his horn be exalted.
I will set his hand also in the sea,
And his right hand in the rivers.
He shall cry unto me, 'Thou art my father,
My God, and the rock of my salvation.'
Also I will make him my firstborn,
Higher than the kings of the earth.
My mercy will I keep for him forevermore,
And my covenant shall stand fast with him.
His seed also will I make to endure forever,
And his throne as the days of heaven.
If his children forsake my law,
And walk not in my judgments;
If they break my statutes,
And keep not my commandments;
Then will I visit their transgression with the rod,
And their iniquity with stripes.
Nevertheless my lovingkindness will I not utterly
　　take from him,
Nor suffer my faithfulness to fail.
My covenant will I not break,
Nor alter the thing that is gone out of my lips.
Once have I sworn by my holiness
That I will not lie unto David.
His seed shall endure forever,
And his throne as the sun before me.
It shall be established forever as the moon,
And as a faithful witness in heaven."

But thou hast cast off and abhorred,
Thou hast been wroth with thine anointed.
Thou hast made void the covenant of thy servant:
Thou hast profaned his crown by casting it to the
　　ground.

Thou hast broken down all his hedges;
Thou hast brought his strongholds to ruin.
All that pass by the way spoil him:
He is a reproach to his neighbours.
Thou hast set up the right hand of his adversaries;
Thou hast made all his enemies to rejoice.
Thou hast also turned the edge of his sword,
And hast not made him to stand in the battle.
Thou hast made his glory to cease,
And cast his throne down to the ground.
The days of his youth hast thou shortened:
Thou hast covered him with shame.

How long, LORD? Wilt thou hide thyself forever?
Shall thy wrath burn like fire?
Remember how short my time is:
Wherefore hast thou made all men in vain?
What man is he that liveth, and shall not see death?
Shall he deliver his soul from the hand of the grave?
LORD, where are thy former lovingkindnesses,
Which thou swarest unto David in thy truth?
Remember, LORD, the reproach of thy servants;
How I do bear in my bosom the reproach of all the
    mighty people;
Wherewith thine enemies have reproached, O LORD;
Wherewith they have reproached the footsteps of
    thine anointed.
Blessed be the LORD forevermore.

Amen, and Amen.   — Psalm 89.

Through All Generations

John Hampden, the great Puritan leader, fell in a skirmish in the early days of the Civil War in England. His soldiers chanted the 90th Psalm as they carried his body to the grave.

LORD, thou hast been our dwelling place
    In all generations.
Before the mountains were brought forth,
Or ever thou hadst formed the earth and the world,
Even from everlasting to everlasting, thou art God.
Thou turnest man to destruction;
And sayest, "Return, ye children of men."
For a thousand years in thy sight
Are but as yesterday when it is past,
And as a watch in the night.
Thou carriest them away as with a flood; they are
    as a sleep:
In the morning they are like grass which groweth up.
In the morning it flourisheth, and groweth up;
In the evening it is cut down, and withereth.

For we are consumed by thine anger,
And by thy wrath are we troubled.
Thou hast set our iniquities before thee,
Our secret sins in the light of thy countenance.
For all our days are passed away in thy wrath:
We spend our years as a tale that is told.
The days of our years are threescore years and ten;
And if by reason of strength they be fourscore years,
Yet is their strength labour and sorrow;
For it is soon cut off, and we fly away.
Who knoweth the power of thine anger?

Even according to thy fear, so is thy wrath.
So teach us to number our days,
That we may apply our hearts unto wisdom.

Return, O LORD, how long?
And let it repent thee concerning thy servants.
O satisfy us early with thy mercy;
That we may rejoice and be glad all our days.
Make us glad according to the days wherein thou
    hast afflicted us,
And the years wherein we have seen evil.
Let thy work appear unto thy servants,
And thy glory unto their children.
And let the beauty of the LORD our God be upon us:
And establish thou the work of our hands upon us;
Yea, the work of our hands establish thou it.

— Psalm 90.

The Great Deliverance of God

Henri de Rohan, one of the most distinguished leaders of the Huguenot cause in France, when threatened with assassination, at the darkest hour of the cause, wrote to his mother that he had no fear, for, he said, "He that dwelleth in the secret place of the most High shall abide under the shadow of the Almighty."

John Calvin's colleague at Geneva was Theodore de Beza. Though religious in his youth, he later became absorbed in worldly interests until a dangerous illness brought him again to devote himself to religion. When he first attended the service of the Reformed Assembly at Geneva, the congregation was singing Psalm 91. The opening words became his constant support, conquering his fears and giving him courage for his many trials.

HE that dwelleth in the secret place of the most High
Shall abide under the shadow of the Almighty.
I will say of the LORD, "He is my refuge and my fortress:
My God; in him will I trust."
Surely he shall deliver thee from the snare of the fowler,
And from the noisome pestilence.
He shall cover thee with his feathers,
And under his wings shalt thou trust:
His truth shall be thy shield and buckler.

Thou shalt not be afraid for the terror by night;
Nor for the arrow that flieth by day;
Nor for the pestilence that walketh in darkness;
Nor for the destruction that wasteth at noonday.
A thousand shall fall at thy side,
And ten thousand at thy right hand;
But it shall not come nigh thee.

Only with thine eyes shalt thou behold
And see the reward of the wicked.

Because thou hast made the LORD, which is my
    refuge,
Even the most High, thy habitation;
There shall no evil befall thee,
Neither shall any plague come nigh thy dwelling.
For he shall give his angels charge over thee,
To keep thee in all thy ways.
They shall bear thee up in their hands,
Lest thou dash thy foot against a stone.
Thou shalt tread upon the lion and adder:
The young lion and the dragon shalt thou trample
    under feet.

Because he hath set his love upon me,
Therefore will I deliver him:
I will set him on high, because he hath known my
    name.
He shall call upon me, and I will answer him:
I will be with him in trouble;
I will deliver him, and honour him.
With long life will I satisfy him,
And shew him my salvation.   — Psalm 91.

Thou, O Lord, Hast Made Me Glad

IT is a good thing to give thanks unto the LORD,
　And to sing praises unto thy name, O most
　　High:
To shew forth thy lovingkindness in the morning,
And thy faithfulness every night,
Upon an instrument of ten strings, and upon the
　　psaltery;
Upon the harp with a solemn sound.
For thou, LORD, hast made me glad through thy
　　work:
I will triumph in the works of thy hands.

O LORD, how great are thy works!
And thy thoughts are very deep.
A brutish man knoweth not;
Neither doth a fool understand this.
When the wicked spring as the grass,
And when all the workers of iniquity do flourish;
It is that they shall be destroyed forever:

But thou, LORD, art most high forevermore.
For, lo, thine enemies, O LORD,
For, lo, thine enemies shall perish;
All the workers of iniquity shall be scattered.
But my horn shalt thou exalt like the horn of an
　　unicorn:
I shall be anointed with fresh oil.
Mine eye also shall see my desire on mine enemies,
And mine ears shall hear my desire of the wicked
　　that rise up against me.

The righteous shall flourish like the palm-tree:
He shall grow like a cedar in Lebanon.
Those that be planted in the house of the LORD
Shall flourish in the courts of our God.
They shall still bring forth fruit in old age;
They shall be fat and flourishing;
To shew that the LORD is upright:
He is my rock, and there is no unrighteousness in
    him.   — Psalm 92.

ROAD FROM JERICHO TO
BETHLEHEM
*Photograph by W. A. Pottenger
expressly for The Book of Life*

The Hospice of St. John is seen in
the distance.

The Lord Reigneth

THE LORD reigneth, he is clothed with majesty;
The LORD is clothed with strength, wherewith
he hath girded himself:
The world also is stablished, that it cannot be moved.
Thy throne is established of old:
Thou art from everlasting.

The floods have lifted up, O LORD,
The floods have lifted up their voice;
The floods lift up their waves.
The LORD on high is mightier than the noise of many
waters,
Yea, than the mighty waves of the sea.

Thy testimonies are very sure:
Holiness becometh thine house,
O LORD, forever. — Psalm 93.

NEAR JERUSALEM
Photograph by W. A. Pottenger expressly for The Book of Life
The Tower of the Hospice of Saint John is seen through the trees.

He That Formed the Eye, Shall He Not See?

O LORD God, to whom vengeance belongeth;
O God, to whom vengeance belongeth, shew
thyself.
Lift up thyself, thou judge of the earth:
Render a reward to the proud.
LORD, how long shall the wicked,
How long shall the wicked triumph?
How long shall they utter and speak hard things?
And all the workers of iniquity boast themselves?
They break in pieces thy people, O LORD,
And afflict thine heritage.
They slay the widow and the stranger,
And murder the fatherless.
Yet they say, "The LORD shall not see,
Neither shall the God of Jacob regard it."

Understand, ye brutish among the people:
And ye fools, when will ye be wise?
He that planted the ear, shall he not hear?
He that formed the eye, shall he not see?
He that chastiseth the heathen, shall not he correct?
He that teacheth man knowledge, shall not he know?
The LORD knoweth the thoughts of man,
That they are vanity.

Blessed is the man whom thou chastenest, O LORD,
And teachest him out of thy law;
That thou mayest give him rest from the days of
adversity,
Until the pit be digged for the wicked.

For the LORD will not cast off his people,
Neither will he forsake his inheritance.
But judgment shall return unto righteousness:
And all the upright in heart shall follow it.

Who will rise up for me against the evildoers?
Or who will stand up for me against the workers of
    iniquity?
Unless the LORD had been my help,
My soul had almost dwelt in silence.
When I said, "My foot slippeth";
Thy mercy, O LORD, held me up.
In the multitude of my thoughts within me
Thy comforts delight my soul.

Shall the throne of iniquity have fellowship with
    thee,
Which frameth mischief by a law?
They gather themselves together against the soul of
    the righteous,
And condemn the innocent blood.
But the LORD is my defence;
And my God is the rock of my refuge.
And he shall bring upon them their own iniquity,
And shall cut them off in their own wickedness;
Yea, the LORD our God shall cut them off.

                                    — Psalm 94.

The Sea Is His and His Hands Formed the Dry Land

The 95th Psalm was the battle-hymn of the Knights Templar.

O COME, let us sing unto the LORD:
    Let us make a joyful noise to the rock of our
      salvation.
Let us come before his presence with thanksgiving,
And make a joyful noise unto him with psalms.
For the LORD is a great God,
And a great King above all gods.
In his hand are the deep places of the earth:
The strength of the hills is his also.
The sea is his, and he made it:
And his hands formed the dry land.
O come, let us worship and bow down:
Let us kneel before the LORD our maker.
For he is our God;
And we are the people of his pasture, and the sheep
    of his hand.

To-day if ye will hear his voice,
Harden not your heart, as in the provocation,
And as in the day of temptation in the wilderness:
When your fathers tempted me,
Proved me, and saw my work.
Forty years long was I grieved with this generation,
And said, "It is a people that do err in their heart,
And they have not known my ways:
Unto whom I sware in my wrath
That they should not enter into my rest."

                                     — Psalm 95

The Beauty of Holiness

O SING unto the LORD a new song:
  Sing unto the LORD, all the earth.
  Sing unto the LORD, bless his name;
Shew forth his salvation from day to day.
Declare his glory among the heathen,
His wonders among all people.
For the LORD is great, and greatly to be praised:
He is to be feared above all gods.
For all the gods of the nations are idols:
But the LORD made the heavens.
Honour and majesty are before him:
Strength and beauty are in his sanctuary.

Give unto the LORD, O ye kindreds of the people,
Give unto the LORD glory and strength.
Give unto the LORD the glory due unto his name:
Bring an offering, and come into his courts.
O worship the LORD in the beauty of holiness:
Fear before him, all the earth.

Say among the heathen that the LORD reigneth:
The world also shall be established that it shall not
      be moved:
He shall judge the people righteously.
Let the heavens rejoice, and let the earth be glad;
Let the sea roar, and the fulness thereof.
Let the field be joyful, and all that is therein:
Then shall all the trees of the wood rejoice
Before the LORD: for he cometh,
For he cometh to judge the earth:
He shall judge the world with righteousness,
And the people with his truth.   — Psalm 96.

Clouds and Darkness Are Round About Him

THE Lord reigneth; let the earth rejoice;
  Let the multitude of isles be glad thereof.
    Clouds and darkness are round about him:
Righteousness and judgment are the habitation of
    his throne.
A fire goeth before him,
And burneth up his enemies round about.
His lightnings enlightened the world:
The earth saw, and trembled.
The hills melted like wax at the presence of the Lord,
At the presence of the Lord of the whole earth.
The heavens declare his righteousness,
And all the people see his glory.

Confounded be all they that serve graven images,
That boast themselves of idols:
Worship him, all ye gods.
Zion heard, and was glad;
And the daughters of Judah rejoiced
Because of thy judgments, O Lord.
For thou, Lord, art high above all the earth:
Thou art exalted far above all gods.

Ye that love the Lord, hate evil:
He preserveth the souls of his saints;
He delivereth them out of the hand of the wicked.
Light is sown for the righteous,
And gladness for the upright in heart.
Rejoice in the Lord, ye righteous;
And give thanks at the remembrance of his holiness.

— Psalm 97.

A Song of the Sea

O SING unto the LORD a new song;
  For he hath done marvellous things:
  His right hand, and his holy arm, hath gotten
    him the victory.
The LORD hath made known his salvation:
His righteousness hath he openly shewed in the
  sight of the heathen.
He hath remembered his mercy and his truth toward
  the house of Israel:
All the ends of the earth have seen the salvation of
  our God.

Make a joyful noise unto the LORD, all the earth:
Make a loud noise, and rejoice, and sing praise.
Sing unto the LORD with the harp;
With the harp, and the voice of a psalm.
With trumpets and sound of cornet
Make a joyful noise before the LORD, the King.

Let the sea roar, and the fulness thereof;
The world, and they that dwell therein.
Let the floods clap their hands:
Let the hills be joyful together
Before the LORD; for he cometh to judge the earth:
With righteousness shall he judge the world,
And the people with equity.   — Psalm 98.

Worship at His Footstool

THE Lord reigneth; let the people tremble:
    He sitteth between the cherubim; let the earth
      be moved.
The Lord is great in Zion;
And he is high above all the people.
Let them praise thy great and terrible name;
For it is holy.

The king's strength also loveth judgment;
Thou dost establish equity,
Thou executest judgment and righteousness in Jacob.
Exalt ye the Lord our God,
And worship at his footstool;
For he is holy.

Moses and Aaron among his priests,
And Samuel among them that call upon his name;
They called upon the Lord, and he answered them.
He spake unto them in the cloudy pillar:
They kept his testimonies, and the ordinance that he
    gave them.
Thou answeredst them, O Lord our God:
Thou wast a God that forgavest them,
Though thou tookest vengeance of their inventions.
Exalt the Lord our God,
And worship at his holy hill;
For the Lord our God is holy.   — Psalm 99.

Make a Joyful Noise Unto the Lord, All Ye Lands

Longfellow, in "The Courtship of Miles Standish," wrote,

"Heard, as he drew near the door, the musical voice of Priscilla
Singing the hundredth Psalm, the grand old Puritan anthem,
Music that Luther sang to the sacred words of the Psalmist,
Full of the breath of the Lord, consoling and comforting many."

MAKE a joyful noise unto the LORD, all ye lands.
Serve the LORD with gladness:
Come before his presence with singing.
Know ye that the LORD he is God:
It is he that hath made us, and not we ourselves;
We are his people, and the sheep of his pasture.

Enter into his gates with thanksgiving,
And into his courts with praise:
Be thankful unto him, and bless his name.
For the LORD is good; his mercy is everlasting;
And his truth endureth to all generations.   — Psalm 100.

𝕴 𝖂𝖎𝖑𝖑 𝕾𝖎𝖓𝖌 𝖔𝖋 𝕸𝖊𝖗𝖈𝖞 𝖆𝖓𝖉 𝕵𝖚𝖉𝖌𝖒𝖊𝖓𝖙

Bacon wrote in his "Mirror for Magistrates," "King David propounded a rule to himself for the choice of his courtiers. He was a wise and good king, and a wise and good king shall do well to follow such a good example: and if he find any to be faulty, which perhaps cannot suddenly be discovered, let him take on him this resolution as King David did, 'There shall no deceitful person dwell in my house.'"—Psalm 101:7.

𝕴 WILL sing of mercy and judgment:
Unto thee, O LORD, will I sing.
I will behave myself wisely in a perfect way.
O when wilt thou come unto me?
I will walk within my house with a perfect heart.
I will set no wicked thing before mine eyes:
I hate the work of them that turn aside;
It shall not cleave to me.
A froward heart shall depart from me:
I will not know a wicked person.

Whoso privily slandereth his neighbour, him will I cut
off:
Him that hath an high look and a proud heart will not
I suffer.
Mine eyes shall be upon the faithful of the land, that
they may dwell with me:
He that walketh in a perfect way, he shall serve me.
He that worketh deceit shall not dwell within my
house:
He that telleth lies shall not tarry in my sight.
I will early destroy all the wicked of the land;
That I may cut off all wicked doers from the city of
the LORD.   — Psalm 101.

My Days Are Like a Shadow

HEAR my prayer, O LORD,
And let my cry come unto thee.
Hide not thy face from me in the day when I
am in trouble;
Incline thine ear unto me:
In the day when I call answer me speedily.
For my days are consumed like smoke,
And my bones are burned as an hearth.
My heart is smitten, and withered like grass;
So that I forget to eat my bread.
By reason of the voice of my groaning
My bones cleave to my skin.
I am like a pelican of the wilderness:
I am like an owl of the desert.
I watch, and am as a sparrow alone upon the house-
top.
Mine enemies reproach me all the day;
And they that are mad against me are sworn against
me.
For I have eaten ashes like bread,
And mingled my drink with weeping,
Because of thine indignation and thy wrath:
For thou hast lifted me up, and cast me down.
My days are like a shadow that declineth;
And I am withered like grass.
But thou, O LORD, shalt endure forever;
And thy remembrance unto all generations.
Thou shalt arise, and have mercy upon Zion:
For the time to favour her, yea, the set time, is come.
For thy servants take pleasure in her stones,
And favour the dust thereof.

So the heathen shall fear the name of the LORD,
And all the kings of the earth thy glory.
When the LORD shall build up Zion,
He shall appear in his glory.
He will regard the prayer of the destitute,
And not despise their prayer.
This shall be written for the generation to come:
And the people which shall be created shall praise the
    LORD.
For he hath looked down from the height of his sanc-
    tuary;
From heaven did the LORD behold the earth;
To hear the groaning of the prisoner;
To loose those that are appointed to death;
To declare the name of the LORD in Zion,
And his praise in Jerusalem;
When the people are gathered together,
And the kingdoms, to serve the LORD.
He weakened my strength in the way;
He shortened my days.
I said, "O my God, take me not away in the midst of
    my days:
Thy years are throughout all generations.
Of old hast thou laid the foundation of the earth:
And the heavens are the work of thy hands.
They shall perish, but thou shalt endure:
Yea, all of them shall wax old like a garment;
As a vesture shalt thou change them, and they shall
    be changed:
But thou art the same,
And thy years shall have no end.
The children of thy servants shall continue,
And their seed shall be established before thee."

— Psalm 102.

Like as a Father Pitieth His Children

When Livingstone disappeared into the jungles of Central Africa in 1866, he was not seen again until he was found by Stanley in 1872, at Ujiji, in a starving condition. Stanley returned to the coast for supplies and provisions, which did not reach Livingstone for five months. At last they came, and the entry in his diary for August 9, 1872, reads: "I do most devoutly thank the Lord for his goodness in bringing my men near to this. Three came to-day and how thankful I am, I cannot express. It is well—the men who were with Mr. Stanley came again to me. 'Bless the Lord, O my soul, and all that is within me, bless his holy name.'"—Psalm 103:1.

BLESS the LORD, O my soul:
And all that is within me, bless his holy name.
Bless the LORD, O my soul,
And forget not all his benefits:
Who forgiveth all thine iniquities;
Who healeth all thy diseases;
Who redeemeth thy life from destruction;
Who crowneth thee with lovingkindness and tender
    mercies;
Who satisfieth thy mouth with good things;
So that thy youth is renewed like the eagle's.

The LORD executeth righteousness
And judgment for all that are oppressed.
He made known his ways unto Moses,
His acts unto the children of Israel.
The LORD is merciful and gracious,
Slow to anger, and plenteous in mercy.
He will not always chide:
Neither will he keep his anger forever.
He hath not dealt with us after our sins;

Nor rewarded us according to our iniquities.
For as the heaven is high above the earth,
So great is his mercy toward them that fear him.
As far as the east is from the west,
So far hath he removed our transgressions from us.
Like as a father pitieth his children,
So the LORD pitieth them that fear him.
For he knoweth our frame;
He remembereth that we are dust.
As for man, his days are as grass:
As a flower of the field, so he flourisheth.
For the wind passeth over it, and it is gone;
And the place thereof shall know it no more.
But the mercy of the LORD is from everlasting to ever-
        lasting upon them that fear him,
And his righteousness unto children's children;
To such as keep his covenant,
And to those that remember his commandments to do
        them.

The LORD hath prepared his throne in the heavens:
And his kingdom ruleth over all.
Bless the LORD, ye his angels,
That excel in strength, that do his commandments,
Hearkening unto the voice of his word.
Bless ye the LORD, all ye his hosts;
Ye ministers of his, that do his pleasure.
Bless the LORD, all his works in all places of his
        dominion:
Bless the LORD, O my soul.   — Psalm 103.

He Covers Himself with Light as with a Garment

Alexander von Humboldt (1769–1859), the scientist, said, "A single Psalm, the 104th, may be said to present a picture of the entire Cosmos. We are astonished to see, within the compass of a poem of such small dimensions, the universe, the heavens and the earth, thus drawn with a few grand strokes."

BLESS the LORD, O my soul.
O LORD my God, thou art very great;
Thou art clothed with honour and majesty.
Who coverest thyself with light as with a garment:
Who stretchest out the heavens like a curtain:
Who layeth the beams of his chambers in the waters:
Who maketh the clouds his chariot:
Who walketh upon the wings of the wind:
Who maketh his angels spirits;
His ministers a flaming fire:
Who laid the foundations of the earth,
That it should not be removed forever.
Thou coveredst it with the deep as with a garment:
The waters stood above the mountains.
At thy rebuke they fled;
At the voice of thy thunder they hasted away.
They go up by the mountains;
They go down by the valleys
Unto the place which thou hast founded for them.
Thou hast set a bound that they may not pass over;
That they turn not again to cover the earth.

He sendeth the springs into the valleys,
Which run among the hills.
They give drink to every beast of the field:

The wild asses quench their thirst.
By them shall the fowls of the heaven have their habi-
  tation,
Which sing among the branches.
He watereth the hills from his chambers:
The earth is satisfied with the fruit of thy works.

He causeth the grass to grow for the cattle,
And herb for the service of man:
That he may bring forth food out of the earth;
And wine that maketh glad the heart of man,
And oil to make his face to shine,
And bread which strengtheneth man's heart.
The trees of the LORD are full of sap;
The cedars of Lebanon, which he hath planted;
Where the birds make their nests:
As for the stork, the fir-trees are her house.
The high hills are a refuge for the wild goats;
And the rocks for the conies.

He appointed the moon for seasons:
The sun knoweth his going down.
Thou makest darkness, and it is night:
Wherein all the beasts of the forest do creep forth.
The young lions roar after their prey,
And seek their meat from God.
The sun ariseth, they gather themselves together,
And lay them down in their dens.
Man goeth forth unto his work
And to his labour until the evening.

O LORD, how manifold are thy works!
In wisdom hast thou made them all:
The earth is full of thy riches.

So is this great and wide sea,
Wherein are things creeping innumerable,
Both small and great beasts.
There go the ships:
There is that leviathan, whom thou hast made to play
    therein.
These wait all upon thee;
That thou mayest give them their meat in due season.
That thou givest them they gather:
Thou openest thine hand, they are filled with good.
Thou hidest thy face, they are troubled:
Thou takest away their breath, they die,
And return to their dust.
Thou sendest forth thy spirit, they are created:
And thou renewest the face of the earth.

The glory of the LORD shall endure forever:
The LORD shall rejoice in his works.
He looketh on the earth, and it trembleth:
He toucheth the hills, and they smoke.
I will sing unto the LORD as long as I live:
I will sing praise to my God while I have my being.
My meditation of him shall be sweet:
I will be glad in the LORD.
Let the sinners be consumed out of the earth,
And let the wicked be no more.
Bless thou the LORD, O my soul.
Praise ye the LORD.   — Psalm 104.

Make Known His Mighty Deeds

O GIVE thanks unto the LORD; call upon his name.
Make known his deeds among the people.
Sing unto him, sing psalms unto him:
Talk ye of all his wondrous works.
Glory ye in his holy name:
Let the heart of them rejoice that seek the LORD.
Seek the LORD, and his strength:
Seek his face evermore.
Remember his marvellous works that he hath done;
His wonders, and the judgments of his mouth;
O ye seed of Abraham, his servant,
Ye children of Jacob his chosen.

He is the LORD our God:
His judgments are in all the earth.
He hath remembered his covenant forever,
The word which he commanded to a thousand genera-
tions.
Which covenant he made with Abraham,
And his oath unto Isaac;
And confirmed the same unto Jacob for a law,
And to Israel for an everlasting covenant:
Saying, "Unto thee will I give the land of Canaan,
The lot of your inheritance":
When they were but a few men in number;
Yea, very few, and strangers in it.
When they went from one nation to another,
From one kingdom to another people;
He suffered no man to do them wrong:
Yea, he reproved kings for their sakes;

Saying, "Touch not mine anointed,
And do my prophets no harm."

Moreover he called for a famine upon the land:
He brake the whole staff of bread.
He sent a man before them, even Joseph,
Who was sold for a servant:
Whose feet they hurt with fetters:
He was laid in iron:
Until the time that his word came:
The word of the LORD tried him.
The king sent and loosed him;
Even the ruler of the people, and let him go free.
He made him lord of his house,
And ruler of all his substance:
To bind his princes at his pleasure;
And teach his senators wisdom.
Israel also came into Egypt;
And Jacob sojourned in the land of Ham.
And he increased his people greatly;
And made them stronger than their enemies.
He turned their heart to hate his people,
To deal subtlely with his servants.
He sent Moses, his servant;
And Aaron whom he had chosen.
They shewed his signs among them,
And wonders in the land of Ham.
He sent darkness, and made it dark;
And they rebelled not against his word.
He turned their waters into blood,
And slew their fish.
Their land brought forth frogs in abundance,
In the chambers of their kings.
He spake, and there came divers sorts of flies,

And lice in all their coasts.
He gave them hail for rain,
And flaming fire in their land.
He smote their vines also and their fig-trees;
And brake the trees of their coasts.
He spake, and the locusts came, and caterpillers,
And that without number,
And did eat up all the herbs in their land,
And devoured the fruit of their ground.
He smote also all the firstborn in their land,
The chief of all their strength.
He brought them forth also with silver and gold:
And there was not one feeble person among their tribes.
Egypt was glad when they departed:
For the fear of them fell upon them.

He spread a cloud for a covering;
And fire to give light in the night.
The people asked, and he brought quails,
And satisfied them with the bread of heaven.
He opened the rock, and the waters gushed out;
They ran in the dry places like a river.
For he remembered his holy promise,
And Abraham his servant.
And he brought forth his people with joy,
And his chosen with gladness:
And gave them the lands of the heathen:
And they inherited the labour of the people;
That they might observe his statutes,
And keep his laws.
Praise ye the LORD.   — Psalm 105.

Blessed Are They that Keep Judgment

Before taking the seat of judgment, Louis IX of France always repeated the words of the 3rd verse of the 106th Psalm: "Blessed are they that keep judgment and he that doeth righteousness at all times."

PRAISE ye the LORD.
O give thanks unto the LORD; for he is good:
For his mercy endureth forever.
Who can utter the mighty acts of the LORD?
Who can shew forth all his praise?
Blessed are they that keep judgment,
And he that doeth righteousness at all times.
Remember me, O LORD, with the favour that thou
bearest unto thy people:
O visit me with thy salvation;
That I may see the good of thy chosen,
That I may rejoice in the gladness of thy nation,
That I may glory with thine inheritance.

We have sinned with our fathers,
We have committed iniquity, we have done wickedly.
Our fathers understood not thy wonders in Egypt;
They remembered not the multitude of thy mercies;
But provoked him at the sea, even at the Red Sea.
Nevertheless he saved them for his name's sake,
That he might make his mighty power to be known.
He rebuked the Red Sea also, and it was dried up:
So he led them through the depths, as through the
wilderness.
And he saved them from the hand of him that hated
them,

And redeemed them from the hand of the enemy.
And the waters covered their enemies:
There was not one of them left.
Then believed they his words;
They sang his praise.

They soon forgat his works;
They waited not for his counsel:
But lusted exceedingly in the wilderness,
And tempted God in the desert.
And he gave them their request;
But sent leanness into their soul
They envied Moses also in the camp,
And Aaron, the saint of the LORD.
The earth opened and swallowed up Dathan,
And covered the company of Abiram.
And a fire was kindled in their company;
The flame burned up the wicked.

They made a calf in Horeb,
And worshiped the molten image.
Thus they changed their glory
Into the similitude of an ox that eateth grass.
They forgat God, their saviour,
Which had done great things in Egypt;
Wondrous works in the land of Ham,
And terrible things by the Red Sea.
Therefore he said that he would destroy them,
Had not Moses his chosen stood before him in the
    breach,
To turn away his wrath,
Lest he should destroy them.

Yea, they despised the pleasant land,
They believed not his word:

But murmured in their tents,
And hearkened not unto the voice of the LORD.
Therefore he lifted up his hand against them,
To overthrow them in the wilderness:
To overthrow their seed also among the nations,
And to scatter them in the lands.
They joined themselves also unto Baal-peor,
And ate the sacrifices of the dead.
Thus they provoked him to anger with their inven-
 tions:
And the plague brake in upon them.
Then stood up Phinehas, and executed judgment:
And so the plague was stayed.
And that was counted unto him for righteousness
Unto all generations forevermore.

They angered him also at the waters of strife,
So that it went ill with Moses for their sakes:
Because they provoked his spirit,
So that he spake unadvisedly with his lips.
They did not destroy the nations,
Concerning whom the LORD commanded them:
But were mingled among the heathen,
And learned their works.
And they served their idols:
Which were a snare unto them.
Yea, they sacrificed their sons and their daughters unto
 devils,
And shed innocent blood, even the blood of their sons
 and of their daughters,
Whom they sacrificed unto the idols of Canaan:
And the land was polluted with blood.
Thus were they defiled with their own works,
And went a whoring with their own inventions.

Therefore was the wrath of the LORD kindled against
    his people,
Insomuch that he abhorred his own inheritance.
And he gave them into the hand of the heathen;
And they that hated them ruled over them.
Their enemies also oppressed them,
And they were brought into subjection under their
    hand.
Many times did he deliver them;
But they provoked him with their counsel,
And were brought low for their iniquity.
Nevertheless he regarded their affliction,
When he heard their cry:
And he remembered for them his covenant,
And repented according to the multitude of his mercies.
He made them also to be pitied
Of all those that carried them captives.

Save us, O LORD our God,
And gather us from among the heathen,
To give thanks unto thy holy name,
And to triumph in thy praise.
Blessed be the LORD God of Israel
From everlasting to everlasting:
And let all the people say, "Amen."
Praise ye the LORD.   — Psalm 106.

They That Go Down to the Sea

O GIVE thanks unto the LORD, for he is good:
For his mercy endureth forever.
Let the redeemed of the LORD say so,
Whom he hath redeemed from the hand of the enemy;
And gathered them out of the lands,
From the east, and from the west,
From the north, and from the south.

They wandered in the wilderness in a solitary way;
They found no city to dwell in.
Hungry and thirsty,
Their soul fainted in them.
Then they cried unto the LORD in their trouble,
And he delivered them out of their distresses.
And he led them forth by the right way,
That they might go to a city of habitation.
O that men would praise the LORD for his goodness,
And for his wonderful works to the children of men!
For he satisfieth the longing soul,
And filleth the hungry soul with goodness.

Such as sit in darkness and in the shadow of death,
Being bound in affliction and iron;
Because they rebelled against the words of God,
And contemned the counsel of the most High:
Therefore he brought down their heart with labour;
They fell down, and there was none to help.
Then they cried unto the LORD in their trouble,
And he saved them out of their distresses.
He brought them out of darkness and the shadow of
death,

SUNSET ON THE MEDITERRANEAN

Photograph by W. A. Pottenger
expressly for The Book of Life

A BEAUTIFUL sunset on the great sea which is so closely connected with Biblical history.

"They that go down to the sea in ships that do business in great waters."

And brake their bands in sunder.
O that men would praise the LORD for his goodness,
And for his wonderful works to the children of men!
For he hath broken the gates of brass,
And cut the bars of iron in sunder.

Fools because of their transgression,
And because of their iniquities, are afflicted.
Their soul abhorreth all manner of meat;
And they draw near unto the gates of death.
Then they cry unto the LORD in their trouble,
And he saveth them out of their distresses.
He sent his word, and healed them,
And delivered them from their destructions.
O that men would praise the LORD for his goodness,
And for his wonderful works to the children of men!
And let them sacrifice the sacrifices of thanksgiving,
And declare his works with rejoicing.

They that go down to the sea in ships,
That do business in great waters;
These see the works of the LORD,
And his wonders in the deep.
For he commandeth, and raiseth the stormy wind,
Which lifteth up the waves thereof.
They mount up to the heaven, they go down again to
      the depths:
Their soul is melted because of trouble.
They reel to and fro, and stagger like a drunken man,
And are at their wit's end.
Then they cry unto the LORD in their trouble,
And he bringeth them out of their distresses.
He maketh the storm a calm,
So that the waves thereof are still.

Then are they glad because they be quiet;
So he bringeth them unto their desired haven.
O that men would praise the LORD for his goodness,
And for his wonderful works to the children of men!
Let them exalt him also in the congregation of the
  people,
And praise him in the assembly of the elders.

He turneth rivers into a wilderness,
And the watersprings into dry ground;
A fruitful land into barrenness,
For the wickedness of them that dwell therein.
He turneth the wilderness into a standing water,
And dry ground into watersprings.
And there he maketh the hungry to dwell,
That they may prepare a city for habitation;
And sow the fields, and plant vineyards,
Which may yield fruits of increase.
He blesseth them also, so that they are multiplied
  greatly;
And suffereth not their cattle to decrease.

Again, they are diminished and brought low
Through oppression, affliction, and sorrow.
He poureth contempt upon princes,
And causeth them to wander in the wilderness, where
  there is no way.
Yet setteth he the poor on high from affliction,
And maketh him families like a flock.
The righteous shall see it, and rejoice:
And all iniquity shall stop her mouth.
Whoso is wise, and will observe these things,
Even they shall understand the lovingkindness of the
  LORD.   — Psalm 107.

Thy Truth Reacheth Unto the Clouds

O GOD, my heart is fixed;
    I will sing and give praise, even with my glory.
    Awake, psaltery and harp:
I myself will awake early.
I will praise thee, O Lord, among the people:
And I will sing praises unto thee among the nations.
For thy mercy is great above the heavens:
And thy truth reacheth unto the clouds.
Be thou exalted, O God, above the heavens:
And thy glory above all the earth;
That thy beloved may be delivered:
Save with thy right hand, and answer me.

God hath spoken in his holiness;
I will rejoice, I will divide Shechem,
And mete out the valley of Succoth.
Gilead is mine; Manasseh is mine;
Ephraim also is the strength of mine head;
Judah is my lawgiver;
Moab is my washpot;
Over Edom will I cast out my shoe;
Over Philistia will I triumph.
Who will bring me into the strong city?
Who will lead me into Edom?
Wilt not thou, O God, who hast cast us off?
And wilt not thou, O God, go forth with our hosts?
Give us help from trouble:
For vain is the help of man.
Through God we shall do valiantly:
For he it is that shall tread down our enemies.

— Psalm 108.

The Fate of the Evil Man

HOLD not thy peace, O God of my praise;
  For the mouth of the wicked and the mouth of
    the deceitful are opened against me:
They have spoken against me with a lying tongue.
They compassed me about also with words of hatred;
And fought against me without a cause.
For my love they are my adversaries:
But I give myself unto prayer.
And they have rewarded me evil for good,
And hatred for my love.
Set thou a wicked man over him:
And let Satan stand at his right hand.
When he shall be judged, let him be condemned:
And let his prayer become sin.
Let his days be few;
And let another take his office.
Let his children be fatherless,
And his wife a widow.
Let his children be continually vagabonds, and beg:
Let them seek their bread also out of their desolate places.
Let the extortioner catch all that he hath;
And let the strangers spoil his labour.
Let there be none to extend mercy unto him:
Neither let there be any to favour his fatherless children.
Let his posterity be cut off;
And in the generation following let their name be
  blotted out.
Let the iniquity of his fathers be remembered with the
  LORD;
And let not the sin of his mother be blotted out.
Let them be before the LORD continually,

That he may cut off the memory of them from the
earth.
Because that he remembered not to shew mercy,
But persecuted the poor and needy man,
That he might even slay the broken in heart.
As he loved cursing, so let it come unto him:
As he delighted not in blessing, so let it be far from him.
As he clothed himself with cursing like as with his
garments,
So let it come into his bowels like water,
And like oil into his bones.
Let it be unto him as the garment which covereth him,
And for a girdle wherewith he is girded continually.
Let this be the reward of mine adversaries from the
LORD,
And of them that speak evil against my soul.
But do thou for me, O GOD the Lord, for thy name's
sake:
Because thy mercy is good, deliver thou me.
For I am poor and needy,
And my heart is wounded within me.
I am gone like the shadow when it declineth:
I am tossed up and down as the locust.
My knees are weak through fasting;
And my flesh faileth of fatness.
I became also a reproach unto them:
When they looked upon me they shaked their heads.
Help me, O LORD my God:
O save me according to thy mercy:
That they may know that this is thy hand;
That thou, LORD, hast done it.
Let them curse, but bless thou:
When they arise, let them be ashamed;
But let thy servant rejoice.

Let mine adversaries be clothed with shame,
And let them cover themselves with their own con-
    fusion, as with a mantle.
I will greatly praise the LORD with my mouth;
Yea, I will praise him among the multitude.
For he shall stand at the right hand of the poor,
To save him from those that condemn his soul.

—Psalm 109.

Sit Thou at My Right Hand

THE LORD said unto my Lord,
    "Sit thou at my right hand,
        Until I make thine enemies thy footstool."
The LORD shall send the rod of thy strength out of
    Zion:
Rule thou in the midst of thine enemies.
Thy people shall be willing in the day of thy power,
In the beauties of holiness from the womb of the
    morning;
Thou hast the dew of thy youth.

The LORD hath sworn, and will not repent,
Thou art a priest forever after the order of Melchizedek.
The Lord at thy right hand
Shall strike through kings in the day of his wrath.
He shall judge among the heathen,
He shall fill the places with the dead bodies;
He shall wound the heads over many countries.
He shall drink of the brook in the way:
Therefore shall he lift up the head.   — Psalm 110.

The Fear of the Lord Is the Beginning of Wisdom

Dunstan (? –988), statesman, man of affairs, teacher, lover of the arts and crafts, Archbishop of Canterbury, died as he was repeating the 4th and 5th verses of the 111th Psalm.

PRAISE ye the LORD.
I will praise the LORD with my whole heart,
In the assembly of the upright, and in the congregation.
The works of the LORD are great,
Sought out of all them that have pleasure therein.
His work is honourable and glorious:
And his righteousness endureth forever.
He hath made his wonderful works to be remembered:
The LORD is gracious and full of compassion.
He hath given meat unto them that fear him:
He will ever be mindful of his covenant.
He hath shewed his people the power of his works,
That he may give them the heritage of the heathen.

The works of his hands are verity and judgment;
All his commandments are sure.
They stand fast forever and ever,
And are done in truth and uprightness,
He sent redemption unto his people:
He hath commanded his covenant forever:
Holy and reverend is his name.

The fear of the LORD is the beginning of wisdom:
A good understanding have all they that do his commandments:
His praise endureth forever. — Psalm 111.

The Reward of the Upright

PRAISE ye the LORD.
   Blessed is the man that feareth the LORD,
   That delighteth greatly in his commandments.
His seed shall be mighty upon earth:
The generation of the upright shall be blessed.
Wealth and riches shall be in his house:
And his righteousness endureth forever.
Unto the upright there ariseth light in the darkness:
He is gracious, and full of compassion, and righteous.
A good man sheweth favour, and lendeth:
He will guide his affairs with discretion.

Surely he shall not be moved forever:
The righteous shall be in everlasting remembrance.
He shall not be afraid of evil tidings:
His heart is fixed, trusting in the LORD.
His heart is established, he shall not be afraid,
Until he see his desire upon his enemies.
He hath dispersed, he hath given to the poor;
His righteousness endureth forever;
His horn shall be exalted with honour.
The wicked shall see it, and be grieved;
He shall gnash with his teeth, and melt away:
The desire of the wicked shall perish.   — Psalm 112.

His Glory Is Above the Heavens

PRAISE ye the Lord.
　　Praise, O ye servants of the Lord,
　　Praise the name of the Lord.
Blessed be the name of the Lord
From this time forth and forevermore.
From the rising of the sun unto the going down of the
　　same
The Lord's name is to be praised.

The Lord is high above all nations,
And his glory above the heavens.
Who is like unto the Lord our God,
Who dwelleth on high,
Who humbleth himself to behold
The things that are in heaven, and in the earth!

He raiseth up the poor out of the dust,
And lifteth the needy out of the dunghill;
That he may set him with princes,
Even with the princes of his people.
He maketh the barren woman to keep house,
And to be a joyful mother of children.
Praise ye the Lord.　　　　　　　　　　　— Psalm 113.

The Earth Shall Tremble in the Presence of the Lord

WHEN Israel went out of Egypt,
  The house of Jacob from a people of strange
    language;
Judah was his sanctuary,
And Israel his dominion.
The sea saw it, and fled:
Jordan was driven back.
The mountains skipped like rams,
And the little hills like lambs.

What ailed thee, O thou sea, that thou fleddest?
Thou Jordan, that thou wast driven back?
Ye mountains, that ye skipped like rams;
And ye little hills, like lambs?
Tremble, thou earth, at the presence of the LORD,
At the presence of the God of Jacob;
Which turned the rock into a standing water,
The flint into a fountain of waters.   — Psalm 114.

The Glory Is the Lord's

At the battle of Agincourt (1415), the English army, after the victory was won, knelt on the field and sang the 1st verse of the 115th Psalm: "Not unto us, O Lord, not unto us, but unto thy name, give glory, for thy mercy and for thy truth's sake."

NOT unto us, O LORD, not unto us,
But unto thy name give glory,
For thy mercy, and for thy truth's sake.
Wherefore should the heathen say,
"Where is now their God?"

But our God is in the heavens:
He hath done whatsoever he hath pleased.
Their idols are silver and gold,
The work of men's hands.
They have mouths, but they speak not:
Eyes have they, but they see not:
They have ears, but they hear not:
Noses have they, but they smell not:
They have hands, but they handle not:
Feet have they, but they walk not:
Neither speak they through their throat.
They that make them are like unto them;
So is every one that trusteth in them.

O Israel, trust thou in the LORD:
He is their help and their shield.
O house of Aaron, trust in the LORD:
He is their help and their shield.

Ye that fear the LORD, trust in the LORD:
He is their help and their shield.

The LORD hath been mindful of us:
He will bless us;
He will bless the house of Israel;
He will bless the house of Aaron.
He will bless them that fear the LORD,
Both small and great.
The LORD shall increase you more and more,
You and your children.
Ye are blessed of the LORD
Which made heaven and earth.
The heaven, even the heavens, are the LORD's:
But the earth hath he given to the children of men.

The dead praise not the LORD,
Neither any that go down into silence.
But we will bless the LORD
From this time forth and forevermore.
Praise the LORD.   — Psalm 115.

A Merciful God

I LOVE the LORD, because he hath heard
My voice and my supplications.
Because he hath inclined his ear unto me,
Therefore will I call upon him as long as I live.
The sorrows of death compassed me,
And the pains of hell gat hold upon me:
I found trouble and sorrow.
Then called I upon the name of the LORD;
O LORD, I beseech thee, deliver my soul.
Gracious is the LORD, and righteous;
Yea, our God is merciful.
The LORD preserveth the simple:
I was brought low, and he helped me.

Return unto thy rest, O my soul;
For the LORD hath dealt bountifully with thee.
For thou hast delivered my soul from death,
Mine eyes from tears,
And my feet from falling.
I will walk before the LORD
In the land of the living.
I believed, therefore have I spoken:
I was greatly afflicted:
I said in my haste,
"All men are liars."

What shall I render unto the LORD
For all his benefits toward me?
I will take the cup of salvation,
And call upon the name of the LORD.
I will pay my vows unto the LORD
Now in the presence of all his people.

Precious in the sight of the LORD
Is the death of his saints.
O LORD, truly I am thy servant;
I am thy servant, and the son of thine handmaid:
Thou hast loosed my bonds.
I will offer to thee the sacrifice of thanksgiving,
And will call upon the name of the LORD.
I will pay my vows unto the LORD
Now in the presence of all his people,
In the courts of the LORD's house,
In the midst of thee, O Jerusalem.
Praise ye the LORD.   — Psalm 116.

The Truth of the Lord Endureth Forever

This is the shortest Psalm. When the lines of the enemy were broken at Dunbar, Cromwell ordered his troopers to stop and chant this Psalm. The great captain was always practical. There was no time to be lost in chanting Psalms when the foe must be pursued.

O PRAISE the LORD, all ye nations:
Praise him, all ye people.
For his merciful kindness is great toward us:
And the truth of the LORD endureth forever.
Praise ye the LORD.   — Psalm 117.

His Mercy Endureth Forever

Luther said of the 118th Psalm· "This is my Psalm, my chosen Psalm. I love them all. I love all Holy Scripture, which is my consolation and my life. But this Psalm is nearest my heart, and I have a familiar right to call it mine. It has saved me from many a passing danger, from which nor emperor, nor kings, nor sages, nor saints could have saved me. It is my friend; dearer to me than all the honors and power of the earth."

Queen Elizabeth, on the death of Queen Mary, by whom she had been constantly threatened with death, quoted the 118th Psalm, the 23rd verse, "This is the Lord's doing and it is marvellous in our eyes."

GIVE thanks unto the LORD; for he is good: because his mercy endureth forever.
Let Israel now say,
That his mercy endureth forever.
Let the house of Aaron now say,
That his mercy endureth forever.
Let them now that fear the LORD say,
That his mercy endureth forever.

I called upon the LORD in distress:
The LORD answered me, and set me in a large place.
The LORD is on my side;
I will not fear:
What can man do unto me?
The LORD taketh my part with them that help me:
Therefore shall I see my desire upon them that hate me.
It is better to trust in the LORD
Than to put confidence in man.
It is better to trust in the LORD
Than to put confidence in princes.

All nations compassed me about:
But in the name of the LORD will I destroy them.
They compassed me about;
Yea, they compassed me about;
But in the name of the LORD I will destroy them.
They compassed me about like bees;
They are quenched as the fire of thorns:
For in the name of the LORD I will destroy them.
Thou hast thrust sore at me that I might fall:
But the LORD helped me.
The LORD is my strength and song,
And is become my salvation.
The voice of rejoicing and salvation is in the taber-
　　nacles of the righteous:
The right hand of the LORD doeth valiantly.
The right hand of the LORD is exalted:
The right hand of the LORD doeth valiantly.

I shall not die, but live,
And declare the works of the LORD.
The LORD hath chastened me sore:
But he hath not given me over unto death.
Open to me the gates of righteousness:
I will go into them, and I will praise the LORD:
This gate of the LORD,
Into which the righteous shall enter.
I will praise thee: for thou hast heard me,
And art become my salvation.

The stone which the builders refused
Is become the head stone of the corner.
This is the LORD's doing;
It is marvellous in our eyes.
This is the day which the LORD hath made:
We will rejoice and be glad in it.

Save now, I beseech thee, O LORD:
O LORD, I beseech thee, send now prosperity.
Blessed be he that cometh in the name of the LORD:

We have blessed you out of the house of the LORD.
God is the LORD, which hath shewed us light:
Bind the sacrifice with cords, even unto the horns of
the altar.

Thou art my God, and I will praise thee:
Thou art my God, I will exalt thee.
O give thanks unto the LORD; for he is good:
For his mercy endureth forever. — Psalm 118.

The Law of the Lord

This is the longest Psalm. It is what is known as an alphabetic Psalm, arranged in short sections of eight couplets, each couplet beginning in the original with the letters of the Hebrew alphabet in succession. It is really, then, not one long Psalm, but a collection of short Psalms, each one magnifying the law of the Lord. It is a beautiful Psalm, a little Psalter within the Psalter, and it has been greatly loved by many people. Livingstone, Ruskin, and Henry Martyn committed it to memory when they were children. Among those who made especial use of it have been David Brainerd, who followed in the steps of John Eliot, the apostle to the American Indians, whose Journal inspired the missionaries, Carey and Martyn, and influenced the decision of Livingstone to become a missionary; Thomas Chalmers, the famous Scotch preacher; Pascal, the French Huguenot; David I, King of Scotland; the Emperor Maurice in the 6th century. Theodosius, Augustine, Izaak Walton, and Dante are others who have loved it.

The sections are indicated by the letters of the Hebrew alphabet.

א ALEPH

BLESSED are the undefiled in the way,
Who walk in the law of the LORD.
Blessed are they that keep his testimonies,
And that seek him with the whole heart.
They also do no iniquity:
They walk in his ways.
Thou hast commanded us to keep thy precepts diligently.
O that my ways were directed to keep thy statutes!
Then shall I not be ashamed,
When I have respect unto all thy commandments.
I will praise thee with uprightness of heart.
When I shall have learned thy righteous judgments.

I will keep thy statutes:
O forsake me not utterly.

‎ב‎ BETH

Wherewithal shall a young man cleanse his way?
By taking heed thereto according to thy word.
With my whole heart have I sought thee:
O let me not wander from thy commandments.
Thy word have I hid in mine heart,
That I might not sin against thee.
Blessed art thou, O LORD:
Teach me thy statutes.
With my lips have I declared
All the judgments of thy mouth.
I have rejoiced in the way of thy testimonies,
As much as in all riches.
I will meditate in thy precepts,
And have respect unto thy ways.
I will delight myself in thy statutes:
I will not forget thy word.

‎ג‎ GIMEL

Deal bountifully with thy servant, that I may live,
And keep thy word.
Open thou mine eyes, that I may behold
Wondrous things out of thy law.
I am a stranger in the earth:
Hide not thy commandments from me.
My soul breaketh for the longing
That it hath unto thy judgments at all times.
Thou hast rebuked the proud that are cursed,
Which do err from thy commandments.
Remove from me reproach and contempt;
For I have kept thy testimonies.

Princes also did sit and speak against me:
But thy servant did meditate in thy statutes.
Thy testimonies also are my delight
And my counsellors.

ד DALETH

My soul cleaveth unto the dust:
Quicken thou me according to thy word.
I have declared my ways, and thou heardest me:
Teach me thy statutes.
Make me to understand the way of thy precepts:
So shall I talk of thy wondrous works.
My soul melteth for heaviness:
Strengthen thou me according unto thy word.
Remove from me the way of lying:
And grant me thy law graciously.
I have chosen the way of truth:
Thy judgments have I laid before me.
I have stuck unto thy testimonies:
O LORD, put me not to shame.
I will run the way of thy commandments,
When thou shalt enlarge my heart.

ה HE

Teach me, O LORD, the way of thy statutes;
And I shall keep it unto the end.
Give me understanding, and I shall keep thy law;
Yea, I shall observe it with my whole heart.
Make me to go in the path of thy commandments;
For therein do I delight.
Incline my heart unto thy testimonies,
And not to covetousness.
Turn away mine eyes from beholding vanity;
And quicken thou me in thy way.

Stablish thy word unto thy servant,
Who is devoted to thy fear.
Turn away my reproach which I fear:
For thy judgments are good.
Behold, I have longed after thy precepts:
Quicken me in thy righteousness.

ו VAU

Let thy mercies come also unto me, O LORD,
Even thy salvation, according to thy word.
So shall I have wherewith to answer him that re-
     proacheth me:
For I trust in thy word.
And take not the word of truth utterly out of my
     mouth;
For I have hoped in thy judgments.
So shall I keep thy law continually
Forever and ever.
And I will walk at liberty:
For I seek thy precepts.
I will speak of thy testimonies also before kings,
And will not be ashamed.
And I will delight myself in thy commandments,
Which I have loved.
My hands also will I lift up unto thy commandments,
Which I have loved;
And I will meditate in thy statutes.

ז ZAIN

Remember the word unto thy servant,
Upon which thou hast caused me to hope.
This is my comfort in my affliction:
For thy word hath quickened me.
The proud have had me greatly in derision:

Yet have I not declined from thy law.
I remembered thy judgments of old, O Lord;
And have comforted myself.
Horror hath taken hold upon me
Because of the wicked that forsake thy law.
Thy statutes have been my songs
In the house of my pilgrimage.
I have remembered thy name,
O Lord, in the night,
And have kept thy law.
This I had,
Because I kept thy precepts.

ה CHETH

Thou art my portion, O Lord:
I have said that I would keep thy words.
I intreated thy favour with my whole heart:
Be merciful unto me according to thy word.
I thought on my ways,
And turned my feet unto thy testimonies.
I made haste, and delayed not
To keep thy commandments.
The bands of the wicked have robbed me:
But I have not forgotten thy law.
At midnight I will rise to give thanks unto thee
Because of thy righteous judgments.
I am a companion of all them that fear thee,
And of them that keep thy precepts.
The earth, O Lord, is full of thy mercy:
Teach me thy statutes.

ט TETH

Thou hast dealt well with thy servant,
O Lord, according unto thy word.
Teach me good judgment and knowledge:

For I have believed thy commandments.
Before I was afflicted I went astray:
But now have I kept thy word.
Thou art good, and doest good;
Teach me thy statutes.
The proud have forged a lie against me:
But I will keep thy precepts with my whole heart.
Their heart is as fat as grease;
But I delight in thy law.
It is good for me that I have been afflicted;
That I might learn thy statutes.
The law of thy mouth is better unto me
Than thousands of gold and silver.

' JOD

Thy hands have made me and fashioned me:
Give me understanding, that I may learn thy com-
    mandments.
They that fear thee will be glad when they see me;
Because I have hoped in thy word.
I know, O LORD, that thy judgments are right,
And that thou in faithfulness hast afflicted me.
Let, I pray thee, thy merciful kindness be for my
    comfort,
According to thy word unto thy servant.
Let thy tender mercies come unto me, that I may live:
For thy law is my delight.
Let the proud be ashamed; for they dealt perversely
    with me without a cause:
But I will meditate in thy precepts.
Let those that fear thee turn unto me,
And those that have known thy testimonies.
Let my heart be sound in thy statutes;
That I be not ashamed.

‫כ‬ CAPH

My soul fainteth for thy salvation:
But I hope in thy word.
Mine eyes fail for thy word,
Saying, "When wilt thou comfort me?"
For I am become like a bottle in the smoke;
Yet do I not forget thy statutes.
How many are the days of thy servant?
When wilt thou execute judgment on them that per-
   secute me?
The proud have digged pits for me,
Which are not after thy law.
All thy commandments are faithful:
They persecute me wrongfully; help thou me.
They had almost consumed me upon earth;
But I forsook not thy precepts.
Quicken me after thy lovingkindness;
So shall I keep the testimony of thy mouth.

‫ל‬ LAMED

Forever, O LORD,
Thy word is settled in heaven.
Thy faithfulness is unto all generations:
Thou hast established the earth, and it abideth.
They continue this day according to thine ordinances:
For all are thy servants.
Unless thy law had been my delights,
I should then have perished in mine affliction.
I will never forget thy precepts:
For with them thou hast quickened me.
I am thine, save me;
For I have sought thy precepts.
The wicked have waited for me to destroy me:
But I will consider thy testimonies.

I have seen an end of all perfection:
But thy commandment is exceeding broad.

‫מ‬ MEM

O how love I thy law!
It is my meditation all the day.
Thou through thy commandments hast made me
    wiser than mine enemies:
For they are ever with me.
I have more understanding than all my teachers:
For thy testimonies are my meditation.
I understand more than the ancients,
Because I keep thy precepts.
I have refrained my feet from every evil way,
That I might keep thy word.
I have not departed from thy judgments:
For thou hast taught me.
How sweet are thy words unto my taste!
Yea, sweeter than honey to my mouth!
Through thy precepts I get understanding:
Therefore I hate every false way.

‫נ‬ NUN

Thy word is a lamp unto my feet,
And a light unto my path.
I have sworn, and I will perform it,
That I will keep thy righteous judgments.
I am afflicted very much:
Quicken me, O LORD, according unto thy word.
Accept, I beseech thee, the freewill offerings of my
    mouth, O LORD,
And teach me thy judgments.
My soul is continually in my hand:
Yet do I not forget thy law.

The wicked have laid a snare for me:
Yet I erred not from thy precepts.
Thy testimonies have I taken as an heritage forever:
For they are the rejoicing of my heart.
I have inclined mine heart to perform thy statutes
    alway,
Even unto the end.

ס SAMECH

I hate vain thoughts:
But thy law do I love.
Thou art my hiding place and my shield:
I hope in thy word.
Depart from me, ye evildoers:
For I will keep the commandments of my God.
Uphold me according unto thy word, that I may live:
And let me not be ashamed of my hope.
Hold thou me up, and I shall be safe:
And I will have respect unto thy statutes continually.
Thou hast trodden down all them that err from thy
    statutes:
For their deceit is falsehood.
Thou puttest away all the wicked of the earth like
    dross:
Therefore I love thy testimonies.
My flesh trembleth for fear of thee;
And I am afraid of thy judgments.

ע AIN

I have done judgment and justice:
Leave me not to mine oppressors.
Be surety for thy servant for good:
Let not the proud oppress me.
Mine eyes fail for thy salvation,
And for the word of thy righteousness.

Deal with thy servant according unto thy mercy,
And teach me thy statutes.
I am thy servant; give me understanding,
That I may know thy testimonies.
It is time for thee, LORD, to work:
For they have made void thy law.
Therefore I love thy commandments above gold;
Yea, above fine gold.
Therefore I esteem all thy precepts
Concerning all things to be right;
And I hate every false way.

פ PE

Thy testimonies are wonderful:
Therefore doth my soul keep them.
The entrance of thy words giveth light;
It giveth understanding unto the simple.
I opened my mouth, and panted:
For I longed for thy commandments.
Look thou upon me, and be merciful unto me,
As thou usest to do unto those that love thy name.
Order my steps in thy word:
And let not any iniquity have dominion over me.
Deliver me from the oppression of man:
So will I keep thy precepts.
Make thy face to shine upon thy servant;
And teach me thy statutes.
Rivers of waters run down mine eyes,
Because they keep not thy law.

צ TZADDI

Righteous art thou, O LORD,
And upright are thy judgments.
Thy testimonies that thou hast commanded are
righteous

And very faithful.
My zeal hath consumed me,
Because mine enemies have forgotten thy words.
Thy word is very pure:
Therefore thy servant loveth it.
I am small and despised:
Yet do not I forget thy precepts.
Thy righteousness is an everlasting righteousness,
And thy law is the truth.
Trouble and anguish have taken hold on me:
Yet thy commandments are my delights.
The righteousness of thy testimonies is everlasting:
Give me understanding, and I shall live.

ק KOPH

I cried with my whole heart; hear me, O LORD:
I will keep thy statutes.
I cried unto thee; save me,
And I shall keep thy testimonies.
I prevented the dawning of the morning, and cried:
I hoped in thy word.
Mine eyes prevent the night watches,
That I might meditate in thy word.
Hear my voice according unto thy lovingkindness:
O LORD, quicken me according to thy judgment.
They draw nigh that follow after mischief:
They are far from thy law.
Thou art near, O LORD;
And all thy commandments are truth.
Concerning thy testimonies, I have known of old
That thou hast founded them forever.

ר RESH

Consider mine affliction, and deliver me:
For I do not forget thy law.

Plead my cause, and deliver me:
Quicken me according to thy word.
Salvation is far from the wicked:
For they seek not thy statutes.
Great are thy tender mercies, O Lord:
Quicken me according to thy judgments.
Many are my persecutors and mine enemies;
Yet do I not decline from thy testimonies.
I beheld the transgressors, and was grieved;
Because they kept not thy word.
Consider how I love thy precepts:
Quicken me, O Lord, according to thy lovingkind-
  ness.
Thy word is true from the beginning:
And every one of thy righteous judgments endureth
  forever.

ש SCHIN

Princes have persecuted me without a cause:
But my heart standeth in awe of thy word.
I rejoice at thy word,
As one that findeth great spoil.
I hate and abhor lying:
But thy law do I love.
Seven times a day do I praise thee
Because of thy righteous judgments.
Great peace have they which love thy law:
And nothing shall offend them.
Lord, I have hoped for thy salvation,
And done thy commandments.
My soul hath kept thy testimonies;
And I love them exceedingly.
I have kept thy precepts and thy testimonies:
For all my ways are before thee.

ת TAU

Let my cry come near before thee, O Lord:
Give me understanding according to thy word.
Let my supplication come before thee:
Deliver me according to thy word.
My lips shall utter praise,
When thou hast taught me thy statutes.
My tongue shall speak of thy word:
For all thy commandments are righteousness.
Let thine hand help me;
For I have chosen thy precepts.
I have longed for thy salvation, O Lord;
And thy law is my delight.
Let my soul live, and it shall praise thee;
And let thy judgments help me.
I have gone astray like a lost sheep; seek thy servant;
For I do not forget thy commandments.   — Psalm 119.

I Am for Peace But They Are for War

IN my distress I cried unto the LORD,
  And he heard me.
    Deliver my soul, O LORD, from lying lips,
And from a deceitful tongue.
What shall be given unto thee?
Or what shall be done unto thee,
Thou false tongue?
Sharp arrows of the mighty,
With coals of juniper.

Woe is me, that I sojourn in Mesech,
That I dwell in the tents of Kedar!
My soul hath long dwelt
With him that hateth peace.
I am for peace:
But when I speak, they are for war.   — Psalm 120.

HARBOR OF HAIFA
Photograph by the Reverend Frederick J. Moore
A ship of peace may be seen in this modern harbor of Palestine which was
opened in 1934. The fast-growing city of Haifa may be seen in the foreground.

I Will Lift Mine Eyes Unto the Hills

I WILL lift up mine eyes unto the hills, from whence
    cometh my help.
  My help cometh from the LORD,
Which made heaven and earth.
He will not suffer thy foot to be moved:
He that keepeth thee will not slumber.
Behold, he that keepeth Israel
Shall neither slumber nor sleep.

The LORD is thy keeper:
The LORD is thy shade upon thy right hand.
The sun shall not smite thee by day,
Nor the moon by night.
The LORD shall preserve thee from all evil:
He shall preserve thy soul.
The LORD shall preserve thy going out and thy coming
    in
From this time forth, and even forevermore.

— Psalm 121.

𝔄 𝔖ong of the 𝔓ilgrims on the 𝔐arch

James Hogg, the Scotch poet, known as the "Ettrick Shepherd," learned the 122d Psalm, before he could read. Later, he learned by heart nearly all the Psalter.

I WAS glad when they said unto me,
"Let us go into the house of the LORD."
Our feet shall stand within thy gates, O Jeru-
salem.
Jerusalem is builded as a city that is compact together:
Whither the tribes go up, the tribes of the LORD,
Unto the testimony of Israel,
To give thanks unto the name of the LORD.
For there are set thrones of judgment,
The thrones of the house of David.

Pray for the peace of Jerusalem:
They shall prosper that love thee.
Peace be within thy walls,
And prosperity within thy palaces.
For my brethren and companions' sakes,
I will now say, "Peace be within thee."
Because of the house of the LORD our God
I will seek thy good. — Psalm 122.

Our Eyes Wait Upon the Lord

UNTO thee lift I up mine eyes,
O thou that dwellest in the heavens.
Behold, as the eyes of servants look unto the
hand of their masters,
And as the eyes of a maiden unto the hand of her mis-
tress;
So our eyes wait upon the LORD our God,
Until that he have mercy upon us.

Have mercy upon us, O LORD, have mercy upon us:
For we are exceedingly filled with contempt.
Our soul is exceedingly filled
With the scorning of those that are at ease,
And with the contempt of the proud. — Psalm 123.

POOL OF THE SULTAN

Photograph by W. A. Pottenger
expressly for The Book of Life

THIS is the lower end of one of the reservoirs just outside of Jerusalem in the valley near the southwest corner of the modern city. It dates back perhaps to the days of the Kings.

My Soul Has Escaped

IF it had not been the LORD who was on our side,
Now may Israel say;
If it had not been the LORD who was on our
side,
When men rose up against us:
Then they had swallowed us up quick,
When their wrath was kindled against us:
Then the waters had overwhelmed us,
The stream had gone over our soul:
Then the proud waters had gone over our soul.

Blessed be the LORD,
Who hath not given us as a prey to their teeth.
Our soul is escaped as a bird out of the snare of the
fowlers:
The snare is broken, and we are escaped.
Our help is in the name of the LORD,
Who made heaven and earth.   —Psalm 124.

As the Mountains Are Round About Jerusalem

THEY that trust in the LORD
Shall be as Mount Zion, which cannot be re-
moved, but abideth forever.
As the mountains are round about Jerusalem,
So the LORD is round about his people
From henceforth even forever.
For the rod of the wicked shall not rest upon the lot
of the righteous;
Lest the righteous put forth their hands unto iniquity.

Do good, O LORD, unto those that be good,
And to them that are upright in their hearts.
As for such as turn aside unto their crooked ways,
The LORD shall lead them forth with the workers of
iniquity:
But peace shall be upon Israel.   — Psalm 125.

They that Sow in Tears Shall Reap in Joy

For twenty years Robert Estienne struggled with the ecclesiastical authorities of Paris who proscribed his edition of the Bible in the common tongue. He writes, "When I recall the war I have waged for twenty years and more, I have been astonished that so small and frail a person as myself could have had strength to continue the struggle. Yet every time that memory reminds me of my deliverance, that voice which in Psalm 126 celebrates the redemption of the church strikes an echo in my heart, 'When the Lord turned again the captivity of Zion, we were like them that dream.'"

WHEN the Lord turned again the captivity of
    Zion,
We were like them that dream.
Then was our mouth filled with laughter,
And our tongue with singing:
Then said they among the heathen,
"The Lord hath done great things for them."
The Lord hath done great things for us;
Whereof we are glad.

Turn again our captivity, O Lord,
As the streams in the south.
They that sow in tears shall reap in joy.
He that goeth forth and weepeth, bearing precious
    seed,
Shall doubtless come again with rejoicing,
Bringing his sheaves with him.   — Psalm 126.

The Lord Must Build the House

In his appeal for the use of prayer in opening the sessions of the committee to frame a constitution for the United States, Benjamin Franklin referred to the Bible three times, and quoted the 1st verse of the 127th Psalm:—

"In the beginning of the contest with Britain, when we were sensible of danger, we had daily prayers in this room for the Divine protection. Our prayers, Sir, were heard, and they were graciously answered. All of us who were engaged in the struggle must have observed frequent instances of a superintending Providence. To that kind Providence we owe this opportunity of consulting in peace on the means of establishing our future national felicity. And have we now forgotten this powerful Friend? or do we imagine that we no longer need His assistance? I have lived for a long time, eighty-one years, and the longer I live the more convincing proof I see of this truth, that God governs in the affairs of men. And if a sparrow cannot fall to the ground without His notice, is it probable that an empire can rise without His aid?

EXCEPT the LORD build the house,
　　They labour in vain that build it:
　　Except the LORD keep the city,
The watchman waketh but in vain.
It is vain for you to rise up early, to sit up late,
To eat the bread of sorrows:
For so he giveth his beloved sleep.

Lo, children are an heritage of the LORD:
And the fruit of the womb is his reward.
As arrows are in the hand of a mighty man;
So are children of the youth.
Happy is the man that hath his quiver full of them:
They shall not be ashamed,
But they shall speak with the enemies in the gate.

— Psalm 127.

The Lord Shall Bless Thee out of Zion

BLESSED is every one that feareth the LORD;
   That walketh in his ways.
   For thou shalt eat the labour of thine hands:
Happy shalt thou be, and it shall be well with thee.
Thy wife shall be as a fruitful vine by the sides of thine
    house:
Thy children like olive plants round about thy table.
Behold, that thus shall the man be blessed
That feareth the LORD.

The LORD shall bless thee out of Zion:
And thou shalt see the good of Jerusalem all the days
   of thy life.
Yea, thou shalt see thy children's children,
And peace upon Israel.   — Psalm 128.

They Have Not Prevailed Against Me

MANY a time have they afflicted me from my
youth,
    May Israel now say:
Many a time have they afflicted me from my youth:
Yet they have not prevailed against me.
The plowers plowed upon my back:
They made long their furrows.
The LORD is righteous:
He hath cut asunder the cords of the wicked.

Let them all be confounded and turned back that hate
    Zion.
Let them be as the grass upon the housetops,
Which withereth afore it groweth up:
Wherewith the mower filleth not his hand;
Nor he that bindeth sheaves his bosom.
Neither do they which go by say,
"The blessing of the LORD be upon you:
We bless you in the name of the LORD."　　— Psalm 129.

Out of the Depths Have I Cried Unto Thee

This Psalm, which he heard chanted in Saint Paul's Cathedral on May 24, 1738, was one of the influences which led to the consecration of John Wesley (1703-1791) to his great task of reformation. For fifty years his personality was one of the great spiritual agencies in England. During that time he laid the foundation of the mighty movement known as Methodism.

OUT of the depths have I cried unto thee, O LORD.
  LORD, hear my voice:
    Let thine ears be attentive to the voice of my
      supplications.
If thou, LORD, shouldest mark iniquities,
O LORD, who shall stand?
But there is forgiveness with thee,
That thou mayest be feared.

I wait for the LORD, my soul doth wait,
And in his word do I hope.
My soul waiteth for the LORD
More than they that watch for the morning:
I say, more than they that watch for the morning.

Let Israel hope in the LORD:
For with the LORD there is mercy,
And with him is plenteous redemption.
And he shall redeem Israel
From all his iniquities.   — Psalm 130.

The Prayer of the Humble

LORD, my heart is not haughty,
Nor mine eyes lofty:
Neither do I exercise myself in great matters,
Or in things too high for me.
Surely I have behaved and quieted myself,
As a child that is weaned of his mother:
My soul is even as a weaned child.

Let Israel hope in the LORD
From henceforth and forever.
— Psalm 131.

A Prayer of the King

LORD, remember David,
And all his afflictions:
How he sware unto the LORD,
And vowed unto the mighty God of Jacob;
"Surely I will not come into the tabernacle of my house,
Nor go up into my bed;
I will not give sleep to mine eyes,
Or slumber to mine eyelids,
Until I find out a place for the LORD,
An habitation for the mighty God of Jacob."

Lo, we heard of it at Ephratah:
We found it in the fields of the wood.
We will go into his tabernacles:
We will worship at his footstool.
Arise, O LORD, into thy rest;
Thou, and the ark of thy strength.

Let thy priests be clothed with righteousness;
And let thy saints shout for joy.
For thy servant David's sake
Turn not away the face of thine anointed.

The LORD hath sworn in truth unto David;
He will not turn from it;
"Of the fruit of thy body will I set upon thy throne.
If thy children will keep my covenant
And my testimony that I shall teach them,
Their children shall also sit upon thy throne forever-
 more.
For the LORD hath chosen Zion;
He hath desired it for his habitation.

This is my rest forever:
Here will I dwell; for I have desired it.
I will abundantly bless her provision:
I will satisfy her poor with bread.
I will also clothe her priests with salvation:
And her saints shall shout aloud for joy.
There will I make the horn of David to bud:
I have ordained a lamp for mine anointed.
His enemies will I clothe with shame:
But upon himself shall his crown flourish."

— Psalm 132.

It Is Pleasant to Dwell in Unity

BEHOLD, how good and how pleasant it is
For brethren to dwell together in unity!
It is like the precious ointment upon the head,
That ran down upon the beard,
Even Aaron's beard:
That went down to the skirts of his garments;
As the dew of Hermon,
And as the dew that descended upon the mountains of
Zion:
For there the LORD commanded the blessing,
Even life forevermore. — Psalm 133.

A Song in the Night

BEHOLD, bless ye the LORD, all ye servants of the
LORD,
Which by night stand in the house of the LORD.
Lift up your hands in the sanctuary,
And bless the LORD.
The LORD that made heaven and earth
Bless thee out of Zion. — Psalm 134.

A Song of Praise

On the day that David Livingstone left home, the family arose at four o'clock. David read the 121st and 135th Psalms. He and his father then walked to Glasgow, where he took the steamer for Liverpool, sailing from that port for Africa. He never saw his father again, but happened to be at home on one of his rare visits when his mother died.

PRAISE ye the LORD.
Praise ye the name of the LORD;
Praise him, O ye servants of the LORD.
Ye that stand in the house of the LORD,
In the courts of the house of our God,
Praise the LORD; for the LORD is good:
Sing praises unto his name; for it is pleasant.
For the LORD hath chosen Jacob unto himself,
And Israel for his peculiar treasure.

For I know that the LORD is great,
And that our LORD is above all gods.
Whatsoever the LORD pleased, that did he in heaven,
And in earth, in the seas, and all deep places.
He causeth the vapours to ascend from the ends of the
    earth;
He maketh lightnings for the rain;
He bringeth the wind out of his treasuries.

Who smote the firstborn of Egypt,
Both of man and beast.
Who sent tokens and wonders into the midst of thee,
    O Egypt,
Upon Pharaoh, and upon all his servants.

Who smote great nations,
And slew mighty kings;
Sihon, King of the Amorites,
And Og, King of Bashan,
And all the kingdoms of Canaan:
And gave their land for an heritage,
An heritage unto Israel, his people.

Thy name, O Lord, endureth forever;
And thy memorial, O Lord, throughout all generations.
For the Lord will judge his people,
And he will repent himself concerning his servants.
The idols of the heathen are silver and gold,
The work of men's hands.
They have mouths, but they speak not;
Eyes have they, but they see not;
They have ears, but they hear not;
Neither is there any breath in their mouths.
They that make them are like unto them:
So is every one that trusteth in them.

Bless the Lord, O house of Israel:
Bless the Lord, O house of Aaron:
Bless the Lord, O house of Levi:
Ye that fear the Lord, bless the Lord.
Blessed be the Lord out of Zion,
Which dwelleth at Jerusalem.
Praise ye the Lord.   — Psalm 135.

The Wailing Place of the Jews

Photograph by W. A. Pottenger
expressly for The Book of Life

THIS is an open space on the west side of the wall of the Temple enclosure, within the city. The Jews long ago bought the place, and gather there, especially on Friday afternoon, as the Sabbath draws on, to mourn over the loss of Jerusalem. The lower courses of great stones go back to Jewish times, when they were part of the wall of the Temple area. These are the oldest stones in their original position above ground in Jerusalem. Prayer-book in hand, the people stand facing the ancient stones, and repeat litanies of prayers and lamentations. Psalm 79 is often on their lips, "O God, the heathen are come into thine inheritance; thy holy temple have they defiled."

His Mercy Endureth Forever

Milton translated a number of the Psalms from the original into poetic form, among them the first eight and the 80th to the 88th inclusive. When he was only fifteen years old, a student at Christ's College, Cambridge, he translated the 14th and the 136th.

> "Let us with a gladsome mind
> Praise the Lord, for he is kind,
> For his mercies aye endure
> Ever faithful, ever sure."

O GIVE thanks unto the LORD; for he is good:
For his mercy endureth forever.
O give thanks unto the God of gods:
For his mercy endureth forever.
O give thanks to the LORD of lords:
For his mercy endureth forever.

To him who alone doeth great wonders:
For his mercy endureth forever.
To him that by wisdom made the heavens:
For his mercy endureth forever.
To him that stretched out the earth above the waters:
For his mercy endureth forever.
To him that made great lights:
For his mercy endureth forever:
The sun to rule by day:
For his mercy endureth forever:
The moon and stars to rule by night:
For his mercy endureth forever.
To him that smote Egypt in their firstborn:
For his mercy endureth forever:
And brought out Israel from among them:
For his mercy endureth forever:

With a strong hand, and with a stretched out arm:
For his mercy endureth forever.
To him which divided the Red Sea into parts:
For his mercy endureth forever:
And made Israel to pass through the midst of it:
For his mercy endureth forever:
But overthrew Pharaoh and his host in the Red Sea:
For his mercy endureth forever.
To him which led his people through the wilderness:
For his mercy endureth forever.

To him which smote great kings:
For his mercy endureth forever:
And slew famous kings:
For his mercy endureth forever:
Sihon, King of the Amorites:
For his mercy endureth forever:
And Og, the king of Bashan:
For his mercy endureth forever:
And gave their land for an heritage:
For his mercy endureth forever:
Even an heritage unto Israel, his servant:
For his mercy endureth forever.

Who remembered us in our low estate:
For his mercy endureth forever:
And hath redeemed us from our enemies:
For his mercy endureth forever.
Who giveth food to all flesh:
For his mercy endureth forever.

O give thanks unto the God of heaven:
For his mercy endureth forever.   — Psalm 136

How Shall We Sing the Lord's Songs in a Strange Land?

Many a weary exile has echoed these words. King John II of France, a captive in England after the battle of Poitiers, replied to a courtier, who asked why he was so sad at a tournament, with the words: "How shall we sing the Lord's songs in a strange land?"

BY the rivers of Babylon,
There we sat down, yea, we wept,
When we remembered Zion.
We hanged our harps
Upon the willows in the midst thereof.
For there they that carried us away captive required
of us a song;
And they that wasted us required of us mirth, saying:
"Sing us one of the songs of Zion."

How shall we sing the LORD's song
In a strange land?
If I forget thee, O Jerusalem,
Let my right hand forget her cunning.
If I do not remember thee,
Let my tongue cleave to the roof of my mouth;
If I prefer not Jerusalem
Above my chief joy.
Remember, O LORD, the children of Edom
In the day of Jerusalem;
Who said, "Rase it, rase it,
Even to the foundation thereof."
O daughter of Babylon, who art to be destroyed;
Happy shall he be, that rewardeth thee
As thou hast served us.
Happy shall he be, that taketh and dasheth thy little ones
Against the stones. — Psalm 137.

All the Kings of the Earth Shall Praise Thee

I WILL praise thee with my whole heart:
Before the gods will I sing praise unto thee.
I will worship toward thy holy temple,
And praise thy name for thy lovingkindness and for
thy truth:
For thou hast magnified thy word above all thy name.
In the day when I cried thou answeredst me,
And strengthenedst me with strength in my soul.

All the kings of the earth shall praise thee, O LORD,
When they hear the words of thy mouth.
Yea, they shall sing in the ways of the LORD:
For great is the glory of the LORD.
Though the LORD be high, yet hath he respect unto the
lowly:
But the proud he knoweth afar off.
Though I walk in the midst of trouble, thou wilt revive
me:
Thou shalt stretch forth thine hand against the wrath
of mine enemies,
And thy right hand shall save me.
The LORD will perfect that which concerneth me:
Thy mercy, O LORD, endureth forever:
Forsake not the works of thine own hands.

— Psalm 138.

The Darkness Hideth Not from Thee

O LORD, thou hast searched me, and known me.
  Thou knowest my downsitting and mine up-
    rising,
Thou understandest my thought afar off.
Thou compassest my path and my lying down,
And art acquainted with all my ways.
For there is not a word in my tongue,
But, lo, O LORD, thou knowest it altogether.
Thou hast beset me behind and before,
And laid thine hand upon me.
Such knowledge is too wonderful for me;
It is high, I cannot attain unto it.

Whither shall I go from thy spirit?
Or whither shall I flee from thy presence?
If I ascend up into heaven, thou art there:
If I make my bed in hell, behold, thou art there.
If I take the wings of the morning,
And dwell in the uttermost parts of the sea;
Even there shall thy hand lead me,
And thy right hand shall hold me.
If I say, "Surely the darkness shall cover me":
Even the night shall be light about me.
Yea, the darkness hideth not from thee;
But the night shineth as the day:
The darkness and the light are both alike to thee.

For thou hast possessed my reins:
Thou hast covered me in my mother's womb.
I will praise thee; for I am fearfully and wonderfully
    made:

Marvellous are thy works;
And that my soul knoweth right well.
My substance was not hid from thee,
When I was made in secret,
And curiously wrought in the lowest parts of the earth.
Thine eyes did see my substance, yet being imperfect;
And in thy book all my members were written,
Which in continuance were fashioned,
When as yet there was none of them.
How precious also are thy thoughts unto me, O God!
How great is the sum of them!
If I should count them, they are more in number than
　　the sand:
When I awake, I am still with thee.

Surely thou wilt slay the wicked, O God:
Depart from me therefore, ye bloody men.
For they speak against thee wickedly,
And thine enemies take thy name in vain.
Do not I hate them, O Lord, that hate thee?
And am not I grieved with those that rise up against
　　thee?
I hate them with perfect hatred:
I count them mine enemies.
Search me, O God, and know my heart:
Try me, and know my thoughts:
And see if there be any wicked way in me,
And lead me in the way everlasting.　　　— Psalm 139.

A Prayer for Deliverance

DELIVER me, O LORD, from the evil man:
 Preserve me from the violent men;
 Who imagine mischiefs in their hearts;
Continually are they gathered together for war.
They have sharpened their tongues like a serpent;
Adders' poison is under their lips.

Keep me, O LORD, from the hands of the wicked;
Preserve me from the violent men;
Who have purposed to overthrow my goings.
The proud have hid a snare for me, and cords;
They have spread a net by the wayside;
They have set gins for me.
I said unto the LORD, "Thou art my God":
Hear the voice of my supplications, O LORD.
O God the LORD, the strength of my salvation,
Thou hast covered my head in the day of battle.
Grant not, O LORD, the desires of the wicked:
Further not their wicked devices; lest they exalt them-
 selves.
As for the head of those that compass me about,
Let the mischief of their own lips cover them.
Let burning coals fall upon them:
Let them be cast into the fire;
Into deep pits, that they rise not up again.
Let not an evil speaker be established in the earth:
Evil shall hunt the violent man to overthrow him.
I know that the LORD will maintain the cause of the
 afflicted,
And the right of the poor.
Surely the righteous shall give thanks unto thy name:
The upright shall dwell in thy presence.   — Psalm 140.

An Evening Sacrifice

The early Christians used the 73rd Psalm for morning worship,
and the 141st for evening prayer.

LORD, I cry unto thee: make haste unto me;
  Give ear unto my voice, when I cry unto thee.
  Let my prayer be set forth before thee as incense;
And the lifting up of my hands as the evening sacrifice.
Set a watch, O LORD, before my mouth;
Keep the door of my lips.
Incline not my heart to any evil thing,
To practise wicked works
With men that work iniquity:
And let me not eat of their dainties.

Let the righteous smite me; it shall be a kindness;
And let him reprove me;
It shall be an excellent oil, which shall not break my
      head;
For yet my prayer also shall be in their calamities.
When their judges are overthrown in stony places,
They shall hear my words;
For they are sweet.
Our bones are scattered at the grave's mouth,
As when one cutteth and cleaveth wood upon the earth.

But mine eyes are unto thee, O God the LORD:
In thee is my trust; leave not my soul destitute.
Keep me from the snares which they have laid for me,
And the gins of the workers of iniquity.
Let the wicked fall into their own nets,
Whilst that I withal escape.   — Psalm 141.

I Cried Unto the Lord with My Voice

This was one of the Psalms which were sung to St. Francis of Assisi as he lay dying.

I CRIED unto the LORD with my voice;
    With my voice unto the LORD did I make my
        supplication.
I poured out my complaint before him;
I shewed before him my trouble.
When my spirit was overwhelmed within me, then
    thou knewest my path.
In the way wherein I walked have they privily laid a
    snare for me.
I looked on my right hand, and beheld, but there was
    no man that would know me:
Refuge failed me; no man cared for my soul.

I cried unto thee, O LORD:
I said, "Thou art my refuge
And my portion in the land of the living.
Attend unto my cry; for I am brought very low:
Deliver me from my persecutors; for they are stronger
    than I.
Bring my soul out of prison, that I may praise thy name:
The righteous shall compass me about;
For thou shalt deal bountifully with me." — Psalm 142.

I Remember the Days of Old

HEAR my prayer, O LORD, give ear to my suppli-
cations:
In thy faithfulness answer me, and in thy
righteousness.
And enter not into judgment with thy servant:
For in thy sight shall no man living be justified.
For the enemy hath persecuted my soul;
He hath smitten my life down to the ground;
He hath made me to dwell in darkness, as those that
have been long dead.
Therefore is my spirit overwhelmed within me;
My heart within me is desolate.

I remember the days of old;
I meditate on all thy works;
I muse on the work of thy hands.
I stretch forth my hands unto thee:
My soul thirsteth after thee, as a thirsty land.
Hear me speedily, O LORD: my spirit faileth:
Hide not thy face from me,
Lest I be like unto them that go down into the pit.
Cause me to hear thy lovingkindness in the morning;
For in thee do I trust:
Cause me to know the way wherein I should walk;
For I lift up my soul unto thee.

Deliver me, O LORD, from mine enemies:
I flee unto thee to hide me.
Teach me to do thy will; for thou art my God:
Thy spirit is good; lead me into the land of upright-
ness.

Quicken me, O Lord, for thy name's sake:
For thy righteousness' sake bring my soul out of
    trouble.
And of thy mercy cut off mine enemies,
And destroy all them that afflict my soul:
For I am thy servant.   — Psalm 143.

Happy Is the People

BLESSED be the Lord my strength,
    Which teacheth my hands to war, and my fin-
        gers to fight:
My goodness, and my fortress;
My high tower, and my deliverer;
My shield, and he in whom I trust;
Who subdueth my people under me.

Lord, what is man, that thou takest knowledge of him!
Or the son of man, that thou makest account of him!
Man is like to vanity:
His days are as a shadow that passeth away.
Bow thy heavens, O Lord, and come down:
Touch the mountains, and they shall smoke.
Cast forth lightning, and scatter them:
Shoot out thine arrows, and destroy them.
Send thine hand from above;
Rid me, and deliver me out of great waters,
From the hand of strange children;
Whose mouth speaketh vanity,
And their right hand is a right hand of falsehood.

I will sing a new song unto thee, O God:
Upon a psaltery and an instrument of ten strings will I
    sing praises unto thee.

It is he that giveth salvation unto kings:

Who delivereth David, his servant, from the hurtful sword.

Rid me, and deliver me from the hand of strange children,

Whose mouth speaketh vanity,

And their right hand is a right hand of falsehood:

That our sons may be as plants grown up in their youth;

That our daughters may be as corner stones, polished after the similitude of a palace:

That our garners may be full, affording all manner of store:

That our sheep may bring forth thousands and ten thousands in our streets:

That our oxen may be strong to labour;

That there be no breaking in, nor going out;

That there be no complaining in our streets.

Happy is that people, that is in such a case:

Yea, happy is that people, whose God is the LORD.

— Psalm 144.

Thy Kingdom Is an Everlasting Kingdom

Damascus was one of the earliest cities to have a Christian church. It was also the first city to be taken by the power of Islam. A great Christian cathedral was built there on the ruins of a heathen temple. This, in turn, was converted into a mosque. The rebuilding destroyed all Christian features except one. On a great stone over the south portal an inscription carved in Greek letters, an adaptation of the 13th verse of the 145th Psalm may still be read: "Thy kingdom, O Christ, is an everlasting kingdom and thy dominion endureth throughout all generations."

I WILL extol thee, my God, O King;
And I will bless thy name forever and ever.
Every day will I bless thee;
And I will praise thy name forever and ever.
Great is the LORD, and greatly to be praised;
And his greatness is unsearchable.
One generation shall praise thy works to another,
And shall declare thy mighty acts.
I will speak of the glorious honour of thy majesty,
And of thy wondrous works.
And men shall speak of the might of thy terrible acts:
And I will declare thy greatness.
They shall abundantly utter the memory of thy great
goodness,
And shall sing of thy righteousness.

The LORD is gracious, and full of compassion;
Slow to anger, and of great mercy.
The LORD is good to all:
And his tender mercies are over all his works.
All thy works shall praise thee, O LORD;

And thy saints shall bless thee.
They shall speak of the glory of thy kingdom,
And talk of thy power;
To make known to the sons of men his mighty acts,
And the glorious majesty of his kingdom.
Thy kingdom is an everlasting kingdom,
And thy dominion endureth throughout all generations.

The LORD upholdeth all that fall,
And raiseth up all those that be bowed down.
The eyes of all wait upon thee;
And thou givest them their meat in due season.
Thou openest thine hand,
And satisfiest the desire of every living thing.
The LORD is righteous in all his ways,
And holy in all his works.
The LORD is nigh unto all them that call upon him,
To all that call upon him in truth.
He will fulfil the desire of them that fear him:
He also will hear their cry, and will save them.
The LORD preserveth all them that love him:
But all the wicked will he destroy.
My mouth shall speak the praise of the LORD:
And let all flesh bless his holy name forever and ever.

— Psalm 145.

Who Giveth Food to the Hungry

PRAISE ye the LORD.
   Praise the LORD, O my soul.
   While I live will I praise the LORD:
I will sing praises unto my God while I have any being.
Put not your trust in princes,
Nor in the son of man, in whom there is no help.
His breath goeth forth, he returneth to his earth;
In that very day his thoughts perish.

Happy is he that hath the God of Jacob for his help,
Whose hope is in the LORD his God:
Which made heaven, and earth,
The sea, and all that therein is:
Which keepeth truth forever:
Which executeth judgment for the oppressed:
Which giveth food to the hungry.

The LORD looseth the prisoners:
The LORD openeth the eyes of the blind:
The LORD raiseth them that are bowed down:
The LORD loveth the righteous:
The LORD preserveth the strangers;
He relieveth the fatherless and the widow:
But the way of the wicked he turneth upside down.
The LORD shall reign forever,
Even thy God, O Zion, unto all generations.
Praise ye the LORD.   — Psalm 146.

Praise Ye the Lord!

The last four Psalms might be grouped together as one great song of praise and thanksgiving to God from all created things.

PRAISE ye the LORD:
  For it is good to sing praises unto our God;
  For it is pleasant; and praise is comely.
The LORD doth build up Jerusalem:
He gathereth together the outcasts of Israel.
He healeth the broken in heart,
And bindeth up their wounds.
He telleth the number of the stars;
He calleth them all by their names.
Great is our LORD, and of great power:
His understanding is infinite.
The LORD lifteth up the meek:
He casteth the wicked down to the ground.
Sing unto the LORD with thanksgiving;
Sing praise upon the harp unto our God:
Who covereth the heaven with clouds,
Who prepareth rain for the earth,
Who maketh grass to grow upon the mountains.
He giveth to the beast his food,
And to the young ravens which cry.
He delighteth not in the strength of the horse:
He taketh not pleasure in the legs of a man.
The LORD taketh pleasure in them that fear him,
In those that hope in his mercy.
Praise the LORD, O Jerusalem;
Praise thy God, O Zion.
For he hath strengthened the bars of thy gates;
He hath blessed thy children within thee.

SNOW STORM AT JERUSALEM

This is a most unusual picture showing a heavy fall of snow at Jerusalem. Snow rarely falls in Palestine, although it is mentioned several times in the Old Testament.

"Snow and hail, stormy winds fulfilling his word."

One of David's captains "slew a lion in a pit" during a snow storm.

He maketh peace in thy borders,
And filleth thee with the finest of the wheat.
He sendeth forth his commandment upon earth:
His word runneth very swiftly.
He giveth snow like wool.
He scattereth the hoarfrost like ashes.
He casteth forth his ice like morsels:
Who can stand before his cold?
He sendeth out his word, and melteth them:
He causeth his wind to blow, and the waters flow.
He sheweth his word unto Jacob,
His statutes and his judgments unto Israel.
He hath not dealt so with any nation:
And as for his judgments, they have not known
    them.
Praise ye the LORD.   — Psalm 147.

PRAISE ye the LORD.
Praise ye the LORD from the heavens:
Praise him in the heights.
Praise ye him, all his angels:
Praise ye him, all his hosts.
Praise ye him, sun and moon:
Praise him, all ye stars of light.
Praise him, ye heavens of heavens,
And ye waters that be above the heavens.
Let them praise the name of the LORD:
For he commanded, and they were created.
He hath also stablished them forever and ever:
He hath made a decree which shall not pass.
Praise the LORD from the earth,
Ye dragons, and all deeps:
Fire and hail; snow and vapours;
Stormy wind fulfilling his word:
Mountains and all hills;
Fruitful trees and all cedars:
Beasts and all cattle;
Creeping things and flying fowl:
Kings of the earth and all people;
Princes and all judges of the earth:
Both young men and maidens;
Old men and children:
Let them praise the name of the LORD:
For his name alone is excellent;
His glory is above the earth and heaven.
He also exalteth the horn of his people,
The praise of all his saints;
Even of the children of Israel,
A people near unto him.
Praise ye the LORD.

—Psalm 148.

CEDAR OF LEBANON

Photograph by Professor Lewis Bayles Paton

"MOUNTAINS, and all hills; fruitful trees, and all cedars."

RAISE ye the LORD.
Sing unto the LORD a new song,
And his praise in the congregation of saints.
Let Israel rejoice in him that made him:
Let the children of Zion be joyful in their King.
Let them praise his name in the dance:
Let them sing praises unto him with the timbrel and harp.
For the LORD taketh pleasure in his people:
He will beautify the meek with salvation.
Let the saints be joyful in glory:
Let them sing aloud upon their beds.
Let the high praises of God be in their mouth,
And a two-edged sword in their hand;
To execute vengeance upon the heathen,
And punishments upon the people;
To bind their kings with chains,
And their nobles with fetters of iron;
To execute upon them the judgment written:
This honour have all his saints.
Praise ye the LORD.   —Psalm 149.

RAISE ye the LORD.
Praise God in his sanctuary:
Praise him in the firmament of his power.
Praise him for his mighty acts:
Praise him according to his excellent greatness.
Praise him with the sound of the trumpet:
Praise him with the psaltery and harp.
Praise him with the timbrel and dance:
Praise him with stringed instruments and organs.
Praise him upon the loud cymbals:
Praise him upon the high sounding cymbals.
Let everything that hath breath praise the LORD.
Praise ye the LORD.   —Psalm 150.

Canticle to the Sun

Saint Francis of Assisi, one of the most beautiful spirits of all Christian history, who loved men and nature because he believed that both man and nature were God's handiwork, wrote in the spirit of the 148th, 149th, and 150th Psalms this beautiful Canticle to the Sun. Perhaps no other piece of literature has so close a resemblance to the Psalms in spirit and in form.

"MOST high, almighty, and excellent LORD, to Thee be praise and glory and honour, and all blessing! To Thee alone, Most High, do they belong, and no man is worthy to name Thy name.

"Praised be Thou, my LORD, with all Thy creatures, and, above all, our Brother the Sun, who brings to us the light and the day. Beautiful is he, and radiant in his glorious splendour; and to us, Most High, he beareth witness of Thee.

"Praised be Thou, my LORD, for our Sister the Moon, and for all the Stars. In the heavens Thou hast set them, bright and precious and beautiful.

"Praised be Thou, my LORD, for our Brother the Wind, for the air, the cloud, the calm, and all weather, whereby Thou sustainest life in all Thy creatures.

"Praised be Thou, my LORD, for our Sister the Water, for manifold are her services, and she is humble, precious, and pure.

"Praised be Thou, my LORD, for our Brother the Fire. By him Thou dost lighten our darkness. Beautiful is he, joyful, very mighty, and strong.

"Praised be Thou, my LORD, for our Sister, Mother Earth, who doth sustain and nourish us, and bringeth forth in abundance divers fruits, flowers of many colours, and grass.

"Praised be Thou, my LORD, for those who for love of Thee, forgive their enemies, and endure weakness and tribulation. Yea, blessed are those who shall continue in peace, for by Thee, Most High, shall they be crowned.

"Praised be Thou, my LORD, for our Sister, the Death of the body, from whom no living man can escape. Woe to those who die in mortal sin! Blessed are they who are conformed to Thy most holy will, for the second death shall have no power to hurt them.

"Praise and bless my LORD! give thanks to Him and serve Him with all humbleness of heart."

The Book of Job

ONCE upon a time a wise man in Israel thought long upon the question, "Why is there suffering in the world?"

Other people asked the same question, and in the time of that wise man there was an answer which many people repeated without much thought. They said people suffered because they had sinned. Now it is very true that sin brings suffering, but when they turned that about and said that all suffering came from sin, this wise man doubted it. Still more did he doubt it when they applied it to particular cases. Can we say, "This man suffers, therefore this man has sinned"? Can we go a step further and say, "This man suffers much, therefore he must have been a great sinner"? This wise man did not believe we could say that. Do not the righteous suffer, as well as the wicked?

As he pondered over the problem his thoughts turned to a story of a righteous man who suffered. Perhaps it was one of the old, old stories, which were told from generation to generation. We do not know its age or its origin. It was the story of Job, a man rich and pious, and who suddenly lost his riches and all his children; but still he kept his piety. Then he was smitten with a hopeless disease, a kind of leprosy, which brought him face to face with a lingering and painful death.

Still he kept his piety and refused to curse God who dealt so harshly with him.

In the story the reason for his suffering is not sin. It is that God is allowing his piety to be tested. He stands the test, and in the end he is rewarded. But the sufferer, Job, did not know that he was being tested. To him, sitting in pain awaiting death, there could have been no explanation for his suffering.

Suppose friends came and said that his sin was the reason for his suffering; what would such a man say to that reason?

So on the basis of this story the wise man wrote a dialogue in poetry. Three friends come to Job, and discuss with him his suffering. They suggest that he suffers because he has sinned. Job indignantly denies it. Each becomes more heated as the debate goes on. At last, Jehovah himself speaks, and gives an entirely different point of view. God is so great, so good, so wise, that men may trust him, even if they find it impossible to solve the hard problems of life. Job accepts this trust. The end of the poem, taken from the old story which furnished the beginning, tells of the reward which finally came to Job.

The arrangement of the book is very systematic:

1. The prose story of Job.
2. The debate; in three cycles of speeches. Each cycle, with one exception in the last, has a speech by each of Job's three friends and an answer by Job.

3. A new speaker, Elihu, is introduced, who tries to help the side of the friends.

4. Two speeches by Jehovah, with short responses by Job.

5. The prose ending of the story.

All except 1 and 5 are in poetry.

The Book of Job is a dramatic poem, but it was not a drama. The Hebrews had no theatre, and the poem was not written to be acted; but the development of the dialogue is dramatic and full of climaxes. The three friends are each different. Eliphaz has a vision, like an old prophet; Bildad relies on the wisdom of the fathers; and Zophar thinks the facts are so plain that they need no authority. Eliphaz is a prophet; Bildad, a traditionalist; Zophar, a dogmatist. Each one is more harsh than the preceding one. Job also grows more bitter, till at the end of each round of speeches he calls his friends liars. The experience of life has shaken him out of the old conceptions of life, and he is searching in agony for a new faith which shall meet the facts of life. At last he finds it, not in an intellectual theory, but in a humble trust in God. His problem is met by a religious experience.

As the Revised Version is clearer in some passages of Job, the former in a few places has been followed.

JOB AND HIS FRIENDS

Painted expressly for The Book of Life by
Helen M. Bennett

"Now when Job's three friends heard of
all this evil that was come upon him, they
came every one from his own place; Eliphaz
the Temanite, and Bildad the Shuhite, and
Zophar the Naamathite: for they had made
an appointment together to come to mourn
with him and to comfort him."   Job 2:11.

The Prologue

THE TESTING OF JOB

Job, a rich man of the East.
Eliphaz, the Temanite,
Bildad, the Shuhite,
Zophar, the Naamathite. } *Friends of Job.*
Elihu, son of Barachel, the Buzite.
The Wife of Job.
The LORD.
Satan.
Sons of God, Messengers, Friends, Spectators.

PLACES

The Land of Uz, a country east of Palestine.
The Court of Heaven.

TIME

The Patriarchal Age.

HOW JOB WAS RICH IN WEALTH AND CHILDREN

THERE was a man in the land of Uz, whose name was Job; and that man was perfect and upright, and one that feared God, and eschewed evil. And there were born unto him seven sons and three daughters. His substance also was seven thousand sheep, and three thousand camels, and five hundred yoke of oxen, and five hundred she asses, and a very great household; so that this man was the greatest of all the men of the east.

And his sons went and feasted in their houses, every one his day; and sent and called for their three sisters to eat and to drink with them. And it was so, when the days of their feasting were gone about, that Job sent and sanctified them, and rose up early in the morning, and offered burnt offerings according to the number of them all: for Job said, "It may be that my sons have sinned, and cursed God in their hearts." Thus did Job continually.

HOW THE ACCUSER DOUBTS JOB'S PIETY

Now there was a day when the sons of God came to present themselves before the LORD, and Satan came also among them.

The LORD: "Whence comest thou?"

Satan: "From going to and fro in the earth, and from walking up and down in it."

The LORD: "Hast thou considered my servant Job, that there is none like him in the earth, a perfect and an upright man, one that feareth God, and escheweth evil?"

Satan: "Doth Job fear God for naught? Hast not thou made an hedge about him, and about his house, and about all that he hath on every side? Thou hast blessed the work of his hands, and his substance is increased in the land. But put forth thine hand now, and touch all that he hath, and he will curse thee to thy face."

The LORD: "Behold, all that he hath is in thy power; only upon himself put not forth thine hand."

So Satan went forth from the presence of the LORD.

HOW DISASTER FELL UPON JOB

And there was a day when his sons and his daughters were eating and drinking wine in their eldest brother's house:

First Messenger: "The oxen were plowing, and the asses feeding beside them: and the Sabeans fell upon them, and took them away; yea, they have slain the servants with the edge of the sword; and I only am escaped alone to tell thee."

While he was yet speaking, there came also another:

Second Messenger: "The fire of God is fallen from heaven, and hath burned up the sheep, and the servants, and consumed them; and I only am escaped alone to tell thee."

While he was yet speaking, there came also another:

Third Messenger: "The Chaldeans made out three bands, and fell upon the camels, and have carried them away, yea, and slain the servants with the edge of the sword; and I only am escaped alone to tell thee."

While he was yet speaking, there came also another:

Fourth Messenger: "Thy sons and thy daughters were eating and drinking wine in their eldest brother's house: and, behold, there came a great wind from the wilderness, and smote the four corners of the house, and it fell upon the young men, and they are dead; and I only am escaped alone to tell thee."

HOW HIS PIETY STOOD THE TEST

Then Job arose, and rent his mantle, and shaved his head, and fell down upon the ground, and worshiped, "Naked came I out of my mother's womb, and naked shall I return thither: the LORD gave, and the LORD hath taken away; blessed be the name of the LORD."

In all this Job sinned not, nor charged God foolishly.

—Job 1.

HOW THE ACCUSER STILL DOUBTED JOB

Again there was a day when the sons of God came to present themselves before the LORD, and Satan came also among them to present himself before the LORD.

The LORD: "From whence comest thou?"

Satan: "From going to and fro in the earth, and from walking up and down in it."

And the LORD said unto Satan, "Hast thou considered my servant Job, that there is none like him in the earth, a perfect and an upright man, one that feareth God, and escheweth evil? And still he holdeth fast his integrity, although thou movedst me against him, to destroy him without cause."

Satan: "Skin for skin, yea, all that a man hath will he give for his life; but put forth thine hand now, and touch his bone and his flesh, and he will curse thee to thy face."

And the LORD said unto Satan, "Behold, he is in thine hand; but save his life."

HOW JOB WAS TESTED BY PAINFUL DISEASE; BUT HIS PIETY STILL REMAINED

So went Satan forth from the presence of the LORD, and smote Job with sore boils from the sole of his foot unto his crown. And he took him a potsherd to scrape himself withal; and he sat down among the ashes.

The wife of Job: "Dost thou still retain thine integrity? Curse God, and die."

Job: "Thou speakest as one of the foolish women speaketh. What? Shall we receive good at the hand of God, and shall we not receive evil?"

In all this did not Job sin with his lips.

HOW JOB'S THREE FRIENDS CAME BUT FOUND NOTHING TO SAY

Now when Job's three friends heard of all this evil that was come upon him, they came every one from his own place; Eliphaz, the Temanite, and Bildad, the Shuhite, and Zophar, the Naamathite: for they had made an

appointment together to come to mourn with him and
to comfort him.   And when they lifted up their eyes
afar off, and knew him not, they lifted up their voice,
and wept;   and they rent every one his mantle, and
sprinkled dust upon their heads toward heaven.   So they
sat down with him upon the ground seven days and seven
nights, and none spake a word unto him: for they saw
that his grief was very great.   —Job 2.

The Debates

JOB'S COMPLAINT: "WOULD I HAD NEVER BEEN BORN"

AFTER this opened Job his mouth, and cursed his day.
And Job spake, and said,

"Let the day perish wherein I was born,
And the night in which it was said,
'There is a man child conceived.'
Let that day be darkness;
Let not God regard it from above,
Neither let the light shine upon it.
Let darkness and the shadow of death stain it;
Let a cloud dwell upon it;
Let the blackness of the day terrify it.
As for that night, let darkness seize upon it;
Let it not be joined unto the days of the year,
Let it not come into the number of the months.
Lo, let that night be solitary,
Let no joyful voice come therein.
Let them curse it that curse the day,
Who are ready to raise up their mourning.
Let the stars of the twilight thereof be dark;
Let it look for light, but have none;
Neither let it see the dawning of the day:
Because it shut not up the doors of my mother's womb,
Nor hid sorrow from mine eyes.

"WOULD I HAD DIED AT BIRTH"

"Why died I not from the womb?
Why did I not give up the ghost when I came out of
the belly?

Why did the knees prevent me?
Or why the breasts that I should suck?
For now should I have lain still and been quiet;
I should have slept: then had I been at rest,
With kings and counsellors of the earth,
Which built desolate places for themselves;
Or with princes that had gold,
Who filled their houses with silver:
Or as an hidden untimely birth I had not been;
As infants which never saw light.
There the wicked cease from troubling;
And there the weary be at rest.
There the prisoners rest together;
They hear not the voice of the oppressor.
The small and great are there;
And the servant is free from his master.

"WOULD I MIGHT DIE NOW"

"Wherefore is light given to him that is in misery,
And life unto the bitter in soul;
Which long for death, but it cometh not;
And dig for it more than for hid treasures;
Which rejoice exceedingly,
And are glad, when they can find the grave?
Why is light given to a man whose way is hid,
And whom God hath hedged in?
For my sighing cometh before I eat,
And my roarings are poured out like the waters.
For the thing which I greatly feared is come upon me,
And that which I was afraid of is come unto me.
I was not in safety, neither had I rest, neither was I
    quiet;
Yet trouble came."   —Job 3.

The First Speech of Eliphaz

"Are you so easily discouraged?"

Then Eliphaz, the Temanite, answered and said,

"If we assay to commune with thee, wilt thou be
    grieved?
But who can withhold himself from speaking?
Behold, thou hast instructed many,
And thou hast strengthened the weak hands.
Thy words have upholden him that was falling,
And thou hast strengthened the feeble knees.
But now it is come upon thee, and thou faintest;
It toucheth thee, and thou art troubled.
Is not this thy fear, thy confidence, thy hope,
And the uprightness of thy ways?

"Remember that the righteous never perish"

"Remember, I pray thee, who ever perished, being
    innocent?
Or where were the righteous cut off?
Even as I have seen, they that plow iniquity,
And sow wickedness, reap the same.
By the blast of God they perish,
And by the breath of his nostrils are they consumed.
The roaring of the lion, and the voice of the fierce lion,
And the teeth of the young lions, are broken.
The old lion perisheth for lack of prey,
And the stout lion's whelps are scattered abroad.

"I heard a voice saying that no man was wholly sinless: so all suffer"

"Now a thing was secretly brought to me,
And mine ear received a little thereof.

In thoughts from the visions of the night,
When deep sleep falleth on men,
Fear came upon me, and trembling,
Which made all my bones to shake.
Then a spirit passed before my face;
The hair of my flesh stood up:
It stood still, but I could not discern the form thereof:
An image was before mine eyes,
There was silence, and I heard a voice, saying,
'Shall mortal man be more just than God?
Shall a man be more pure than his maker?
Behold, he put no trust in his servants;
And his angels he charged with folly:
How much less in them that dwell in houses of clay,
Whose foundation is in the dust,
Which are crushed before the moth?
They are destroyed from morning to evening:
They perish forever without any regarding it.
Doth not their excellency which is in them go away?
They die, even without wisdom.'   —Job 4.

"BUT ONLY THE WICKED PERISH"

"Call now, if there be any that will answer thee;
And to which of the saints wilt thou turn?
For wrath killeth the foolish man, and envy slayeth
    the silly one.
I have seen the foolish taking root:
But suddenly I cursed his habitation.
His children are far from safety,
And they are crushed in the gate,
Neither is there any to deliver them.
Whose harvest the hungry eateth up,
And taketh it even out of the thorns,
And the robber swalloweth up their substance.

Although affliction cometh not forth of the dust,
Neither doth trouble spring out of the ground;
Yet man is born unto trouble,
As the sparks fly upward.

"IF I WERE YOU, I WOULD SEEK GOD"

"I would seek unto God,
  And unto God would I commit my cause:
Which doeth great things and unsearchable;
  Marvellous things without number:
Who giveth rain upon the earth,
  And sendeth waters upon the fields:
To set up on high those that be low;
  That those which mourn may be exalted to safety.
He disappointeth the devices of the crafty,
  So that their hands cannot perform their enterprise.
He taketh the wise in their own craftiness:
  And the counsel of the froward is carried headlong.
They meet with darkness in the daytime,
  And grope in the noonday as in the night.
But he saveth the poor from the sword of their mouth,
  And from the hand of the mighty.
So the poor hath hope,
  And iniquity stoppeth her mouth.

"YOU SHOULD REJOICE THAT GOD CORRECTS YOU"

"Behold, happy is the man whom God correcteth;
  Therefore despise not thou the chastening of the Al-
      mighty:
For he maketh sore, and bindeth up:
  He woundeth, and his hands make whole.
He shall deliver thee in six troubles:
  Yea, in seven there shall no evil touch thee.
In famine he shall redeem thee from death:

And in war from the power of the sword.
Thou shalt be hid from the scourge of the tongue:
Neither shalt thou be afraid of destruction when it
  cometh.
At destruction and famine thou shalt laugh:
Neither shalt thou be afraid of the beasts of the earth.

"IF YOU SUBMIT, GOD WILL YET BLESS YOU"

"For thou shalt be in league with the stones of the field:
And the beasts of the field shall be at peace with thee.
And thou shalt know that thy tabernacle shall be in
  peace;
And thou shalt visit thy habitation, and shalt not sin.
Thou shalt know also that thy seed shall be great,
And thine offspring as the grass of the earth.
Thou shalt come to thy grave in a full age,
Like as a shock of corn cometh in in his season.
Lo, this, we have searched it, so it is;
Hear it, and know thou it for thy good."   —Job 5.

THE FIRST REPLY OF JOB

"SURELY I HAVE REASON FOR COMPLAINT"

But Job answered and said,

"Oh that my grief were but weighed,
And my calamity laid in the balances together!
For now it would be heavier than the sand of the sea:
Therefore my words are swallowed up.
For the arrows of the Almighty are within me,
The poison whereof drinketh up my spirit:
The terrors of God do set themselves in array against
  me.
Doth the wild ass bray when he hath grass?

Or loweth the ox over his fodder?
Can that which is unsavoury be eaten without salt?
Or is there any taste in the white of an egg?
The things that my soul refused to touch
Are as my sorrowful meat.

"EVEN DEATH WOULD BE WELCOME"

"Oh that I might have my request;
And that God would grant me the thing that I long
    for!
Even that it would please God to destroy me;
That he would let loose his hand, and cut me off!
Then should I yet have comfort;
Yea, I would harden myself in sorrow:
Let him not spare; for I have not concealed the words
    of the Holy One.
What is my strength, that I should hope?
And what is mine end, that I should prolong my life?
Is my strength the strength of stones?
Or is my flesh of brass?
Is not my help in me?
And is wisdom driven quite from me?

"YOU HAVE NOT SHOWN THE SYMPATHY I HOPED"

"To him that is afflicted pity should be shewed from his
    friend;
But he forsaketh the fear of the Almighty.
My brethren have dealt deceitfully as a brook,
And as the stream of brooks they pass away;
Which are blackish by reason of the ice,
And wherein the snow is hid:
What time they wax warm, they vanish:
When it is hot, they are consumed out of their place.

The paths of their way are turned aside;
They go to nothing, and perish.
The troops of Tema looked,
The companies of Sheba waited for them.
They were confounded because they had hoped;
They came thither, and were ashamed.
For now ye are nothing;
Ye see my casting down, and are afraid.
Did I say, 'Bring unto me'?
Or, 'Give a reward for me of your substance'?
Or, 'Deliver me from the enemy's hand'?
Or, 'Redeem me from the hand of the mighty'?

"HOW HAVE I SINNED TO DESERVE THIS SUFFERING?"

"Teach me, and I will hold my tongue:
And cause me to understand wherein I have erred.
How forcible are right words!
But what doth your arguing reprove?
Do ye imagine to reprove words,
And the speeches of one that is desperate, which are as
    wind?
Yea, ye overwhelm the fatherless,
And ye dig a pit for your friend.
Now therefore be content, look upon me;
For it is evident unto you if I lie.
Return, I pray you, let it not be iniquity;
Yea, return again, my righteousness is in it.
Is there iniquity in my tongue?
Cannot my taste discern perverse things?   —Job 6.

"ALL MY LIFE IS SUFFERING"

"Is there not an appointed time to man upon earth?
Are not his days also like the days of an hireling?
As a servant earnestly desireth the shadow,

And as an hireling looketh for the reward of his work:
So am I made to possess months of vanity,
And wearisome nights are appointed to me.
When I lie down, I say,
'When shall I arise, and the night be gone?'
And I am full of tossings to and fro unto the dawning
    of the day.
My flesh is clothed with worms and clods of dust;
My skin is broken, and become loathsome.
My days are swifter than a weaver's shuttle,
And are spent without hope.
O remember that my life is wind:
Mine eye shall no more see good.
The eye of him that hath seen me shall see me no
    more:
Thine eyes are upon me, and I am not.
As the cloud is consumed and vanisheth away:
So he that goeth down to the grave shall come up no
    more.
He shall return no more to his house,
Neither shall his place know him any more.

"WHY DOES GOD TORMENT ME?"

"Therefore I will not refrain my mouth;
I will speak in the anguish of my spirit;
I will complain in the bitterness of my soul.
Am I a sea, or a whale,
That thou settest a watch over me?
When I say, 'My bed shall comfort me,
My couch shall ease my complaint';
Then thou scarest me with dreams,
And terrifiest me through visions:
So that my soul chooseth strangling,
And death rather than my life.

I loathe it; I would not live alway:
Let me alone; for my days are vanity.
What is man, that thou shouldest magnify him?
And that thou shouldest set thine heart upon him?
And that thou shouldest visit him every morning,
And try him every moment?
How long wilt thou not depart from me,
Nor let me alone till I swallow down my spittle?

"IF I HAVE SINNED, WHY DOES NOT GOD FORGIVE?"

"If I have sinned; what do I unto thee, O thou watcher
    of men?
Why hast thou set me as a mark against thee,
So that I am a burden to myself?
And why dost thou not pardon my transgression, and
    take away mine iniquity?
For now shall I sleep in the dust;
And thou shalt seek me in the morning, but I shall
    not be." —Job 7.

THE FIRST SPEECH OF BILDAD

"DO YOU THINK TO CHARGE GOD WITH INJUSTICE?"

Then answered Bildad, the Shuhite, and said,

"How long wilt thou speak these things?
And how long shall the words of thy mouth be like a
    strong wind?
Doth God pervert judgment?
Or doth the Almighty pervert justice?
If thy children have sinned against him,
And he have cast them away for their transgression;
If thou wouldest seek unto God betimes,
And make thy supplication to the Almighty;
If thou wert pure and upright;

Surely now he would awake for thee,
And make the habitation of thy righteousness pros-
　　perous.
Though thy beginning was small,
Yet thy latter end should greatly increase.

"HAVE NOT THE FATHERS TAUGHT THAT SUFFERING GROWS OUT OF SIN?"

"For enquire, I pray thee, of the former age,
And prepare thyself to the search of their fathers:

For we are but of yesterday, and know nothing,
Because our days upon earth are a shadow:
Shall not they teach thee, and tell thee,
And utter words out of their heart?
Can the rush grow up without mire?　Can the flag
　　grow without water?
Whilst it is yet in its greenness, and not cut down,
It withereth before any other herb.
So are the paths of all that forget God;
And the hypocrite's hope shall perish:
Whose hope shall be cut off,
And whose trust shall be a spider's web.
He shall lean upon his house, but it shall not stand:
He shall hold it fast, but it shall not endure.
He is green before the sun,
And his branch shooteth forth in his garden.
His roots are wrapped about the heap,
And seeth the place of stones.
If he destroy it from its place,
Then it shall deny him, saying, 'I have not seen thee.'
Behold, this is the joy of his way,
And out of the earth shall others grow.

"TURN TO GOD; HE WILL YET RESTORE YOU"

"Behold, God will not cast away a perfect man,
   Neither will he help the evil doers:
Till he fill thy mouth with laughing,
And thy lips with rejoicing.
They that hate thee shall be clothed with shame;
And the dwelling place of the wicked shall come to
   naught."   —Job 8.

THE SECOND REPLY OF JOB

"HOW CAN A MAN PROVE HIS RIGHTEOUSNESS? GOD
   IS GREAT, AND DOES AS HE WILL"

Then Job answered and said,

"I know it is so of a truth:
But how should man be just with God?
If he will contend with him,
He cannot answer him one of a thousand.
He is wise in heart, and mighty in strength:
Who hath hardened himself against him, and hath
   prospered?
Which removeth the mountains, and they know not:
Which overturneth them in his anger.
Which shaketh the earth out of her place,
And the pillars thereof tremble.
Which commandeth the sun, and it riseth not;
And sealeth up the stars.
Which alone spreadeth out the heavens,
And treadeth upon the waves of the sea.
Which maketh Arcturus, Orion, and Pleiades,
And the chambers of the south.
Which doeth great things past finding out;
Yea, and wonders without number.
Lo, he goeth by me, and I see him not:

He passeth on also, but I perceive him not.
Behold, he taketh away. Who can hinder him?
Who will say unto him, 'What doest thou?'
If God will not withdraw his anger,
The proud helpers do stoop under him.
How much less shall I answer him,
And choose out my words to reason with him,
Whom, though I were righteous, yet would I not
    answer,
But I would make supplication to my judge.
If I had called, and he had answered me;
Yet would I not believe that he had hearkened unto
    my voice.
For he breaketh me with a tempest,
And multiplieth my wounds without cause.
He will not suffer me to take my breath,
But filleth me with bitterness.
If I speak of strength, lo, he is strong:
And if of judgment, who shall set me a time to plead?
If I justify myself, mine own mouth shall condemn
    me:
If I say, "I am perfect," it shall also prove me perverse.
Though I were perfect, yet would I not know my
    soul:
I would despise my life.

"HE DESTROYS THE GOOD AND THE EVIL ALIKE"

"This is one thing, therefore I said it,
'He destroyeth the perfect and the wicked.'
If the scourge slay suddenly,
He will laugh at the trial of the innocent.
The earth is given into the hand of the wicked:
He covereth the faces of the judges thereof;
If not, where, and who is he?

"SWIFTLY SPEEDS MY LIFE, AND GOD WILL NOT ANSWER MY CRY"

"Now my days are swifter than a post:
They flee away, they see no good.
They are passed away as the swift ships:
As the eagle that hasteth to the prey.
If I say, "I will forget my complaint,
I will leave off my heaviness, and comfort myself":
I am afraid of all my sorrows,
I know that thou wilt not hold me innocent.
If I be wicked,
Why then labour I in vain?
If I wash myself with snow water,
And make my hands never so clean;
Yet shalt thou plunge me in the ditch,
And mine own clothes shall abhor me.
For he is not a man, as I am, that I should answer him,
And we should come together in judgment.
Neither is there any daysman betwixt us,
That might lay his hand upon us both.
Let him take his rod away from me,
And let not his fear terrify me:
Then would I speak, and not fear him;
But it is not so with me. —Job 9.

"WHY DOES GOD TORTURE ME?"

"My soul is weary of my life;
I will leave my complaint upon myself;
I will speak in the bitterness of my soul.
I will say unto God, 'Do not condemn me;
Shew me wherefore thou contendest with me.
Is it good unto thee that thou shouldest oppress,
That thou shouldest despise the work of thine hands,
And shine upon the counsel of the wicked?

Hast thou eyes of flesh?
Or seest thou as man seeth?
Are thy days as the days of man?
Are thy years as man's days,
That thou enquirest after mine iniquity,
And searchest after my sin?
Thou knowest that I am not wicked;
And there is none that can deliver out of thine hand.
Thine hands have made me and fashioned me together
    round about;
Yet thou dost destroy me.
Remember, I beseech thee, that thou hast made me
    as the clay;
And wilt thou bring me into dust again?
Hast thou not poured me out as milk,
And curdled me like cheese?
Thou hast clothed me with skin and flesh,
And hast fenced me with bones and sinews.
Thou hast granted me life and favour,
And thy visitation hath preserved my spirit.
And these things hast thou hid in thine heart:
I know that this is with thee.
If I sin, then thou markest me,
And thou wilt not acquit me from mine iniquity.
If I be wicked, woe unto me;
And if I be righteous, yet will I not lift up my head.
I am full of confusion;
Therefore see thou mine affliction;
For it increaseth. Thou huntest me as a fierce lion:
And again thou shewest thyself marvellous upon me.
Thou renewest thy witnesses against me,
And increasest thine indignation upon me;
Changes and war are against me.

"WHY DID GOD EVER CALL ME INTO LIFE?"

" 'Wherefore then hast thou brought me forth out of the
      womb?
   O that I had given up the ghost, and no eye had seen
      me!
   I should have been as though I had not been;
   I should have been carried from the womb to the grave.

"LET HIM GIVE ME A LITTLE RESPITE FROM SUFFERING;
      THEN WELCOME, DEATH!"

" 'Are not my days few?   Cease then,
   And let me alone, that I may take comfort a little,
   Before I go whence I shall not return,
   Even to the land of darkness and the shadow of death;
   A land of darkness, as darkness itself;
   And of the shadow of death, without any order,
   And where the light is as darkness.' " —Job 10.

THE FIRST SPEECH OF ZOPHAR

"DO YOU DARE TO CLAIM INNOCENCE?"

Then answered Zophar, the Naamathite, and said,

"Should not the multitude of words be answered?
   And should a man full of talk be justified?
   Should thy lies make men hold their peace?
   And when thou mockest, shall no man make thee
      ashamed?
   For thou hast said, 'My doctrine is pure,
   And I am clean in thine eyes.'

"WOULD THAT GOD WOULD SHOW YOUR WICKEDNESS!"

"But O that God would speak,
   And open his lips against thee;

And that he would shew thee the secrets of wisdom,
That they are double to that which is!
Know, therefore, that God exacteth of thee less than
    thine iniquity deserveth.

"DO YOU DARE QUESTION GOD'S JUSTICE?"

"Canst thou by searching find out God?
Canst thou find out the Almighty unto perfection?
It is as high as heaven; what canst thou do?
Deeper than hell; what canst thou know?
The measure thereof is longer than the earth,
And broader than the sea.
If he cut off, and shut up,
Or gather together, then who can hinder him?
For he knoweth vain men:
He seeth wickedness also; will he not then consider it?
But an empty man will get understanding,
Yea, man is born as a wild ass's colt.

"BUT HUMBLE YOURSELF AND GOD WILL YET RESTORE YOU"

"If thou prepare thine heart,
And stretch out thine hands toward him;
If iniquity be in thine hand, put it far away,
And let not wickedness dwell in thy tabernacles.
For then shalt thou lift up thy face without spot;
Yea, thou shalt be stedfast, and shalt not fear:
Because thou shalt forget thy misery,
And remember it as waters that pass away:
And thine age shall be clearer than the noonday;
Thou shalt shine forth, thou shalt be as the morning.
And thou shalt be secure, because there is hope;
Yea, thou shalt dig about thee, and thou shalt take thy
    rest in safety.

Also thou shalt lie down, and none shall make thee
    afraid;
Yea, many shall make suit unto thee.
But the eyes of the wicked shall fail,
And they shall not escape,
And their hope shall be as the giving up of the ghost."

—Job 11.

The Third Reply of Job

"HOW WISE YOU THINK YOU ARE! I KNOW SOME THINGS TOO"

And Job answered and said,

"No doubt but ye are the people,
    And wisdom shall die with you.
But I have understanding as well as you;
I am not inferior to you:
Yea, who knoweth not such things as these?
I am as one mocked of his neighbour,
Who calleth upon God, and he answereth him:
The just upright man is laughed to scorn.
He that is ready to slip with his feet
Is as a lamp despised in the thought of him that is at
    ease.
The tabernacles of robbers prosper,
And they that provoke God are secure;
Into whose hand God bringeth abundantly.

"THE VERY BEASTS KNOW WHAT YOU CALL WISDOM"

"But ask now the beasts, and they shall teach thee;
And the fowls of the air, and they shall tell thee:
Or speak to the earth, and it shall teach thee:
And the fishes of the sea shall declare unto thee.
Who knoweth not in all these
That the hand of the LORD hath wrought this?

In whose hand is the soul of every living thing,
And the breath of all mankind.
Doth not the ear try words?
And the mouth taste his meat?

"I CAN PARROT THE ANCIENT WISDOM AS WELL AS YOU."

"With the ancient is wisdom;
And in length of days understanding.
With him is wisdom and strength,
He hath counsel and understanding.
Behold, he breaketh down, and it cannot be built
    again:
He shutteth up a man, and there can be no opening.
Behold, he withholdeth the waters, and they dry up:
Also he sendeth them out, and they overturn the earth.
With him is strength and wisdom:
The deceived and the deceiver are his.
He leadeth counsellors away spoiled,
And maketh the judges fools.
He looseth the bond of kings,
And girdeth their loins with a girdle.
He leadeth princes away spoiled,
And overthroweth the mighty.
He removeth away the speech of the trusty,
And taketh away the understanding of the aged.
He poureth contempt upon princes,
And weakeneth the strength of the mighty.
He discovereth deep things out of darkness,
And bringeth out to light the shadow of death.
He increaseth the nations, and destroyeth them:
He enlargeth the nations, and straiteneth them again.
He taketh away the heart of the chief of the people of
    the earth.

And causeth them to wander in a wilderness where
    there is no way.
They grope in the dark without light,
And he maketh them to stagger like a drunken man.

                             —Job 12.

"SEE! I KNOW AS MUCH OF IT AS YOU"

"Lo, mine eye hath seen all this,
Mine ear hath heard and understood it.
What ye know, the same do I know also:
I am not inferior unto you.

"YOU TELL LIES TO DEFEND GOD"

"Surely I would speak to the Almighty,
And I desire to reason with God.
But ye are forgers of lies,
Ye are all physicians of no value.
O that ye would altogether hold your peace!
And it should be your wisdom.
Hear now my reasoning,
And hearken to the pleadings of my lips.
Will ye speak wickedly for God?
And talk deceitfully for him?
Will ye accept his person?
Will ye contend for God?
Is it good that he should search you out?
Or as one man mocketh another, do ye so mock him?
He will surely reprove you,
If ye do secretly accept persons.
Shall not his excellency make you afraid?
And his dread fall upon you?
Your remembrances are like unto ashes,
Your bodies to bodies of clay.

"KEEP STILL NOW AND LET ME SPEAK.

"Hold your peace, let me alone,
That I may speak, and let come on me what will.
Wherefore do I take my flesh in my teeth,
And put my life in mine hand?
Though he slay me, yet will I trust in him:
But I will maintain mine own ways before him.
He also shall be my salvation:
For an hypocrite shall not come before him.
Hear diligently my speech,
And my declaration with your ears.
Behold now, I have ordered my cause;
I know that I shall be justified.
Who is he that will plead with me?
For now, if I hold my tongue, I shall give up the ghost.
Only do not two things unto me:
Then will I not hide myself from thee.
Withdraw thine hand far from me:
And let not thy dread make me afraid.
Then call thou, and I will answer:
Or let me speak, and answer thou me.

"IF I HAVE SINNED, WHAT HAVE I DONE?"

"How many are mine iniquities and sins?
Make me to know my transgression and my sin.
Wherefore hidest thou thy face,
And holdest me for thine enemy?
Wilt thou break a leaf driven to and fro?
And wilt thou pursue the dry stubble?
For thou writest bitter things against me,
And makest me to possess the iniquities of my youth.
Thou puttest my feet also in the stocks,
And lookest narrowly unto all my paths;
Thou settest a print upon the heels of my feet.

And he, as a rotten thing, consumeth,
As a garment that is moth eaten.

"MINE IS THE COMMON LOT"

"Man that is born of a woman
Is of few days, and full of trouble.
He cometh forth like a flower, and is cut down:
He fleeth also as a shadow, and continueth not.
And dost thou open thine eyes upon such an one,
And bringest me into judgment with thee?
Who can bring a clean thing out of an unclean?   Not
    one.
Seeing his days are determined,
The number of his months are with thee,
Thou hast appointed his bounds that he cannot pass;
Turn from him, that he may rest,
Till he shall accomplish, as an hireling, his day.

"A TREE CUT DOWN WILL SPROUT AGAIN, BUT MAN HAS NO HOPE"

"For there is hope of a tree,
If it be cut down, that it will sprout again,
And that the tender branch thereof will not cease.
Though the root thereof wax old in the earth,
And the stock thereof die in the ground;
Yet through the scent of water it will bud,
And bring forth boughs like a plant.
But man dieth, and wasteth away:
Yea, man giveth up the ghost, and where is he?
As the waters fail from the sea,
And the flood decayeth and drieth up:
So man lieth down, and riseth not:
Till the heavens be no more, they shall not awake,
Nor be raised out of their sleep.

"THE GRAVE WILL HIDE ME FROM GOD, BUT BRING NO JUSTICE"

"O that thou wouldest hide me in the grave,
  That thou wouldest keep me secret, until thy wrath
    be past,
  That thou wouldest appoint me a set time, and re-
    member me!
  If a man die, shall he live again?
  All the days of my appointed time will I wait,
  Till my change come.
  Thou shalt call, and I will answer thee:
  Thou wilt have a desire to the work of thine hands.
  For now thou numberest my steps:
  Dost thou not watch over my sin?
  My transgression is sealed up in a bag,
  And thou sewest up mine iniquity.
  And surely the mountain falling cometh to naught,
  And the rock is removed out of his place.
  The waters wear the stones:
  Thou washest away the things which grow out of the
    dust of the earth;
  And thou destroyest the hope of man.
  Thou prevailest forever against him, and he passeth:
  Thou changest his countenance, and sendest him away.
  His sons come to honour, and he knoweth it not;
  And they are brought low, but he perceiveth it not of
    them.
  But his flesh upon him shall have pain,
  And his soul within him shall mourn."   —Job 13, 14.

The first round of speeches is closed. The debate has been about God. The friends have maintained that he is always just; therefore, if Job suffers, he must have sinned. Job sees no justice, only power, in God's action. At last he accuses them of lying about God in order to defend him.

That side of the argument is closed. But the friends wish to show Job his error. If they can compel him to see the peril in which the wicked man stands, they may move him to penitence. So they hold up a mirror in which they expect Job to see himself.

The friends speak in the same order as in the first round of speeches.

The Second Round of Speeches
The Second Speech of Eliphaz

"EMPTY WORDS AND A GODLESS HEART!"

Then answered Eliphaz, the Temanite, and said,

"Should a wise man utter vain knowledge,
And fill his belly with the east wind?
Should he reason with unprofitable talk?
Or with speeches wherewith he can do no good?
Yea, thou castest off fear,
And restrainest prayer before God.
For thy mouth uttereth thine iniquity,
And thou choosest the tongue of the crafty.
Thine own mouth condemneth thee, and not I:
Yea, thine own lips testify against thee.

"DO YOU THINK TO UNDERSTAND GOD, THAT YOU THROW AWAY HIS COMFORT?"

"Art thou the first man that was born?
Or wast thou made before the hills?
Hast thou heard the secret of God?
And dost thou restrain wisdom to thyself?
What knowest thou, that we know not?
What understandest thou, which is not in us?
With us are both the grayheaded and very aged men,
Much older than thy father.
Are the consolations of God small with thee?

Is there any secret thing with thee?
Why doth thine heart carry thee away?
And what do thine eyes wink at,
That thou turnest thy spirit against God,
And lettest such words go out of thy mouth?

"NO MAN CAN BE PURE"

"What is man, that he should be clean?
And he which is born of a woman, that he should be
    righteous?
Behold, he putteth no trust in his saints;
Yea, the heavens are not clean in his sight.
How much more abominable and filthy is man,
Which drinketh iniquity like water?

"THE WICKED NEVER PROSPER"

"I will shew thee, hear me;
And that which I have seen I will declare;
Which wise men have told
From their fathers and have not hid it:
Unto whom alone the earth was given,
And no stranger passed among them.
The wicked man travaileth with pain all his days,
And the number of years is hidden to the oppressor.

"HIS BAD CONSCIENCE MAKES HIM AFRAID"

"A dreadful sound is in his ears:
In prosperity the destroyer shall come upon him.
He believeth not that he shall return out of darkness,
And he is waited for of the sword.
He wandereth abroad for bread, saying, 'Where is it?'
He knoweth that the day of darkness is ready at his
    hand.
Trouble and anguish shall make him afraid;

They shall prevail against him, as a king ready to the
battle.

"HE STRENGTHENETH HIMSELF AGAINST THE ALMIGHTY"

"For he stretcheth out his hand against God,
And strengtheneth himself against the Almighty.
He runneth upon him, even on his neck,
Upon the thick bosses of his bucklers:
Because he covereth his face with his fatness,
And maketh collops of fat on his flanks.
And he dwelleth in desolate cities,
And in houses which no man inhabiteth,
Which are ready to become heaps.

"DISASTER MARKS HIS END"

"He shall not be rich, neither shall his substance con-
tinue,
Neither shall he prolong the perfection thereof upon
the earth.
He shall not depart out of darkness;
The flame shall dry up his branches,
And by the breath of his mouth shall he go away.
Let not him that is deceived trust in vanity:
For vanity shall be his recompence.
It shall be accomplished before his time,
And his branch shall not be green.
He shall shake off his unripe grape as the vine,
And shall cast off his flower as the olive.
For the congregation of hypocrites shall be desolate,
And fire shall consume the tabernacles of bribery.
They conceive mischief, and bring forth vanity,
And their belly prepareth deceit."

—Job 15.

The Fourth Reply of Job

"I HAVE HEARD ENOUGH FROM YOU. IF WE COULD
CHANGE PLACES, I WOULD SPEAK COMFORT,
NOT CONDEMNATION"

Then Job answered and said,

"I have heard many such things:
Miserable comforters are ye all.
Shall vain words have an end?
Or what emboldeneth thee that thou answerest?
I also could speak as ye do:
If your soul were in my soul's stead,
I could heap up words against you, and shake mine
head at you.
But I would strengthen you with my mouth,
And the moving of my lips should assuage your
grief.

"GOD HIMSELF IS MY ENEMY"

"Though I speak, my grief is not assuaged:
And though I forbear, what am I eased?
But now he hath made me weary:
Thou hast made desolate all my company.
And thou hast filled me with wrinkles, which is a wit-
ness against me:
And my leanness rising up in me beareth witness to
my face.
He teareth me in his wrath, who hateth me:
He gnasheth upon me with his teeth;
Mine enemy sharpeneth his eyes upon me.
They have gaped upon me with their mouth;
They have smitten me upon the cheek reproachfully;
They have gathered themselves together against me.

God hath delivered me to the ungodly,
And turned me over into the hands of the wicked.
I was at ease, but he hath broken me asunder:
He hath also taken me by my neck, and shaken me to
      pieces,
And set me up for his mark.
His archers compass me round about,
He cleaveth my reins asunder, and doth not spare;
He poureth out my gall upon the ground.
He breaketh me with breach upon breach,
He runneth upon me like a giant.

"I HAVE NOT SINNED TO MERIT THIS SUFFERING.
I APPEAL TO GOD"

"I have sewed sackcloth upon my skin,
And defiled my horn in the dust.
My face is foul with weeping,
And on my eyelids is the shadow of death;
Not for any injustice in mine hands:
Also my prayer is pure.
O earth, cover not thou my blood,
And let my cry have no place.
Also now, behold, my witness is in heaven,
And my record is on high.
My friends scorn me:
But mine eye poureth out tears unto God.
O that one might plead for a man with God,
As a man pleadeth for his neighbour!
When a few years are come,
Then I shall go the way whence I shall not return.
My breath is corrupt, my days are extinct,
The graves are ready for me.
Are there not mockers with me?
And doth not mine eye continue in their provocation?

"HEAR ME, O GOD. I HAVE NO OTHER HOPE"

"Lay down now, put me in a surety with thee;
Who is he that will strike hands with me?
For thou hast hid their heart from understanding:
Therefore shalt thou not exalt them.
He that speaketh flattery to his friends,
Even the eyes of his children shall fail.
He hath made me also a byword of the people;
And aforetime I was as a tabret.
Mine eye also is dim by reason of sorrow,
And all my members are as a shadow.
Upright men shall be astonied at this,
And the innocent shall stir up himself against the
  hypocrite.
The righteous also shall hold on his way,
And he that hath clean hands shall be stronger and
  stronger.

"YOU, MY FRIENDS, HAVE NO WISDOM. ONLY DEATH AWAITS ME"

"But as for you all, do ye return, and come now:
For I cannot find one wise man among you.
My days are past, my purposes are broken off,
Even the thoughts of my heart.
They change the night unto day:
The light is short because of darkness.
If I wait, the grave is mine house:
I have made my bed in the darkness.
I have said to corruption, 'Thou art my father;'
To the worm, 'Thou art my mother, and my sister.'
And where is now my hope?
As for my hope, who shall see it?
They shall go down to the bars of the pit,
When our rest together is in the dust." —Job 16: 17.

The Second Speech of Bildad

"DO YOU THINK THE MORAL ORDER OF THE WORLD
WILL BE TURNED UPSIDE DOWN FOR YOU?"

Then answered Bildad, the Shuhite, and said,

"How long will it be ere ye make an end of words?
Mark, and afterwards we will speak.
Wherefore are we counted as beasts,
And reputed vile in your sight?
Thou that teareth thyself in thine anger. Shall the
earth be forsaken for thee?
Shall the rock be removed out of his place?

"NATURE ITSELF WORKS AGAINST THE WICKED"

"Yea, the light of the wicked shall be put out,
And the spark of his fire shall not shine.
The light shall be dark in his tabernacle,
And his candle shall be put out with him.
The steps of his strength shall be straitened,
And his own counsel shall cast him down.
For he is cast into a net by his own feet,
And he walketh upon a snare.
The gin shall take him by the heel,
And the robber shall prevail against him.
The snare is laid for him in the ground,
And a trap for him in the way.
Terrors shall make him afraid on every side,
And shall drive him to his feet.
His strength shall be hungerbitten,
And destruction shall be ready at his side.
It shall devour the strength of his skin:
Even the firstborn of death shall devour his strength.
His confidence shall be rooted out of his tabernacle,

And it shall bring him to the king of terrors.
It shall dwell in his tabernacle,
Because it is none of his:
Brimstone shall be scattered upon his habitation.
His roots shall be dried up beneath,
And above shall his branch be cut off.

"AND HIS VERY MEMORY SHALL ROT"

"His remembrance shall perish from the earth,
And he shall have no name in the street.
He shall be driven from light into darkness,
And chased out of the world.
He shall neither have son nor nephew among his
    people,
Nor any remaining in his dwellings.
They that come after him shall be astonied at his day,
As they that went before were affrighted.
Surely such are the dwellings of the wicked,
And this is the place of him that knoweth not God."

—Job 18.

THE FIFTH REPLY OF JOB

"HOW LONG MUST I ENDURE YOU?"

Then Job answered and said,

"How long will ye vex my soul,
And break me in pieces with words?
These ten times have ye reproached me:
Ye are not ashamed that ye make yourselves strange
    to me.
And be it indeed that I have erred,
Mine error remaineth with myself.

"GOD HIMSELF IS MY ENEMY"

"If indeed ye will magnify yourselves against me,
And plead against me my reproach:
Know now that God hath overthrown me,
And hath compassed me with his net.
Behold, I cry out of wrong, but I am not heard:
I cry aloud, but there is no judgment.
He hath fenced up my way that I cannot pass,
And he hath set darkness in my paths.
He hath stripped me of my glory,
And taken the crown from my head.
He hath destroyed me on every side, and I am gone:
And mine hope hath he removed like a tree.
He hath also kindled his wrath against me,
And he counteth me unto him as one of his enemies.
His troops come together, and raise up their way against
      me,
And encamp round about my tabernacle.

"IT IS HE WHO ARRAYS MY FRIENDS AGAINST ME"

"He hath put my brethren far from me,
And mine acquaintance are verily estranged from me.
My kinsfolk have failed,
And my familiar friends have forgotten me.
They that dwell in mine house, and my maids, count
      me for a stranger:
I am an alien in their sight.
I called my servant, and he gave me no answer;
I intreated him with my mouth.
My breath is strange to my wife,
Though I intreated for the children's sake of mine own
      body.
Yea, young children despised me;
I arose, and they spake against me.

All my inward friends abhorred me:
And they whom I loved are turned against me.
My bone cleaveth to my skin and to my flesh,
And I am escaped with the skin of my teeth.

"PITY ME, PITY ME, O MY FRIENDS!"

"Have pity upon me, have pity upon me, O ye my
friends;
For the hand of God hath touched me.
Why do ye persecute me as God,
And are not satisfied with my flesh?

"O THAT MY CLAIMS OF INNOCENCE WERE MADE TO ENDURE! BUT I KNOW THAT GOD WILL YET DECLARE MY INNOCENCE"

"O that my words were now written!
O that they were printed in a book!
That they were graven with an iron pen and lead,
In the rock forever!
For I know that my redeemer liveth,
And that he shall stand at the latter day upon the
earth:
And though after my skin worms destroy this body,
Yet in my flesh shall I see God:
Whom I shall see for myself,
And mine eyes shall behold, and not another;
Though my reins be consumed within me.

"THEN BEWARE HIS VENGEANCE ON MY BEHALF"

"But ye should say, 'Why persecute we him?'
Seeing the root of the matter is found in me;
Be ye afraid of the sword:
For wrath bringeth the punishments of the sword,
That ye may know there is a judgment." —Job 19.

The Second Speech of Zophar

"I am driven to answer"

Then answered Zophar, the Naamathite, and said,

"Therefore do my thoughts cause me to answer,
  And for this I make haste.
I have heard the check of my reproach,
  And the spirit of my understanding causeth me to
    answer.

"do you know that the wicked always suffer?"

"Knowest thou not this of old,
  Since man was placed upon earth,
That the triumphing of the wicked is short,
  And the joy of the hypocrite but for a moment?
Though his excellency mount up to the heavens,
  And his head reach unto the clouds;
Yet he shall perish forever like his own dung:
  They which have seen him shall say, 'Where is he?'
He shall fly away as a dream, and shall not be found:
  Yea, he shall be chased away as a vision of the night.
The eye also which saw him shall see him no more;
  Neither shall his place any more behold him.
His children shall seek to please the poor,
  And his hands shall restore their goods.
His bones are full of the sin of his youth,
  Which shall lie down with him in the dust.

"according to his sin will be his retribution"

"Though wickedness be sweet in his mouth,
  Though he hide it under his tongue;
Though he spare it, and forsake it not;
  But keep it still within his mouth:

Yet his meat in his bowels is turned,
It is the gall of asps within him.
He hath swallowed down riches, and he shall vomit
    them up again:
God shall cast them out of his belly.
He shall suck the poison of asps:
The viper's tongue shall slay him.
He shall not see the rivers,
The floods, the brooks of honey and butter.
That which he laboured for shall he restore, and shall
    not swallow it down:
According to his substance shall the restitution be,
    and he shall not rejoice therein.
Because he hath oppressed and hath forsaken the
    poor;
Because he hath violently taken away an house which
    he builded not;
Surely he shall not feel quietness in his belly,
He shall not save of that which he desired.
There shall none of his meat be left;
Therefore shall no man look for his goods.
In the fulness of his sufficiency he shall be in straits:
Every hand of the wicked shall come upon him.
When he is about to fill his belly,
God shall cast the fury of his wrath upon him,
And shall rain it upon him while he is eating.
He shall flee from the iron weapon,
And the bow of steel shall strike him through.
It is drawn, and cometh out of the body;
Yea, the glittering sword cometh out of his gall:
Terrors are upon him.
All darkness shall be hid in his secret places:
A fire not blown shall consume him;
It shall go ill with him that is left in his tabernacle.

"HEAVEN AND EARTH CONSPIRE AGAINST HIM"

"The heaven shall reveal his iniquity;
And the earth shall rise up against him.
The increase of his house shall depart,
And his goods shall flow away in the day of his wrath.
This is the portion of a wicked man from God,
And the heritage appointed unto him by God."

—Job 20.

THE SIXTH REPLY OF JOB

"LISTEN TO ME!"

But Job answered and said,

"Hear diligently my speech,
And let this be your consolations.
Suffer me that I may speak;
And after that I have spoken, mock on.
As for me, is my complaint to man?
And if it were so, why should not my spirit be troubled?
Mark me, and be astonished,
And lay your hand upon your mouth.

"IT IS NOT TRUE THAT THE WICKED SUFFER. THEY PROSPER, LIVE TO OLD AGE, AND DIE HONOURED"

"Even when I remember I am afraid,
And trembling taketh hold on my flesh.
Wherefore do the wicked live,
Become old, yea, are mighty in power?
Their seed is established in their sight with them,
And their offspring before their eyes.
Their houses are safe from fear,
Neither is the rod of God upon them.
Their bull gendereth, and faileth not;
Their cow calveth, and casteth not her calf.

They send forth their little ones like a flock,
And their children dance.
They take the timbrel and harp,
And rejoice at the sound of the organ.
They spend their days in wealth,
And in a moment go down to the grave.
Therefore they say unto God, 'Depart from us;
For we desire not the knowledge of thy ways.
What is the Almighty, that we should serve him?
And what profit should we have, if we pray unto him?'
Lo, their good is not in their hand:
The counsel of the wicked is far from me.
How oft is the candle of the wicked put out?
And how oft cometh their destruction upon them?
God distributeth sorrows in his anger.
They are as stubble before the wind,
And as chaff that the storm carrieth away.
Ye say, 'God layeth up his iniquity for his children':
Let him recompense it unto himself, that he may
    know it.
Let his own eyes see his destruction,
And let him drink of the wrath of the Almighty.
For what careth he for his house after him,
When the number of his months is cut off in the midst?
Shall any teach God knowledge,
Seeing he judgeth those that are high?
One dieth in his full strength,
Being wholly at ease and quiet.
His breasts are full of milk,
And his bones are moistened with marrow.
And another dieth in the bitterness of his soul,
And never eateth with pleasure.
They shall lie down alike in the dust,
And the worms shall cover them.

"I KNOW YOUR CONDEMNATION OF ME. BUT IT IS TRUE
THAT THE WICKED SUFFER NO MORE THAN THE
RIGHTEOUS. WHEN YOU DENY IT, YOU LIE"

"Behold, I know your thoughts,
And the devices which ye wrongfully imagine against
    me.
For ye say, 'Where is the house of the prince?
And where are the dwelling places of the wicked?'
Have ye not asked them that go by the way?
And do ye not know their tokens,
That the wicked is reserved to the day of destruction?
They shall be brought forth to the day of wrath?
Who shall declare his way to his face?
And who shall repay him what he hath done?
Yet shall he be brought to the grave,
And shall remain in the tomb.
The clods of the valley shall be sweet unto him,
And every man shall draw after him,
As there are innumerable before him.
How then comfort ye me in vain,
Seeing in your answers there remaineth falsehood?"
—Job 21.

Thus ends the second round of speeches. Eliphaz has said that the wicked suffer from conscience; Bildad, that they suffer from the very order of nature; and Zophar, that any prosperity of the wicked is short. Each has drawn a picture of the wicked man in which he expects Job to see himself.

Job continues his complaints without regard to their arguments till Zophar's harshness draws the fire of his answer. He denies that the wicked suffer any more than the righteous, and ends with "You lie."

The first round of speeches was about God; God is just, and so the wicked suffer. Job denied it. The second, about man; the wicked always suffer. Job denied it. There is nothing more to be said on general principles. Perhaps if they charge Job with specific sins, they may move him.

The Third Round of Speeches
The Third Speech of Eliphaz

"You must have been wicked"

Then Eliphaz, the Temanite, answered and said,

"Can a man be profitable unto God,
As he that is wise may be profitable unto himself?
Is it any pleasure to the Almighty, that thou art right-
eous?
Or is it gain to him, that thou makest thy ways perfect?
Will he reprove thee for fear of thee?
Will he enter with thee into judgment?
Is not thy wickedness great,
And thine iniquities infinite?

"You have oppressed the poor and flattered the rich"

"For thou hast taken a pledge from thy brother for
naught,
And stripped the naked of their clothing.
Thou hast not given water to the weary to drink,
And thou hast withholden bread from the hungry.
But as for the mighty man, he had the earth;
And the honourable man dwelt in it.
Thou hast sent widows away empty,
And the arms of the fatherless have been broken.
Therefore snares are round about thee,
And sudden fear troubleth thee;
Or darkness, that thou canst not see;
And abundance of waters cover thee.

"Doubtless you thought God did not see"

"Is not God in the height of heaven?
And behold the height of the stars, how high they are!

And thou sayest, 'How doth God know?
Can he judge through the dark cloud?
Thick clouds are a covering to him, that he seeth not;
And he walketh in the circuit of heaven'.
Hast thou marked the old way
Which wicked men have trodden?
Which were cut down out of time,
Whose foundation was overflown with a flood:
Which said unto God, 'Depart from us':
And what can the Almighty do for them?
Yet he filled their houses with good things:
But the counsel of the wicked is far from me.
The righteous see it, and are glad:
And the innocent laugh them to scorn.
Whereas our substance is not cut down,
But the remnant of them the fire consumeth.

"BUT NOW REPENT, AND HE EVEN YET SHALL HEAR YOU"

"Acquaint now thyself with him, and be at peace:
Thereby good shall come unto thee.
Receive, I pray thee, the law from his mouth,
And lay up his words in thine heart.
If thou return to the Almighty, thou shalt be built up,
Thou shalt put away iniquity far from thy tabernacles.
Then shalt thou lay up gold as dust,
And the gold of Ophir as the stones of the brooks.
Yea, the Almighty shall be thy defence,
And thou shalt have plenty of silver.
For then shalt thou have thy delight in the Almighty,
And shalt lift up thy face unto God.
Thou shalt make thy prayer unto him,
And he shall hear thee, and thou shalt pay thy vows.
Thou shalt also decree a thing,
And it shall be established unto thee:

And the light shall shine upon thy ways.
When men are cast down, then thou shalt say, 'There
    is lifting up';
And he shall save the humble person.
He shall deliver the island of the innocent:
And it is delivered by the pureness of thine hands."

                                                      —Job 22.

THE SEVENTH REPLY OF JOB

"WOULD THAT I COULD FIND GOD!"

Then Job answered and said,

"Even to-day is my complaint bitter:
My stroke is heavier than my groaning.
Oh that I knew where I might find him!
That I might come even to his seat!
I would order my cause before him,
And fill my mouth with arguments.
I would know the words which he would answer me,
And understand what he would say unto me.
Will he plead against me with his great power?
No; but he would put strength in me.
There the righteous might dispute with him;
So should I be delivered forever from my judge.
Behold, I go forward, but he is not there;
And backward, but I cannot perceive him:
On the left hand, where he doth work, but I cannot
    behold him:
He hideth himself on the right hand, that I cannot see
    him.

"HE KNOWS I AM INNOCENT; YET IT PLEASES HIM TO TORTURE ME"

"But he knoweth the way that I take:
When he hath tried me, I shall come forth as gold.

My foot hath held his steps,
His way have I kept, and not declined.
Neither have I gone back from the commandment of
his lips;
I have esteemed the words of his mouth more than my
necessary food.
But he is in one mind, and who can turn him?
And what his soul desireth, even that he doeth.
For he performeth the thing that is appointed for me:
And many such things are with him.
Therefore am I troubled at his presence:
When I consider, I am afraid of him.
For God maketh my heart soft,
And the Almighty troubleth me:
Because I was not cut off before the darkness,
Neither hath he covered the darkness from my face.

—Job 23.

"SEE HOW THE WICKED FLOURISH, AND GOD GIVES NO HEED"

"Why, seeing times are not hidden from the Almighty,
Do they that know him not see his days?
Some remove the landmarks;
They violently take away flocks, and feed thereof.
They drive away the ass of the fatherless,
They take the widow's ox for a pledge.
They turn the needy out of the way:
The poor of the earth hide themselves together.
Behold, as wild asses in the desert,
Go they forth to their work;
Rising betimes for a prey:
The wilderness yieldeth food for them and for their
children.
They reap every one his corn in the field;
And they gather the vintage of the wicked.

They cause the naked to lodge without clothing,
That they have no covering in the cold.
They are wet with the showers of the mountains,
And embrace the rock for want of a shelter.
They pluck the fatherless from the breast,
And take a pledge of the poor.
They cause him to go naked without clothing,
And they take away the sheaf from the hungry;
Which make oil within their walls,
And tread their wine-presses, and suffer thirst.
Men groan from out of the city,
And the soul of the wounded crieth out:
Yet God layeth not folly to them.
And if it be not so now, who will make me a liar,
And make my speech nothing worth?"   —Job 24.

THE THIRD SPEECH OF BILDAD

"NO MAN CAN BE PURE BEFORE GOD"

(Compare the vision in the first speech of Eliphaz)

Then answered Bildad, the Shuhite, and said,
"Dominion and fear are with him,
He maketh peace in his high places.
Is there any number of his armies?
And upon whom doth not his light arise?
How then can man be justified with God?
Or how can he be clean that is born of a woman?
Behold even to the moon, and it shineth not;
Yea, the stars are not pure in his sight.
How much less man, that is a worm?
And the son of man, which is a worm?"   —Job 25.

The Eighth Reply of Job

"little have you helped me"

But Job answered and said,

"How hast thou helped him that is without power?
How savest thou the arm that hath no strength?
How hast thou counselled him that hath no wisdom?
And how hast thou plentifully declared the thing as it
    is?
To whom hast thou uttered words?
And whose spirit came from thee?

"i also can speak of the power of god"

"They that are deceased tremble under the waters,
And the inhabitants thereof.
Hell is naked before him,
And destruction hath no covering.
He stretcheth out the north over the empty place,
And hangeth the earth upon nothing.
He bindeth up the waters in his thick clouds;
And the cloud is not rent under them.
He holdeth back the face of his throne,
And spreadeth his cloud upon it.
He hath compassed the waters with bounds,
Until the day and night come to an end.
The pillars of heaven tremble
And are astonished at his reproof.
He divideth the sea with his power,
And by his understanding he smiteth through the proud.
By his spirit he hath garnished the heavens;
His hand hath formed the crooked serpent.
Lo, these are but the outskirts of his ways:
But how small a whisper do we hear of him!
But the thunder of his power who can understand?"

Moreover Job continued his parable, and said,

"I AM GUILTLESS OF THE SINS YOU CHARGE"

"As God liveth, who hath taken away my judgment;
And the Almighty, who hath vexed my soul;
All the while my breath is in me,
And the spirit of God is in my nostrils,
My lips shall not speak wickedness,
Nor my tongue utter deceit.
God forbid that I should justify you:
Till I die I will not remove mine integrity from me.
My righteousness I hold fast, and will not let it go:
My heart shall not reproach me so long as I live."

(What follows is strangely like Zophar's last speech and unlike what Job has said before. Many think it is the missing third speech of Zophar.)

"EVERY ONE CAN SEE THAT THE PROSPERITY OF THE WICKED IS SHORT"

"Let mine enemy be as the wicked,
And he that riseth up against me as the unrighteous.
For what is the hope of the hypocrite,
Though he hath gained, when God taketh away his soul?
Will God hear his cry
When trouble cometh upon him?
Will he delight himself in the Almighty?
Will he always call upon God?
I will teach you by the hand of God:
That which is with the Almighty will I not conceal.
Behold, all ye yourselves have seen it;
Why then are ye thus altogether vain?
This is the portion of a wicked man with God,
And the heritage of oppressors, which they shall receive
    of the Almighty.

If his children be multiplied, it is for the sword:
And his offspring shall not be satisfied with bread.
Those that remain of him shall be buried in death:
And his widows shall not weep.
Though he heap up silver as the dust,
And prepare raiment as the clay;
He may prepare it, but the just shall put it on,
And the innocent shall divide the silver.
He buildeth his house as a moth,
And as a booth that the keeper maketh.
The rich man shall lie down, but he shall not be gathered:
He openeth his eyes, and he is not.
Terrors take hold on him as waters,
A tempest stealeth him away in the night.
The east wind carrieth him away, and he departeth:
And as a storm hurleth him out of his place.
For God shall cast upon him, and not spare:
He would fain flee out of his hand.
Men shall clap their hands at him,
And shall hiss him out of his place."   —Job 26; 27.

"Where Can Wisdom Be Found?"

(This beautiful poem is not a part of the argument
of Job.   It should be read as an independent poem.)

"Men mine for precious metals—they buy jewels in the bazaars"

"Surely there is a vein for the silver,
  And a place for gold where they refine it.
  Iron is taken out of the earth,
  And brass is molten out of the stone.
  He setteth an end to darkness,
  And searcheth out all perfection:
  The stones of darkness, and the shadow of death.

The flood breaketh out from the inhabitant;
Even the waters forgotten of the foot:
They are dried up, they are gone away from men.
As for the earth, out of it cometh bread:
And under it is turned up as it were fire.
The stones of it are the place of sapphires:
And it hath dust of gold.
There is a path which no fowl knoweth,
And which the vulture's eye hath not seen:
The lion's whelps have not trodden it,
Nor the fierce lion passed by it.
He putteth forth his hand upon the rock;
He overturneth the mountains by the roots.
He cutteth out rivers among the rocks;
And his eye seeth every precious thing.
He bindeth the floods from overflowing;
And the thing that is hid bringeth he forth to light.
But where shall wisdom be found?
And where is the place of understanding?
Man knoweth not the price thereof;
Neither is it found in the land of the living.
The depth saith, 'It is not in me':
And the sea saith, 'It is not with me.'
It cannot be gotten for gold,
Neither shall silver be weighed for the price thereof.
It cannot be valued with the gold of Ophir,
With the precious onyx, or the sapphire.
The gold and the crystal cannot equal it:
And the exchange of it shall not be for jewels of fine
    gold.
No mention shall be made of coral, or of pearls:
For the price of wisdom is above rubies.
The topaz of Ethiopia shall not equal it,
Neither shall it be valued with pure gold.

"BUT ONLY GOD HAS WISDOM"

"Whence then cometh wisdom?
  And where is the place of understanding?
  Seeing it is hid from the eyes of all living,
  And kept close from the fowls of the air.
  Destruction and death say,
  'We have heard the fame thereof with our ears.'
  God understandeth the way thereof,
  And he knoweth the place thereof.
  For he looketh to the ends of the earth,
  And seeth under the whole heaven;
  To make the weight for the winds;
  And he weigheth the waters by measure.
  When he made a decree for the rain,
  And a way for the lightning of the thunder:
  Then did he see it, and declare it;
  He prepared it, yea, and searched it out.

"MAN'S WISDOM IS TO FEAR GOD"

"And unto man he said,
  'Behold, the fear of the LORD, that is wisdom;
  And to depart from evil is understanding.'" —Job 28.

THE FINAL DEFENCE OF JOB

"I RECALL THE DAYS OF MY PAST PROSPERITY"

Moreover Job continued his parable, and said,

"O that I were as in months past,
  As in the days when God preserved me;
  When his candle shined upon my head,
  And when by his light I walked through darkness;
  As I was in the days of my youth,
  When the secret of God was upon my tabernacle;
  When the Almighty was yet with me,

When my children were about me;
When I washed my steps with butter,
And the rock poured me out rivers of oil;
When I went out to the gate through the city,
When I prepared my seat in the street!
The young men saw me, and hid themselves:
And the aged arose, and stood up.
The princes refrained talking,
And laid their hand on their mouth.
The nobles held their peace,
And their tongue cleaved to the roof of their mouth.

"MY HONOR WAS FOUNDED ON MY CHARITY"

"When the ear heard me, then it blessed me;
And when the eye saw me, it gave witness to me:
Because I delivered the poor that cried,
And the fatherless, and him that had none to help him.
The blessing of him that was ready to perish came upon
    me:
And I caused the widow's heart to sing for joy.
I put on righteousness, and it clothed me:
My judgment was as a robe and a diadem.
I was eyes to the blind,
And feet was I to the lame.
I was a father to the poor:
And the cause which I knew not I searched out.
And I brake the jaws of the wicked,
And plucked the spoil out of his teeth.
Then I said, 'I shall die in my nest,
And I shall multiply my days as the sand.'
My root was spread out by the waters,
And the dew lay all night upon my branch.
My glory was fresh in me,
And my bow was renewed in my hand.

Unto me men gave ear,
And waited, and kept silence at my counsel.
After my words they spake not again;
And my speech dropped upon them.
And they waited for me as for the rain;
And they opened their mouth wide as for the latter rain.
If I laughed on them, they believed it not;
And the light of my countenance they cast not down.
I chose out their way, and sat chief,
And dwelt as a king in the army,
As one that comforteth the mourners. —Job 29.

"BUT NOW——HOW DIFFERENT! I AM ABANDONED BY GOD AND MAN"

"But now they that are younger than I have me in derision,
Whose fathers I would have disdained to have set with the dogs of my flock.
Yea, whereto might the strength of their hands profit me,
In whom old age was perished?
For want and famine they were solitary;
Fleeing into the wilderness in former time desolate and waste,
Who cut up mallows by the bushes,
And juniper roots for their meat.
They were driven forth from among men,
They cried after them as after a thief;
To dwell in the cliffs of the valleys,
In caves of the earth, and in the rocks.
Among the bushes they brayed;
Under the nettles they were gathered together.
They were children of fools, yea, children of base men:
They were viler than the earth.

And now am I their song,
Yea, I am their byword.
They abhor me, they flee far from me,
And spare not to spit in my face.
Because he hath loosed my cord, and afflicted me,
They have also let loose the bridle before me.
Upon my right hand rise the youth;
They push away my feet,
And they raise up against me the ways of their de-
    struction.
They mar my path,
They set forward my calamity,
They have no helper.
They came upon me as a wide breaking in of waters:
In the desolation they rolled themselves upon me.
Terrors are turned upon me:
They pursue my soul as the wind:
And my welfare passeth away as a cloud.
And now my soul is poured out upon me;
The days of affliction have taken hold upon me.
My bones are pierced in me in the night season:
And my sinews take no rest.
By the great force of my disease is my garment
    changed:
It bindeth me about as the collar of my coat.
He hath cast me into the mire,
And I am become like dust and ashes.
I cry unto thee, and thou dost not hear me:
I stand up, and thou regardest me not.
Thou art become cruel to me:
With thy strong hand thou opposest thyself against me.
Thou liftest me up to the wind;
Thou causest me to ride upon it, and dissolvest my
    substance.

For I know that thou wilt bring me to death,
And to the house appointed for all living.
Howbeit he will not stretch out his hand to the grave,
Though they cry in his destruction.
Did not I weep for him that was in trouble?
Was not my soul grieved for the poor?
When I looked for good, then evil came unto me:
And when I waited for light, there came darkness.
My bowels boiled, and rested not:
The days of affliction prevented me.
I went mourning without the sun:
I stood up, and I cried in the congregation.
I am a brother to dragons,
And a companion to owls.
My skin is black upon me,
And my bones are burned with heat.
My harp also is turned to mourning,
And my organ into the voice of them that weep.

—Job 30.

"YOU CHARGE ME WITH SPECIFIC SINS. I SWEAR BEFORE GOD I DID NOT COMMIT THEM"

"I made a covenant with mine eyes;
Why then should I think upon a maid?
For what portion of God is there from above?
And what inheritance of the Almighty from on high?
Is not destruction to the wicked?
And a strange punishment to the workers of iniquity?
Doth not he see my ways,
And count all my steps?

If I have walked with vanity,
Or if my foot hath hasted to deceit;
Let me be weighed in an even balance,
That God may know mine integrity.

If my step hath turned out of the way,
And mine heart walked after mine eyes,
And if any blot hath cleaved to mine hands;
Then let me sow, and let another eat;
Yea, let my offspring be rooted out.

If I did despise the cause of my manservant or of my
      maidservant,
When they contended with me;
What then shall I do when God riseth up?
And when he visiteth, what shall I answer him?
Did not he that made me in the womb make him?
And did not one fashion us in the womb?

If I have withheld the poor from their desire,
Or have caused the eyes of the widow to fail;
Or have eaten my morsel myself alone,
And the fatherless hath not eaten thereof;
(For from my youth he was brought up with me, as
      with a father,
And I have guided her from my mother's womb;)
If I have seen any perish for want of clothing,
Or any poor without covering;
If his loins have not blessed me,
And if he were not warmed with the fleece of my sheep;
If I have lifted up my hand against the fatherless,
When I saw my help in the gate:
Then let mine arm fall from my shoulder blade,
And mine arm be broken from the bone.
For destruction from God was a terror to me,
And by reason of his highness I could not endure.

If I have made gold my hope,
Or have said to the fine gold, 'Thou art my confi-
      dence';
If I rejoiced because my wealth was great,

And because mine hand had gotten much;
If I beheld the sun when it shined,
Or the moon walking in brightness;
And my heart hath been secretly enticed,
Or my mouth hath kissed my hand:
This also were an iniquity to be punished by the judge:
For I should have denied the God that is above.
If I rejoiced at the destruction of him that hated
    me,
Or lifted up myself when evil found him:
Neither have I suffered my mouth to sin
By wishing a curse to his soul.
If the men of my tent said not,
'Who can find one that hath not been filled with his
    meat?'
The stranger did not lodge in the street:
But I opened my doors to the traveler.
If I covered my transgressions as Adam,
By hiding mine iniquity in my bosom:
Did I fear a great multitude,
Or did the contempt of families terrify me,
That I kept silence, and went not out of the door?
O that one would hear me!
Behold, my desire is that the Almighty would answer
    me,
And that mine adversary had written a book.
Surely I would take it upon my shoulder,
And bind it as a crown to me.
I would declare unto him the number of my steps;
As a prince would I go near unto him.

If my land cry against me,
Or that the furrows likewise thereof complain;
If I have eaten the fruits thereof without money,

Or have caused the owners thereof to lose their life:
Let thistles grow instead of wheat, and
Cockle instead of barley.
The words of Job are ended." —Job 31.

Thus the third round of speeches ends. Eliphaz has charged Job
with greed and oppressions. Job calls down the curse of God if that
is true. On the contrary, justice and generosity have guided his life.

But we have had no solution of the problem of suffering; only a
denial that the solution of the friends is correct. The debate has
come to no positive conclusion.

Then a new character, Elihu, is introduced. He adds so little
that some think he does not belong in the original poem.

SPEECH OF ELIHU

So these three men ceased to answer Job, because he
was righteous in his own eyes. Then was kindled the
wrath of Elihu, the son of Barachel, the Buzite, of the
kindred of Ram: against Job was his wrath kindled,
because he justified himself rather than God; also
against his three friends was his wrath kindled, because
they had found no answer, and yet had condemned Job.

Now Elihu had waited till Job had spoken, because
they were elder than he. When Elihu saw that there
was no answer in the mouth of these three men, then
his wrath was kindled, and Elihu, the son of Barachel,
the Buzite, answered and said,

"I APOLOGIZE FOR SPEAKING; YET I HAVE WISDOM TO OFFER"

"I am young, and ye are very old;
Wherefore I was afraid, and durst not shew you mine
    opinion.
I said, 'Days should speak,
And multitude of years should teach wisdom.'

But there is a spirit in man:
And the inspiration of the Almighty giveth them
    understanding.
Great men are not always wise:
Neither do the aged understand judgment.
Therefore I said, 'Hearken to me;
I also will shew mine opinion.'
Behold, I waited for your words;
I gave ear to your reasons,
Whilst ye searched out what to say.
Yea, I attended unto you,
And behold, there was none of you that convinced Job,
Or that answered his words:
Lest ye should say, 'We have found out wisdom':
Now he hath not directed his words against me:
Neither will I answer him with your speeches.
They were amazed, they answered no more:
They left off speaking.
When I had waited, for they spake not,
But stood still, and answered no more;
I said, 'I will answer also my part,
I also will shew mine opinion.
For I am full of matter,
The spirit within me constraineth me.'
Behold, my belly is as wine which hath no vent;
It is ready to burst like new bottles.
I will speak, that I may be refreshed:
I will open my lips and answer.
Let me not, I pray you, accept any man's person,
Neither let me give flattering titles unto man.
For I know not to give flattering titles;
In so doing my maker would soon take me away.

                      —Job 32.

"LISTEN, JOB, I WISH TO HELP YOU"

"Wherefore, Job, I pray thee, hear my speeches,
And hearken to all my words.
Behold, now I have opened my mouth,
My tongue hath spoken in my mouth.
My words shall be of the uprightness of my heart:
And my lips shall utter knowledge clearly.
The Spirit of God hath made me,
And the breath of the Almighty hath given me life.
If thou canst answer me,
Set thy words in order before me, stand up.
Behold, I am according to thy wish in God's stead:
I also am formed out of the clay.
Behold, my terror shall not make thee afraid,
Neither shall my hand be heavy upon thee.

"YOU CLAIM TO BE INNOCENT. THAT CANNOT BE"

"Surely thou hast spoken in mine hearing,
And I have heard the voice of thy words, saying,
'I am clean without transgression; I am innocent;
Neither is there iniquity in me.
Behold, he findeth occasions against me,
He counteth me for his enemy,
He putteth my feet in the stocks,
He marketh all my paths.'
Behold, in this thou art not just:
I will answer thee, that God is greater than man.
Why dost thou strive against him?
For he giveth not account of any of his matters.

"YOU WISH GOD WOULD SPEAK; HE HAS SPOKEN"

"For God speaketh once, yea twice,
Yet man perceiveth it not.
In a dream, in a vision of the night,

When deep sleep falleth upon men,
In slumberings upon the bed;
Then he openeth the ears of men,
And sealeth their instruction,
That he may withdraw man from his purpose,
And hide pride from man.
He keepeth back his soul from the pit,
And his life from perishing by the sword.
He is chastened also with pain upon his bed,
And the multitude of his bones with strong pain:
So that his life abhorreth bread,
And his soul dainty meat.
His flesh is consumed away, that it cannot be seen;
And his bones that were not seen stick out.
Yea, his soul draweth near unto the grave,
And his life to the destroyers.
If there be a messenger with him,
An interpreter, one among a thousand,
To shew unto man his uprightness:
Then he is gracious unto him, and saith,
'Deliver him from going down to the pit:
I have found a ransom.'
His flesh shall be fresher than a child's:
He shall return to the days of his youth:
He shall pray unto God, and he will be favourable
    unto him:
And he shall see his face with joy:
For he will render unto man his righteousness.
He looketh upon men, and if any say,
'I have sinned, and perverted that which was right,
And it profited me not';
He will deliver his soul from going into the pit,
And his life shall see the light.

"YOUR SUFFERING WAS INTENDED TO BRING YOU BACK TO GOD"

"Lo, all these things worketh God
    Oftentimes with man,
To bring back his soul from the pit,
To be enlightened with the light of the living.

    Mark well, O Job, hearken unto me:
Hold thy peace, and I will speak.
If thou hast anything to say, answer me:
Speak, for I desire to justify thee.
If not, hearken unto me:
Hold thy peace, and I shall teach thee wisdom."

—Job 33.

"LISTEN, FRIENDS OF JOB. YOU SHOULD HAVE SAID, 'GOD ALWAYS DOES RIGHT'"

Furthermore Elihu answered and said,

"Hear my words, O ye wise men;
    And give ear unto me, ye that have knowledge.
For the ear trieth words,
As the mouth tasteth meat.
Let us choose to us judgment:
Let us know among ourselves what is good.
For Job hath said, 'I am righteous:
And God hath taken away my judgment.
Should I lie against my right?
My wound is incurable without transgression.'
What man is like Job,
Who drinketh up scorning like water?
Which goeth in company with the workers of iniquity,
And walketh with wicked men.
For he hath said, 'It profiteth a man nothing
That he should delight himself with God.'

Therefore hearken unto me, ye men of understanding:
Far be it from God, that he should do wickedness;
And from the Almighty, that he should commit iniquity.
For the work of a man shall he render unto him,
And cause every man to find according to his ways.
Yea, surely God will not do wickedly,
Neither will the Almighty pervert judgment.
Job hath spoken without knowledge,
And his words were without wisdom.
My desire is that Job may be tried unto the end
Because of his answers for wicked men.
For he addeth rebellion unto his sin,
He clappeth his hands among us,
And multiplieth his words against God."

"LISTEN AGAIN, JOB. GOD NEVER HEARS AN ARROGANT PRAYER"

Elihu spake moreover, and said,

"Thinkest thou this to be right, that thou saidst,
  'My righteousness is more than God's'?
For thou saidst, 'What advantage will it be unto thee?'
And, 'What profit shall I have, if I be cleansed from
      my sin?'
I will answer thee,
And thy companions with thee.
Look unto the heavens, and see;
And behold the clouds which are higher than thou.
If thou sinnest, what doest thou against him?
Or if thy transgressions be multiplied, what doest thou
      unto him?
If thou be righteous, what givest thou him?
Or what receiveth he of thine hand?
Thy wickedness may hurt a man as thou art;

And thy righteousness may profit the son of man.
By reason of the multitude of oppressions they make
　　　the oppressed to cry:
They cry out by reason of the arm of the mighty.
But none saith, 'Where is God my maker,
Who giveth songs in the night;
Who teacheth us more than the beasts of the earth,
And maketh us wiser than the fowls of heaven?'
There they cry, but none giveth answer,
Because of the pride of evil men.
Surely God will not hear vanity,
Neither will the Almighty regard it.
Although thou sayest thou shalt not see him,
Yet judgment is before him; therefore trust thou in him.
But now, because it is not so,
He hath visited in his anger; yet he knoweth it not in
　　　great extremity:
Therefore doth Job open his mouth in vain;
He multiplieth words without knowledge."

—Job 34 in part; 35.

"GOD ALWAYS DOES RIGHT. HE AFFLICTS TO KEEP MEN FROM FUTURE SINS"

Elihu also proceeded, and said,

"Suffer me a little, and I will shew thee
　That I have yet to speak on God's behalf.
　I will fetch my knowledge from afar,
　And will ascribe righteousness to my Maker.
　For truly my words shall not be false:
　He that is perfect in knowledge is with thee.
　Behold, God is mighty, and despiseth not any:
　He is mighty in strength and wisdom.
　He preserveth not the life of the wicked:
　But giveth right to the poor.

He withdraweth not his eyes from the righteous:
But with kings are they on the throne;
Yea, he doth establish them forever, and they are
    exalted.
And if they be bound in fetters,
And be holden in cords of affliction;
Then he sheweth them their work,
And their transgressions that they have exceeded.
He openeth also their ear to discipline,
And commandeth that they return from iniquity.
If they obey and serve him,
They shall spend their days in prosperity,
And their years in pleasures.
But if they obey not, they shall perish by the sword,
And they shall die without knowledge.
But the hypocrites in heart heap up wrath:
They cry not when he bindeth them.
They die in youth,
And their life is among the unclean.
He delivereth the poor in his affliction,
And openeth their ears in oppression.
Even so would he have removed thee out of the strait
Into a broad place, where there is no straitness;
And that which should be set on thy table should be
    full of fatness.

(A storm begins to arise.)

"SEE GOD IN THE STORM. HEAR HIS VOICE IN
THE THUNDER"

"With clouds he covereth the light;
And commandeth it not to shine by the cloud that
    cometh betwixt.
The noise thereof sheweth concerning it,
The cattle also concerning the storm.

At this also my heart trembleth,
And is moved out of his place.
Hear attentively the noise of his voice,
And the sound that goeth out of his mouth.
He directeth it under the whole heaven,
And his lightning unto the ends of the earth.
After it a voice roareth:
He thundereth with the voice of his excellency;
And he will not stay them when his voice is heard.
God thundereth marvellously with his voice;
Great things doeth he, which we cannot comprehend.
For he saith to the snow, 'Be thou on the earth';
Likewise to the small rain, and to the great rain of his
    strength.
He sealeth up the hand of every man;
That all men may know his work.
Then the beasts go into dens,
And remain in their places.
Out of the south cometh the whirlwind:
And cold out of the north.
By the breath of God frost is given:
And the breadth of the waters is straitened.
Also by watering he wearieth the thick cloud:
He scattereth his bright cloud:
And it is turned round about by his counsels:
That they may do whatsoever he commandeth them
Upon the face of the world in the earth.
He causeth it to come,
Whether for correction, or for his land, or for mercy.

"CAN YOU UNDERSTAND THE GOD OF THE STORM?"

"Hearken unto this, O Job:
Stand still, and consider the wondrous works of God.
Dost thou know when God disposed them,

And caused the light of his cloud to shine?
Dost thou know the balancings of the clouds,
The wondrous works of him which is perfect in knowl-
    edge?
How thy garments are warm,
When he quieteth the earth by the south wind?
Hast thou with him spread out the sky,
Which is strong, and as a molten looking-glass?
Teach us what we shall say unto him;
For we cannot order our speech by reason of darkness.
Shall it be told him that I speak?
If a man speak, surely he shall be swallowed up.
And now men see not the bright light which is in the
    clouds:
But the wind passeth, and cleanseth them.
Fair weather cometh out of the north:
With God is terrible majesty.
Touching the Almighty, we cannot find him out:
He is excellent in power, and in judgment,
And in plenty of justice: he will not afflict.
Men do therefore fear him:
He respecteth not any that are wise of heart."

—Job 36; 37 in part.

THE SPEECHES OF JEHOVAH

THE VOICE OF JEHOVAH IN THE STORM

"DOST THOU KNOW THE SECRETS OF NATURE?"

Then the LORD answered Job out of the whirlwind,
and said,

"Who is this that darkeneth counsel
By words without knowledge?
Gird up now thy loins like a man;
For I will demand of thee, and answer thou me.

Where wast thou when I laid the foundations of the
    earth?
Declare, if thou hast understanding.
Who hath laid the measures thereof, if thou knowest?
Or who hath stretched the line upon it?
Whereupon are the foundations thereof fastened?
Or who laid the corner stone thereof;
When the morning stars sang together,
And all the sons of God shouted for joy?
Or who shut up the sea with doors, when it brake forth,
As if it had issued out of the womb?
When I made the cloud the garment thereof,
And thick darkness a swaddling band for it,
And brake up for it my decreed place,
And set bars and doors,
And said, 'Hitherto shalt thou come, but no further:
And here shall thy proud waves be stayed'?

Hast thou commanded the morning since thy days;
And caused the dayspring to know his place;
That it might take hold of the ends of the earth,
That the wicked might be shaken out of it?
It is turned as clay to the seal;
And they stand as a garment.
And from the wicked their light is withholden,
And the high arm shall be broken.

Hast thou entered into the springs of the sea?
Or hast thou walked in the search of the depth?
Have the gates of death been opened unto thee?
Or hast thou seen the doors of the shadow of death?
Hast thou perceived the breadth of the earth?
Declare if thou knowest it all.

Where is the way where light dwelleth?
And as for darkness, where is the place thereof,

That thou shouldest take it to the bound thereof,
And that thou shouldest know the paths to the house
    thereof?
Knowest thou it, because thou wast then born?
Or because the number of thy days is great?

Hast thou entered into the treasures of the snow?
Or hast thou seen the treasures of the hail,
Which I have reserved against the time of trouble,
Against the day of battle and war?

By what way is the light parted,
Which scattereth the east wind upon the earth?
Who hath divided a watercourse for the overflowing
    of waters,
Or a way for the lightning of thunder;
To cause it to rain on the earth, where no man is;
On the wilderness, wherein there is no man;
To satisfy the desolate and waste ground;
And to cause the bud of the tender herb to spring forth?

Hath the rain a father?
Or who hath begotten the drops of dew?
Out of whose womb came the ice?
And the hoary frost of heaven, who hath gendered it?
The waters are hid as with a stone,
And the face of the deep is frozen.
Canst thou bind the sweet influences of Pleiades,

Or loose the bands of Orion?
Canst thou bring forth Mazzaroth in his season?
Or canst thou guide Arcturus with his sons?
Knowest thou the ordinances of heaven?
Canst thou set the dominion thereof in the earth?
Canst thou lift up thy voice to the clouds,
That abundance of waters may cover thee?

Canst thou send lightnings, that they may go,
And say unto thee, 'Here we are'?

Who hath put wisdom in the inward parts?
Or who hath given understanding to the heart?
Who can number the clouds in wisdom?
Or who can stay the bottles of heaven,
When the dust groweth into hardness,
And the clods cleave fast together?

"CANST THOU UNDERSTAND THE INSTINCTS OF ANIMALS?"
"Wilt thou hunt the prey for the lion?
Or fill the appetite of the young lions,
When they couch in their dens,
And abide in the covert to lie in wait?

Who provideth for the raven his food?
When his young ones cry unto God, they wander for
lack of meat.
Knowest thou the time when the wild goats of the
rock bring forth?
Or canst thou mark when the hinds do calve?
Canst thou number the months that they fulfil?
Or knowest thou the time when they bring forth?
They bow themselves, they bring forth their young ones,
They cast out their sorrows.
Their young ones are in good liking, they grow up
with corn;
They go forth, and return not unto them.

Who hath sent out the wild ass free?
Or who hath loosed the bands of the wild ass?
Whose house I have made the wilderness,
And the barren land his dwellings.
He scorneth the multitude of the city,
Neither regardeth he the shouting of the driver.

The range of the mountains is his pasture,
And he searcheth after every green thing.

Will the unicorn be willing to serve thee,
Or abide by thy crib?
Canst thou bind the unicorn with his band in the
    furrow?
Or will he harrow the valleys after thee?
Wilt thou trust him, because his strength is great?
Or wilt thou leave thy labour to him?
Wilt thou believe him, that he will bring home thy
    seed,
And gather it into thy barn?

Gavest thou the goodly wings unto the peacocks?
Or wings and feathers unto the ostrich?
Which leaveth her eggs in the earth,
And warmeth them in dust,
And forgetteth that the foot may crush them,
Or that the wild beast may break them.
She is hardened against her young ones, as though they
    were not hers:
Her labour is in vain without fear;
Because God hath deprived her of wisdom,
Neither hath he imparted to her understanding.
What time she lifteth up herself on high,
She scorneth the horse and his rider.

Hast thou given the horse strength?
Hast thou clothed his neck with thunder?
Canst thou make him afraid as a grasshopper?
The glory of his nostrils is terrible.
He paweth in the valley, and rejoiceth in his strength:
He goeth on to meet the armed men.
He mocketh at fear, and is not affrighted;

Neither turneth he back from the sword.
The quiver rattleth against him,
The glittering spear and the shield.
He swalloweth the ground with fierceness and rage:
Neither believeth he that it is the sound of the trumpet.
He saith among the trumpets, 'Ha, ha';
And he smelleth the battle afar off,
The thunder of the captains, and the shouting.

Doth the hawk fly by thy wisdom,
And stretch her wings toward the south?
Doth the eagle mount up at thy command,
And make her nest on high?
She dwelleth and abideth on the rock,
Upon the crag of the rock, and the strong place.
From thence she seeketh the prey,
And her eyes behold afar off.
Her young ones also suck up blood:
And where the slain are, there is she."

Moreover the LORD answered Job, and said,

"Shall he that contendeth with the Almighty instruct
          him?
He that reproveth God, let him answer it."
                                    —Job 38; 39; 40:1-2.

THE ANSWER OF JOB
"I HOLD MY PEACE"

Then Job answered the LORD, and said,

"Behold, I am vile; what shall I answer thee?
I will lay mine hand upon my mouth.
Once have I spoken; but I will not answer:
Yea, twice; but I will proceed no further."   —Job 40: 3-5.

Again the Voice of Jehovah Speaks from the Storm

"CANST THOU SIT ON THE THRONE OF GOD AND RULE THE UNIVERSE?"

Then answered the LORD unto Job out of the whirlwind, and said,

"Gird up thy loins now like a man:
I will demand of thee, and declare thou unto me.
Wilt thou also disannul my judgment?
Wilt thou condemn me, that thou mayest be righteous?
Hast thou an arm like God?
Or canst thou thunder with a voice like him?
Deck thyself now with majesty and excellency;
And array thyself with glory and beauty.
Cast abroad the rage of thy wrath:
And behold every one that is proud, and abase him.
Look on every one that is proud, and bring him low;
And tread down the wicked in their place.
Hide them in the dust together;
And bind their faces in secret.
Then will I also confess unto thee
That thine own right hand can save thee.

"CANST THOU UNDERSTAND ONE OF GOD'S GREAT BEASTS, THE HIPPOPOTAMUS?"

"Behold now behemoth, which I made with thee;
He eateth grass as an ox.
Lo, now his strength is in his loins,
And his force is in the navel of his belly.
He moveth his tail like a cedar:
The sinews of his stones are wrapped together.
His bones are as strong pieces of brass;
His bones are like bars of iron.

He is the chief of the ways of God:
He that made him can make his sword to approach
    unto him.
Surely the mountains bring him forth food,
Where all the beasts of the field play.
He lieth under the shady trees,
In the covert of the reed, and fens,
The shady trees cover him with their shadow;
The willows of the brook compass him about.
Behold, he drinketh up a river, and hasteth not:
He trusteth that he can draw up Jordan into his mouth.
He taketh it with his eyes:
His nose pierceth through snares.   —Job 40:6–24.

"CANST THOU CONTROL THE CROCODILE?"

"Canst thou draw out leviathan with an hook?
Or his tongue with a cord which thou lettest down?
Canst thou put an hook into his nose?
Or bore his jaw through with a thorn?
Will he make many supplications unto thee?
Will he speak soft words unto thee?
Will he make a covenant with thee?
Wilt thou take him for a servant forever?
Wilt thou play with him as with a bird?
Or wilt thou bind him for thy maidens?
Shall the companions make a banquet of him?
Shall they part him among the merchants?
Canst thou fill his skin with barbed irons?
Or his head with fish spears?
Lay thine hand upon him,
Remember the battle, do no more.
Behold, the hope of him is in vain:
Shall not one be cast down even at the sight of him?
None is so fierce that dare stir him up:

Who then is able to stand before me?
Who hath prevented me, that I should repay him?
Whatsoever is under the whole heaven is mine.
I will not conceal his parts,
Nor his power,
Nor his comely proportion.
Who can discover the face of his garment?
Or who can come within his jaws?
Who can open the doors of his face?
His teeth are terrible round about.
His scales are his pride,
Shut up together as with a close seal.
One is so near to another,
That no air can come between them.
They are joined one to another, they stick together,
That they cannot be sundered.
By his sneezings a light doth shine,
And his eyes are like the eyelids of the morning.
Out of his mouth go burning lamps,
And sparks of fire leap out.
Out of his nostrils goeth smoke,
As out of a seething pot or caldron.
His breath kindleth coals,
And a flame goeth out of his mouth.
In his neck remaineth strength,
And sorrow is turned into joy before him.
The flakes of his flesh are joined together:
They are firm in themselves; they cannot be moved.
His heart is as firm as a stone;
Yea, as hard as a piece of the nether millstone.
When he raiseth up himself, the mighty are afraid:
By reason of breakings they purify themselves.
The sword of him that layeth at him cannot hold:
The spear, the dart, nor the habergeon.

He esteemeth iron as straw,
And brass as rotten wood.
The arrow cannot make him flee:
Slingstones are turned with him into stubble.
Darts are counted as stubble:
He laugheth at the shaking of a spear.
Sharp stones are under him:
He spreadeth sharp pointed things upon the mire.
He maketh the deep to boil like a pot:
He maketh the sea like a pot of ointment.
He maketh a path to shine after him;
One would think the deep to be hoary.
Upon earth there is not his like,
Who is made without fear.
He beholdeth all high things:
He is a king over all the children of pride." —Job 41.

Job's Second Answer to God

"I have spoken foolishly. I see God now as never before"

Then Job answered the Lord, and said,

"I know that thou canst do everything,
And that no thought can be withholden from thee.
'Who is he that hideth counsel without knowledge?'
Therefore have I uttered that I understood not;
Things too wonderful for me, which I knew not.
'Hear, I beseech thee, and I will speak:
I will demand of thee, and declare thou unto me.'
I have heard of thee by the hearing of the ear:
But now mine eye seeth thee.
Wherefore I abhor myself,
And repent in dust and ashes." —Job 42: 1-6.

The Epilogue

The Condemnation of Job's Friends and the Reward of Job

AND it was so, that after the LORD had spoken these words unto Job, the LORD said to Eliphaz, the Temanite, "My wrath is kindled against thee, and against thy two friends: for ye have not spoken of me the thing that is right, as my servant Job hath. Therefore take unto you now seven bullocks and seven rams, and go to my servant Job, and offer up for yourselves a burnt offering; and my servant Job shall pray for you: for him will I accept: lest I deal with you after your folly, in that ye have not spoken of me the thing which is right, like my servant Job." So Eliphaz, the Temanite, and Bildad, the Shuhite, and Zophar, the Naamathite, went, and did according as the LORD commanded them: the LORD also accepted Job.

And the LORD turned the captivity of Job, when he prayed for his friends: also the LORD gave Job twice as much as he had before. Then came there unto him all his brethren, and all his sisters, and all they that had been of his acquaintance before, and did eat bread with him in his house: and they bemoaned him, and comforted him over all the evil that the LORD had brought upon him: every man also gave him a piece of money, and every one an earring of gold. So the LORD blessed the latter end of Job more than his beginning: for he had fourteen thousand sheep, and six thousand camels, and a thousand yoke of oxen, and a thousand she asses.

He had also seven sons and three daughters; and he called the name of the first, "Jemima"; and the name of the second, "Kezia"; and the name of the third, "Keren-happuch." And in all the land were no women found so fair as the daughters of Job: and their father gave them inheritance among their brethren.

After this lived Job an hundred and forty years, and saw his sons, and his sons' sons, even four generations.

So Job died, being old and full of days.   —Job 42: 7-17.

What is the solution to the problem of suffering? There is no solution. God speaking in the storm does not tell Job why he has suffered; but he says, "Look about you in nature. See the wisdom and goodness of God. Can you not trust God with your problem?"

There is a confidence in God which demands no solution of problems; which is willing to trust God's wisdom where it cannot see. That confidence the Book of Job offers in place of the solution of the problem of suffering.

NOTES ON JOB

Land of Uz is mentioned a few other times in the Bible, but its locality is not clear. It probably lay southeast of Palestine, bordering on the desert.

Job. The name is not Hebrew. The name and the story of his piety and his disaster came doubtless from an old tale familiar to all the eastern peoples. In Ezek. 14:20, he is coupled with Noah as one of the ancient heroes.

Satan is not yet in "Job" the Satan of the New Testament, the enemy of God. Rather he is a member of God's court, a "prosecuting attorney," whose business it is to test the sincerity of the righteous. He is represented as doubtful of the genuineness of good men, and as quite willing to find them deceivers. The word is used, not as a proper name, but as a title, "The Accuser." Compare Zech. 3:1 where "the Satan" accuses the high priest.

Sore boils. The disease of Job was a kind of leprosy called elephantiasis, still common in the East. It was very painful and the people knew no cure. Job was driven to the rubbish heap outside the village, for leprosy was considered to be contagious.

The three friends said nothing because, had they spoken, they could only have said, "What a great sinner Job must be!" Job knew why they kept silent.

Eliphaz is the most friendly of the three. He is a prophet, and has had a dream, which said that all men sinned, so Job has sinned; but if he will repent, all will be well.

Bildad is a traditionalist. Note how he refers to the wisdom of the fathers as his authority.

Zophar has no authority for his belief. "Any fool knows that God makes the wicked suffer." He is the least sympathetic of the three.

Chap. 26:5–14; see p. 337. The description of the power of God is one of the finest passages in the book. It begins with the shades of the dead, who in the lower regions tremble before the gaze of God; then speaks, in poetic language, of how God controls the world and the great sea; and even the serpent which was thought to lie wrapped around the outer ocean. The poet concludes with a fine climax: all the universe to its farthest bounds only whispers of God's power; the thunder of it who could understand?

Elihu is not mentioned before Chap. 32; see p. 348. Many think his speeches are not part of the original poem. He is wordy and tiresome, and adds little that is new to the ideas of the friends. In this volume some of the speeches of Elihu are omitted, as not necessary for the understanding of the book of Job.

Whirlwind. Rather, "storm." Some have thought that the opening of Jehovah's speech imitates the thunder peals of the storm—sharp, short sentences, growing longer as the rolls of thunder die away in the distance.

Pleiades—Orion 38:31; see p. 359. The reference to these constellations reveals an understanding of astronomy.

Mazzaroth—38:32; see p. 359. The signs of the Zodiac or the planets.

Arcturus—38:32; see p. 359. Revised Version. "Canst thou guide the bear with her train?" ——the constellation of the Great Bear.

Chap. 39:19–25; see p. 361, 362. The horse was in ancient times mostly used in warfare. The writer thinks of him as having by a curious, God-given instinct, a love for battle.

Behemoth and Leviathan. Probably the hippopotamus and the crocodile. That was the guess of the ancient rabbis, and no one has ever made a better guess. The descriptions are highly idealized.

Doubtless the writer had never seen either of these animals. His point is that Job cannot control even one of God's great animals; how then will he hope to understand the problems of life, such as why men suffer?

Chap. 42:7-17; see p. 367. The prose epilogue goes back to the prose prologue, Chaps. 1 and 2; see p. 289. If the prologue rests on an old tale of a rich and pious man who lost his riches but retained his piety, the story doubtless told of the reward for his faithfulness. With no conception of a future life, must not God have rewarded him in this life?

QUESTIONS ON JOB

What question does the Book of Job discuss?

What does the Prologue tell about Job?

Why did the disasters come on Job?

Did Job stand the test placed on him in the Prologue?

What do the friends say about the reason for suffering in the first round of speeches?

What do they say in the second round?

What does the last speech of Job in the second round say about the theory that the wicked suffer because they have sinned?

What does Eliphaz say about why Job must have suffered, in the first speech of the third round?

What does Job reply in the last speech of that round?

What does Jehovah say in his speeches?

Does he explain suffering?

The message of the book is, "All things are a mystery. You trust God with what you cannot understand. Can you not trust him with suffering also?" Is that a solution of the problem of suffering? Is it an attitude toward life which is better than a solution?

How is Job a great lesson in trust?

The Book of Proverbs

THE Book of Proverbs is a little library. It is made up of a preface and eight pamphlets, written in different forms of verse and coming from various authors. They are alike in all being poetry, and in being gathered to teach morals and good living. They belong to what is called Wisdom Literature. They are not all composed of proverbs. Some of them contain short poems.

The brief Preface 1:1-6; see p. 373, states that the book is gathered to teach youth how to live. Then follow the eight divisions, mostly marked by headings:

1. The Praise of Wisdom, Chaps. 1-9; see pp. 373-385.

2. The Proverbs of Solomon, Chaps. 10-22:16; see pp. 386-388.

3. The Words of the Wise, Chaps. 22:17-24:22.

4. More Words of the Wise, Chaps. 24:23-34.

5. A Second Collection of Proverbs of Solomon, Chaps. 25-29; see pp. 417-419.

6. The Words of Agur, Chap. 30; see pp. 420-421.

7. The Words of King Lemuel, Chap. 31: 1-9.

8. The Praise of a Good Woman, Chap. 31: 10-31; see pp. 422, 423.

The Praise of Wisdom is made up, not of Proverbs, but of short poems, many of which personify Wisdom, and tell how she calls to men to choose the better way.

The Proverbs of Solomon is the typical collection of proverbs. Each is composed (in Hebrew), of two lines of exactly the same meter. They are on all sorts of subjects, and are not arranged in order.

The Second Collection of the Proverbs of Solomon is not so regular in form. The proverbs often have more than two lines, but they too deal with many subjects and are not arranged in order.

All the other divisions are very short, and are composed of proverbs, advice, and short poems.

Many of the Proverbs probably came from common life. Sometimes they have a touch of humor, like the proverb about bargaining: "'It's nothing. It's nothing,' the buyer says. When he has gone away, then he brags." There is much about industry and honesty, much about the profit of doing right and the folly of doing wrong. The fool is the one who thinks to find pleasure in wickedness. Back of all the comments on life stands the sense of responsibility to God, for "the fear of the Lord is the beginning of wisdom." The book is a wonderful book of wise counsels for life, useful for any race and any age.

The Proverbs of Solomon, the Son of David, King of Israel

THE PREFACE

TO know wisdom and instruction;
> To perceive the words of understanding;
> To receive the instruction of wisdom,
> Justice, and judgment, and equity;

To give subtilty to the simple,
To the young man knowledge and discretion.
A wise man will hear, and will increase learning;
And a man of understanding shall attain unto wise
    counsels:
To understand a proverb, and the interpretation;
The words of the wise, and their dark sayings.

— Proverbs 1: 2–6.

Poems From the First Section of Proverbs

THE PRAISE OF WISDOM

THE fear of the LORD is the beginning of knowl-
> edge:
> But fools despise wisdom and instruction.
> My son, hear the instruction of thy father,

And forsake not the law of thy mother:
For they shall be an ornament of grace unto thy head,
And chains about thy neck.

KEEP OUT OF BAD COMPANY

My son, if sinners entice thee,
Consent thou not.
If they say, "Come with us,
Let us lay wait for blood,
Let us lurk privily for the innocent without cause:
Let us swallow them up alive as the grave;
And whole, as those that go down into the pit:
We shall find all precious substance,
We shall fill our houses with spoil:
Cast in thy lot among us;
Let us all have one purse":
My son, walk not thou in the way with them;
Refrain thy foot from their path:
For their feet run to evil,
And make haste to shed blood.

Surely in vain the net is spread
In the sight of any bird.
And they lay wait for their own blood;
They lurk privily for their own lives.
So are the ways of every one that is greedy of gain;
Which taketh away the life of the owners thereof.

—Proverbs 1:7–19.

THE PROFIT OF WISDOM

Wisdom crieth without;
She uttereth her voice in the streets:
She crieth in the chief place of concourse,
In the openings of the gates:
In the city she uttereth her words, saying,
"How long, ye simple ones, will ye love simplicity?
And the scorners delight in their scorning, and fools
hate knowledge?

Turn you at my reproof:
Behold, I will pour out my spirit unto you,
I will make known my words unto you.
Because I have called, and ye refused;
I have stretched out my hand, and no man regarded;
But ye have set at naught all my counsel,
And would none of my reproof:
I also will laugh at your calamity;
I will mock when your fear cometh;
When your fear cometh as desolation,
And your destruction cometh as a whirlwind;
When distress and anguish cometh upon you.
Then shall they call upon me, but I will not answer;
They shall seek me early, but they shall not find me:
For that they hated knowledge,
And did not choose the fear of the Lord:
They would none of my counsel:
They despised all my reproof.
Therefore shall they eat of the fruit of their own way,
And be filled with their own devices.
For the turning away of the simple shall slay them,
And the prosperity of fools shall destroy them.
But whoso hearkeneth unto me shall dwell safely,
And shall be quiet from fear of evil."   — Proverbs 1:20–33.

How Wisdom Delivers from Evil

MY son, if thou wilt receive my words,
And hide my commandments with thee;
So that thou incline thine ear unto wisdom,
And apply thine heart to understanding;
Yea, if thou criest after knowledge,
And liftest up thy voice for understanding;
If thou seekest her as silver,
And searchest for her as for hid treasures;

Then shalt thou understand the fear of the Lord,
And find the knowledge of God.
For the Lord giveth wisdom:
Out of his mouth cometh knowledge and understanding.
He layeth up sound wisdom for the righteous:
He is a buckler to them that walk uprightly.
He keepeth the paths of judgment,
And preserveth the way of his saints.
Then shalt thou understand righteousness, and judg-
     ment,
And equity; yea, every good path.

When wisdom entereth into thine heart,
And knowledge is pleasant unto thy soul;
Discretion shall preserve thee,
Understanding shall keep thee:
To deliver thee from the way of the evil man,
From the man that speaketh froward things;
Who leave the paths of uprightness,
To walk in the ways of darkness;
Who rejoice to do evil,
And delight in the frowardness of the wicked;
Whose ways are crooked,
And they froward in their paths:
That thou mayest walk in the way of good men,
And keep the paths of the righteous.
For the upright shall dwell in the land,
And the perfect shall remain in it.
But the wicked shall be cut off from the earth,
And the transgressors shall be rooted out of it.

—Proverbs 2:1–15, 20–22.

A Father's Advice

My son, forget not my law;
But let thine heart keep my commandments:
For length of days, and long life,
And peace, shall they add to thee.

Let not mercy and truth forsake thee:
Bind them about thy neck;
Write them upon the table of thine heart:
So shalt thou find favour and good understanding
In the sight of God and man.

TRUST IN THE LORD

Trust in the LORD with all thine heart;
And lean not unto thine own understanding.
In all thy ways acknowledge him,
And he shall direct thy paths.

BE HUMBLE

Be not wise in thine own eyes:
Fear the LORD, and depart from evil.
It shall be health to thy navel,
And marrow to thy bones.
Honour the LORD with thy substance,
And with the firstfruits of all thine increase:
So shall thy barns be filled with plenty,
And thy presses shall burst out with new wine.

ACCEPT GOD'S CHASTENING

My son, despise not the chastening of the LORD;
Neither be weary of his correction:
For whom the LORD loveth he correcteth;
Even as a father the son in whom he delighteth.

SEEK WISDOM

Happy is the man that findeth wisdom,
And the man that getteth understanding.
For the merchandise of it is better than the merchandise
    of silver,
And the gain thereof than fine gold.
She is more precious than rubies:
And all the things thou canst desire are not to be
    compared unto her.
Length of days is in her right hand;
And in her left hand riches and honour.
Her ways are ways of pleasantness,
And all her paths are peace.
She is a tree of life to them that lay hold upon her:
And happy is every one that retaineth her.

HE WHO FINDS WISDOM UNDERSTANDS GOD

The LORD by wisdom hath founded the earth;
By understanding hath he established the heavens.
By his knowledge the depths are broken up,
And the clouds drop down the dew.
My son, let not them depart from thine eyes:
Keep sound wisdom and discretion:
So shall they be life unto thy soul,
And grace to thy neck.
Then shalt thou walk in thy way safely,
And thy foot shall not stumble.
When thou liest down, thou shalt not be afraid:
Yea, thou shalt lie down, and thy sleep shall be sweet.
Be not afraid of sudden fear,
Neither of the desolation of the wicked, when it cometh.
For the LORD shall be thy confidence,
And shall keep thy foot from being taken.

BE JUST AND GENEROUS

Withhold not good from them to whom it is due,
When it is in the power of thine hand to do it.

Say not unto thy neighbour, "Go, and come again,
And to-morrow I will give,"
When thou hast it by thee.
Devise not evil against thy neighbour,
Seeing he dwelleth securely by thee.
Strive not with a man without cause,
If he have done thee no harm.
Envy thou not the oppressor,
And choose none of his ways.
For the froward is abomination to the LORD:
But his secret is with the righteous.
The curse of the LORD is in the house of the wicked:
But he blesseth the habitation of the just.
Surely he scorneth the scorners:
But he giveth grace unto the lowly.
The wise shall inherit glory:
But shame shall be the promotion of fools.
— Proverbs 3:1–35.

THE ADVICE OF A FATHER, WHO PASSES ON WHAT HIS FATHER TAUGHT HIM

Hear, ye children, the instruction of a father,
And attend to know understanding,
For I give you good doctrine;
Forsake ye not my law.
For I was my father's son,
Tender and only beloved in the sight of my mother.
He taught me also, and said unto me,
"Let thine heart retain my words:
Keep my commandments, and live.
Get wisdom, get understanding:

Forget not, neither decline from the words of my mouth.
Forsake her not, and she shall preserve thee:
Love her, and she shall keep thee.
Wisdom is the principal thing; therefore get wisdom:
And with all thy getting get understanding.
Exalt her, and she shall promote thee:
She shall bring thee to honour, when thou dost embrace
    her.
She shall give to thine head an ornament of grace:
A crown of glory shall she deliver to thee."

WISDOM BRINGS REWARD

Hear, O my son, and receive my sayings;
And the years of thy life shall be many.
I have taught thee in the way of wisdom;
I have led thee in right paths.
When thou goest, thy steps shall not be straitened;
And when thou runnest, thou shalt not stumble.
Take fast hold of instruction; let her not go:
Keep her; for she is thy life.
Enter not into the path of the wicked,
And walk not in the way of evil men.
Avoid it, pass not by it,
Turn from it, and pass on,
For they sleep not except they have done mischief;
And their sleep is taken away unless they cause some
    to fall.
For they eat the bread of wickedness,
And drink the wine of violence.
But the path of the just is as the shining light,
That shineth more and more unto the perfect day.
The way of the wicked is as darkness:
They know not at what they stumble.

My son, attend to my words; incline thine ear unto my sayings.

Let them not depart from thine eyes; keep them in the midst of thine heart.

For they are life unto those that find them, and health to all their flesh.

KEEP THY HEART, AND THY LIFE WILL BE PURE

Keep thy heart with all diligence; for out of it are the issues of life.

Put away from thee a froward mouth, and perverse lips put far from thee.

Let thine eyes look right on, and let thine eyelids look straight before thee.

Ponder the path of thy feet, and let all thy ways be established.

Turn not to the right hand nor to the left: remove thy foot from evil. —Proverbs 4:1–27.

WHAT THE ANT MAY TEACH THE LAZY MAN

Go to the ant, thou sluggard;
Consider her ways, and be wise:
Which having no guide,
Overseer, or ruler,
Provideth her meat in the summer,
And gathereth her food in the harvest.
How long wilt thou sleep, O sluggard?
When wilt thou arise out of thy sleep?
"Yet a little sleep, a little slumber, a little folding of the hands to sleep."—
So shall thy poverty come as a robber,
And thy want as an armed man. — Proverbs. 6: 6–11.

Things the Lord Hates

These six things doth the Lord hate:
Yea, seven are an abomination unto him:
 A proud look, a lying tongue,
 And hands that shed innocent blood,
 An heart that deviseth wicked imaginations,
 Feet that be swift in running to mischief,
 A false witness that speaketh lies,
 And he that soweth discord among brethren.
— Proverbs 6:16–19.

The Call of Wisdom

Doth not wisdom cry?
And understanding put forth her voice?
She standeth in the top of high places,
By the way in the places of the paths.
She crieth at the gates,
At the entry of the city,
At the coming in at the doors.

"Unto you, O men, I call;
And my voice is to the sons of man.
O ye simple, understand wisdom:
And, ye fools, be ye of an understanding heart.
Hear; for I will speak of excellent things;
And the opening of my lips shall be right things.
For my mouth shall speak truth;
And wickedness is an abomination to my lips.
All the words of my mouth are in righteousness;
There is nothing froward or perverse in them.
They are all plain to him that understandeth,
And right to them that find knowledge.
Receive my instruction, and not silver;
And knowledge rather than choice gold.

For wisdom is better than rubies;
And all the things that may be desired are not to be
    compared to it.

HOW WISDOM CAN WORK WITH MEN

"I, wisdom, dwell with prudence, and find out knowledge
    of witty inventions.
The fear of the LORD is to hate evil:
Pride, and arrogancy, and the evil way,
And the froward mouth, do I hate.
Counsel is mine, and sound wisdom:
I am understanding; I have strength.
By me kings reign,
And princes decree justice.
By me princes rule, and nobles,
Even all the judges of the earth.
I love them that love me;
And those that seek me early shall find me.
Riches and honour are with me;
Yea, durable riches and righteousness.
My fruit is better than gold, yea, than fine gold;
And my revenue than choice silver.
I lead in the way of righteousness,
In the midst of the paths of judgment:
That I may cause those that love me to inherit sub-
    stance;
And I will fill their treasures.

HOW WISDOM WORKED WITH GOD

"The LORD possessed me in the beginning of his way,
Before his works of old.
I was set up from everlasting, from the beginning,
Or ever the earth was.
When there were no depths, I was brought forth;

When there were no fountains abounding with water.
Before the mountains were settled,
Before the hills was I brought forth:
While as yet he had not made the earth, nor the fields,
Nor the highest part of the dust of the world.
When he prepared the heavens, I was there:
When he set a compass upon the face of the depth:
When he established the clouds above:
When he strengthened the fountains of the deep:
When he gave to the sea his decree,
That the waters should not pass his commandment:
When he appointed the foundations of the earth:
Then I was by him, as one brought up with him:
And I was daily his delight, rejoicing always before
　　him;
Rejoicing in the habitable part of his earth;
And my delights were with the sons of men.

BLESSED IS THE MAN WHO HEARS WISDOM'S CALL

"Now therefore hearken unto me, O ye children:
For blessed are they that keep my ways.
Hear instruction, and be wise,
And refuse it not.
Blessed is the man that heareth me,
Watching daily at my gates,
Waiting at the posts of my doors.
For whoso findeth me findeth life,
And shall obtain favour of the LORD.
But he that sinneth against me wrongeth his own soul:
All they that hate me love death." 　　　— Proverbs 8:1-36.

THE FEAST OF WISDOM

Wisdom hath builded her house,
She hath hewn out her seven pillars:

She hath killed her beasts;
She hath mingled her wine;
She hath also furnished her table.
She hath sent forth her maidens:
She crieth upon the highest places of the city,

"Whoso is simple, let him turn in hither:"
As for him that wanteth understanding, she saith to
 him,
"Come, eat of my bread,
And drink of the wine which I have mingled.
Forsake the foolish, and live;
And go in the way of understanding.
He that reproveth a scorner getteth to himself shame:
And he that rebuketh a wicked man getteth himself a
 blot.
Reprove not a scorner, lest he hate thee:
Rebuke a wise man, and he will love thee.
Give instruction to a wise man, and he will be yet wiser:
Teach a just man, and he will increase in learning.
The fear of the LORD is the beginning of wisdom:
And the knowledge of the holy is understanding.
For by me thy days shall be multiplied,
And the years of thy life shall be increased.
If thou be wise, thou shalt be wise for thyself:
But if thou scornest, thou alone shalt bear it."

— Proverbs 9:1–12.

Proverbs from the Second Section

In the following selection from the second section headed "The Proverbs of Solomon" notice how each proverb is of two verses, and how they follow each other without order of subject. They are a splendid group of proverbs, very true to life.

THE way of a fool is right in his own eyes:
But he that hearkeneth unto counsel is wise.

A fool's wrath is presently known:
But a prudent man covereth shame.

He that speaketh truth sheweth forth righteousness:
But a false witness, deceit.

There is that speaketh like the piercings of a sword:
But the tongue of the wise is health.

The lip of truth shall be established forever:
But a lying tongue is but for a moment.

Deceit is in the heart of them that imagine evil:
But to the counsellors of peace is joy.

There shall no evil happen to the just:
But the wicked shall be filled with mischief.

A prudent man concealeth knowledge:
But the heart of fools proclaimeth foolishness.

The hand of the diligent shall bear rule:
But the slothful shall be under tribute.

Heaviness in the heart of man maketh it stoop:
But a good word maketh it glad.

The righteous is more excellent than his neighbour:
But the way of the wicked seduceth them.

The slothful man roasteth not that which he took in
   hunting:
But the substance of a diligent man is precious.

In the way of righteousness is life;
And in the pathway thereof there is no death.

A wise son heareth his father's instruction:
But a scorner heareth not rebuke.

A man shall eat good by the fruit of his mouth:
But the soul of the transgressors shall eat violence.

He that keepeth his mouth keepeth his life:
But he that openeth wide his lips shall have destruction.

The soul of the sluggard desireth, and hath nothing:
But the soul of the diligent shall be made fat.

A righteous man hateth lying:
But a wicked man is loathsome, and cometh to shame.

Righteousness keepeth him that is upright in the way:
But wickedness overthroweth the sinner.

There is that maketh himself rich, yet hath nothing:
There is that maketh himself poor, yet hath great
   riches.

Only by pride cometh contention:
But with the well advised is wisdom.

Wealth gotten by vanity shall be diminished:
But he that gathereth by labour shall increase.

Hope deferred maketh the heart sick:
But when the desire cometh, it is a tree of life.

Whoso despiseth the word shall be destroyed:
But he that feareth the commandment shall be rewarded.

The law of the wise is a fountain of life,
To depart from the snares of death.

Good understanding giveth favour:
But the way of transgressors is hard.

Every prudent man dealeth with knowledge:
But a fool layeth open his folly.

A wicked messenger falleth into mischief:
But a faithful ambassador is health.

Poverty and shame shall be to him that refuseth
instruction:
But he that regardeth reproof shall be honoured.

The desire accomplished is sweet to the soul:
But it is abomination to fools to depart from evil.

He that walketh with wise men shall be wise:
But a companion of fools shall be destroyed.

Evil pursueth sinners:
But to the righteous good shall be repaid.

—Proverbs 12:15–28; 13; 1–7, 10–21.

Classified Proverbs from Various Sections

"THE FEAR OF THE LORD IS THE BEGINNING OF WISDOM"

BUY the truth, and sell it not;
Also wisdom, and instruction, and understanding.

— Proverbs 23:23.

The heart of the prudent getteth knowledge;
And the ear of the wise seeketh knowledge.

— Proverbs 18:15.

He that getteth wisdom loveth his own soul:
He that keepeth understanding shall find good.

— Proverbs 19:8.

A good name is rather to be chosen than great riches,
And loving favour rather than silver and gold.

— Proverbs 22:1.

How much better is it to get wisdom than gold!
And to get understanding rather to be chosen than silver

— Proverbs 16:16.

There is gold, and a multitude of rubies:
But the lips of knowledge are a precious jewel.

— Proverbs 20:15.

The fear of the LORD is the instruction of wisdom;
And before honour is humility.

— Proverbs 15:33.

He that walketh in his uprightness feareth the LORD:
But he that is perverse in his ways despiseth him.

— Proverbs 14:2.

My son, if thine heart be wise,
My heart shall rejoice, even mine.
Yea, my reins shall rejoice,
When thy lips speak right things.
Let not thine heart envy sinners:
But be thou in the fear of the LORD all the day long,
For surely there is an end;
And thine expectation shall not be cut off.

— Proverbs 23:15–18.

In the fear of the LORD is strong confidence:
And his children shall have a place of refuge.
The fear of the LORD is a fountain of life,
To depart from the snares of death.

— Proverbs 14:26,27.

The fear of the LORD prolongeth days:
But the years of the wicked shall be shortened.

— Proverbs 10:27.

The fear of the LORD tendeth to life:
And he that hath it shall abide satisfied;
He shall not be visited with evil.

— Proverbs 19:23

By humility and the fear of the LORD
Are riches, and honour, and life.

— Proverbs 22:4.

There is no wisdom nor understanding
Nor counsel against the LORD.

— Proverbs 21:30.

The eyes of the LORD are in every place,
Beholding the evil and the good.

— Proverbs 15:3.

GOD RULES OVER LIFE

The hearing ear and the seeing eye,
The LORD hath made even both of them.

— Proverbs 20:12.

There are many devices in a man's heart;
Nevertheless the counsel of the LORD, that shall stand.
— Proverbs 19:21.

Man's goings are of the LORD;
How can a man then understand his own way?
— Proverbs 20:24.

Hell and destruction are before the LORD:
How much more then the hearts of the children of men?
— Proverbs 15:11.

The spirit of man is the candle of the LORD,
Searching all his innermost parts.
— Proverbs 20:27.

The king's heart is in the hand of the LORD, as the
    rivers of water:
He turneth it whithersoever he will.   —Proverbs 21:1.

Every way of a man is right in his own eyes:
But the LORD pondereth the hearts.
— Proverbs 21: 2.

The fining pot is for silver, and the furnace for gold:
But the LORD trieth the hearts.
— Proverbs 17:3.

The preparations of the heart in man,
And the answer of the tongue, is from the LORD.
All the ways of a man are clean in his own eyes;
But the LORD weigheth the spirits.
Commit thy works unto the LORD,
And thy thoughts shall be established.
The LORD hath made all things for himself:
Yea, even the wicked for the day of evil.
Every one that is proud in heart is an abomination
    to the LORD:
Though hand join in hand, he shall not be unpunished.
By mercy and truth iniquity is purged:

And by the fear of the LORD men depart from evil.
When a man's ways please the LORD,
He maketh even his enemies to be at peace with him.
Better is a little with righteousness
Than great revenues without right.
A man's heart deviseth his way:
But the LORD directeth his steps.

—Proverbs 16:1–9.

The lot is cast into the lap;
But the whole disposing thereof is of the LORD.

—Proverbs 16:33.

GOD HATES EVIL

THINGS WHICH ARE ABOMINATIONS TO GOD

The sacrifice of the wicked is abomination:
How much more, when he bringeth it with a wicked
mind?

—Proverbs 21:27.

He that turneth away his ear from hearing the law,
Even his prayer shall be an abomination.

—Proverbs 28:9.

The sacrifice of the wicked is an abomination to the
LORD:
But the prayer of the upright is his delight.

—Proverbs 15:8.

Lying lips are abomination to the LORD:
But they that deal truly are his delight.

—Proverbs 12:22.

They that are of a froward heart are abomination to
the LORD:
But such as are upright in their way are his delight.

—Proverbs 11:20.

He that justifieth the wicked, and he that condemneth
the just,
Even they both are abomination to the LORD.

—Proverbs 17:15.

GOD REWARDS THE GOOD AND PUNISHES THE EVIL

Righteousness exalteth a nation:
But sin is a reproach to any people.

— Proverbs 14:34.

Where there is no vision, the people perish:
But he that keepeth the law, happy is he.

— Proverbs 29:18.

He that handleth a matter wisely shall find good:
And whoso trusteth in the LORD, happy is he.

— Proverbs 16:20.

The name of the LORD is a strong tower:
The righteous runneth into it, and is safe.

— Proverbs 18:10.

The labour of the righteous tendeth to life:
The fruit of the wicked to sin.

— Proverbs 10:16.

He that walketh uprightly walketh surely:
But he that perverteth his ways shall be known.

— Proverbs 10:9.

Whoso walketh uprightly shall be saved:
But he that is perverse in his ways shall fall at once.

— Proverbs 28:18.

The just man walketh in his integrity:
His children are blessed after him.

— Proverbs 20:7.

The integrity of the upright shall guide them:
But the perverseness of transgressors shall destroy
them.

— Proverbs 11:3.

The highway of the upright is to depart from evil:
He that keepeth his way preserveth his soul.

— Proverbs 16:17.

In the house of the righteous is much treasure:
But in the revenues of the wicked is trouble.

— Proverbs 15:6.

The righteous man wisely considereth the house of the
    wicked:
But God overthroweth the wicked for their wickedness.
— Proverbs 21:12.

The way of the LORD is strength to the upright:
But destruction shall be to the workers of iniquity.
The righteous shall never be removed:
But the wicked shall not inhabit the earth.
— Proverbs 10:29, 30.

The righteousness of the perfect shall direct his way:
But the wicked shall fall by his own wickedness.
The righteousness of the upright shall deliver them:
But transgressors shall be taken in their own naughti-
    ness.
When a wicked man dieth, his expectation shall perish:
And the hope of unjust men perisheth.
—Proverbs 11:5-7.

He that diligently seeketh good procureth favour:
But he that seeketh mischief, it shall come unto him.
— Proverbs 11:27.

Judgments are prepared for scorners,
And stripes for the back of fools.
—Proverbs 19:29.

Whoso rewardeth evil for good,
Evil shall not depart from his house.
— Proverbs 17:13.

The eyes of the LORD preserve knowledge,
And he overthroweth the words of the transgressor.
— Proverbs 22:12.

The LORD is far from the wicked:
But he heareth the prayer of the righteous.
— Proverbs 15:29.

Evil men understand not judgment:
But they that seek the LORD understand all things.
— Proverbs 28:5

The LORD will destroy the house of the proud:
But he will establish the border of the widow.
The thoughts of the wicked are an abomination to the
    LORD:
But the words of the pure are pleasant words.
He that is greedy of gain troubleth his own house;
But he that hateth gifts shall live.

— Proverbs 15:25–27.

Though hand join in hand, the wicked shall not be
    unpunished:
But the seed of the righteous shall be delivered.

— Proverbs 11:21.

The wicked worketh a deceitful work:
But to him that soweth righteousness shall be a sure
    reward.
As righteousness tendeth to life:
So he that pursueth evil pursueth it to his own death.

— Proverbs 11:18,19.

Whoso causeth the righteous to go astray in an evil
    way, he shall fall himself into his own pit:
But the upright shall have good things in possession.

— Proverbs 28:10.

He that covereth his sins shall not prosper:
But whoso confesseth and forsaketh them shall have
    mercy.

— Proverbs 28:13.

The wicked flee when no man pursueth:
But the righteous are bold as a lion.

— Proverbs 28:1.

He that soweth iniquity shall reap vanity:
And the rod of his anger shall fail.

— Proverbs 22:8.

Bread of deceit is sweet to a man;
But afterwards his mouth shall be filled with gravel.
— Proverbs 20:17.

There is a way which seemeth right unto a man,
But the end thereof are the ways of death.
— Proverbs 14:12.

The wicked is driven away in his wickedness:
But the righteous hath hope in his death.
— Proverbs 14:32.

To do justice and judgment
Is more acceptable to the LORD than sacrifice.
— Proverbs 21:3.

The way of the wicked is an abomination unto the LORD.
But he loveth him that followeth after righteousness.
— Proverbs 15:9

He that is of a proud heart stirreth up strife:
But he that putteth his trust in the LORD shall be made
     fat.
He that trusteth in his own heart is a fool:
But whoso walketh wisely, he shall be delivered.
— Proverbs 28:25, 26.

A good man obtaineth favour of the LORD:
But a man of wicked devices will he condemn.
— Proverbs 12:2.

The LORD will not suffer the soul of the righteous to
     famish:
But he casteth away the substance of the wicked.
— Proverbs 10:3.

THE WISE MAN AND THE FOOL

Through wisdom is an house builded:
And by understanding it is established:
And by knowledge shall the chambers be filled with all
     precious and pleasant riches.
A wise man is strong;
Yea, a man of knowledge increaseth strength.

For by wise counsel thou shalt make thy war:
And in multitude of counsellors there is safety.
— Proverbs 24:3–6.

The crown of the wise is their riches:
But the foolishness of fools is folly.
— Proverbs 14:24.

The wise in heart will receive commandments:
But a prating fool shall fall.
— Proverbs 10:8.

A wise man feareth, and departeth from evil:
But the fool rageth, and is confident.
— Proverbs 14:16.

Fools make a mock at sin:
But among the righteous there is favour.
— Proverbs 14:9.

A prudent man foreseeth the evil, and hideth himself;
But the simple pass on, and are punished.
— Proverbs 27:12.

Wisdom is before him that hath understanding;
But the eyes of a fool are in the ends of the earth.
— Proverbs 17:24.

Understanding is a wellspring of life unto him that
    hath it:
But the instruction of fools is folly.
— Proverbs 16:22.

The heart of him that hath understanding seeketh
    knowledge:
But the mouth of fools feedeth on foolishness.
— Proverbs 15:14.

Folly is joy to him that is destitute of wisdom:
But a man of understanding walketh uprightly.
— Proverbs 15:21.

Wherefore is there a price in the hand of a fool to get
    wisdom,
Seeing he hath no heart to it?
— Proverbs 17:16.

The thought of foolishness is sin:
And the scorner is an abomination to men.

— Proverbs 24:9.

A scorner seeketh wisdom, and findeth it not:
But knowledge is easy unto him that understandeth.

— Proverbs 14:6.

Wise men lay up knowledge:
But the mouth of the foolish is near destruction.

— Proverbs 10:14.

Speak not in the ears of a fool:
For he will despise the wisdom of thy words.

— Proverbs 23:9.

If a wise man contendeth with a foolish man,
Whether he rage or laugh, there is no rest.

— Proverbs 29:9.

A fool uttereth all his mind,
But a wise man keepeth it in till afterwards.

— Proverbs 29:11.

A fool's lips enter into contention,
And his mouth calleth for strokes.
A fool's mouth is his destruction,
And his lips are the snare of his soul.

— Proverbs 18:6–7.

Though thou shouldest bray a fool in a mortar among
wheat with a pestle,
Yet will not his foolishness depart from him.

— Proverbs 27:22.

It is as sport to a fool to do mischief:
But a man of understanding hath wisdom.

— Proverbs 10:23.

THE RIGHTEOUS AND THE WICKED

It is joy to the just to do judgment:
But destruction shall be to the workers of iniquity.

—Proverbs 21:15.

An unjust man is an abomination to the just:
And he that is upright in the way is abomination to the
    wicked.
—Proverbs 29:27.

The mouth of a righteous man is a well of life:
But violence covereth the mouth of the wicked.
—Proverbs 10:11.

The tongue of the just is as choice silver:
The heart of the wicked is little worth.
The lips of the righteous feed many:
But fools die for want of wisdom.
—Proverbs 10:20, 21.

The fruit of the righteous is a tree of life;
And he that winneth souls is wise.
—Proverbs 11:30.

The hope of the righteous shall be gladness:
But the expectation of the wicked shall perish.
—Proverbs 10:28.

The light of the righteous rejoiceth:
But the lamp of the wicked shall be put out.
—Proverbs 13:9.

Fret not thyself because of evil men,
Neither be thou envious at the wicked;
For there shall be no reward to the evil man;
The candle of the wicked shall be put out.
—Proverbs 24:19, 20.

Blessings are upon the head of the just:
But violence covereth the mouth of the wicked.
The memory of the just is blessed:
But the name of the wicked shall rot.
—Proverbs 10:6, 7.

The righteous is delivered out of trouble,
And the wicked cometh in his stead.
—Proverbs 11:8.

He that followeth after righteousness and mercy
Findeth life, righteousness, and honour.

—Proverbs 21:21.

Be not thou envious against evil men,
Neither desire to be with them.
For their heart studieth destruction,
And their lips talk of mischief.

—Proverbs 24:1, 2.

Lay not wait, O wicked man, against the dwelling of
    the righteous;
Spoil not his resting place:
For a just man falleth seven times, and riseth up again:
But the wicked shall fall into mischief.

—Proverbs 24:15, 16.

When the righteous are in authority, the people rejoice:
But when the wicked beareth rule, the people mourn.

—Proverbs 29:2.

When the wicked rise, men hide themselves:
But when they perish, the righteous increase.

—Proverbs 28:28.

When the wicked are multiplied, transgression in-
    creaseth:
But the righteous shall see their fall.

—Proverbs 29:16.

The simple inherit folly:
But the prudent are crowned with knowledge.
The evil bow before the good;
And the wicked at the gates of the righteous.

—Proverbs 14:18,19.

The wicked is snared by the transgression of his lips:
But the just shall come out of trouble.

—Proverbs 12:13.

Thorns and snares are in the way of the froward:
He that doth keep his soul shall be far from them.

—Proverbs 22:5.

In the transgression of an evil man there is a snare:
But the righteous doth sing and rejoice.

— Proverbs 29:6.

Even a child is known by his doings,
Whether his work be pure, and whether it be right.

— Proverbs 20:11.

THE RICH AND THE POOR

He that hasteth to be rich hath an evil eye;
And considereth not that poverty shall come upon him.

— Proverbs 28:22.

The rich man's wealth is his strong city,
And as an high wall in his own conceit.

— Proverbs 18:11.

The rich man's wealth is his strong city:
The destruction of the poor is their poverty.

— Proverbs 10:15.

Wealth maketh many friends;
But the poor is separated from his neighbour.

— Proverbs 19:4.

The rich ruleth over the poor,
And the borrower is servant to the lender.

— Proverbs 22:7.

The poor is hated even of his own neighbour:
But the rich hath many friends.

— Proverbs 14:20.

The rich and poor meet together:
The Lord is the maker of them all.

— Proverbs 22:2.

The poor and the deceitful man meet together:
The Lord lighteneth both their eyes.

— Proverbs 29:13.

The righteous considereth the cause of the poor:
But the wicked regardeth not to know it.

— Proverbs 29:7.

He that giveth unto the poor shall not lack:
But he that hideth his eyes shall have many a curse.
—Proverbs 28:27.

Whoso stoppeth his ears at the cry of the poor,
He also shall cry himself, but shall not be heard.
—Proverbs 21:13.

Better is the poor that walketh in his integrity,
Than he that is perverse in his lips, and is a fool.
—Proverbs 19:1.

The desire of a man is his kindness:
And a poor man is better than a liar.
—Proverbs 19:22.

There is that scattereth, and yet increaseth;
And there is that withholdeth more than is meet, but
　　it tendeth to poverty.
—Proverbs 11:24.

Rob not the poor, because he is poor:
Neither oppress the afflicted in the gate:
For the LORD will plead their cause,
And spoil the soul of those that spoiled them.
—Proverbs 22:22, 23.

The rich man is wise in his own conceit;
But the poor that hath understanding searcheth him
　　out.
—Proverbs 28:11.

As a roaring lion, and a ranging bear;
So is a wicked ruler over the poor people.
—Proverbs 28:15

He that hath a bountiful eye shall be blessed;
For he giveth of his bread to the poor.
—Proverbs 22:9.

He that hath pity upon the poor lendeth unto the LORD;
And that which he hath given will he pay him again.
—Proverbs 19:17.

The liberal soul shall be made fat:
And he that watereth shall be watered also himself.
He that withholdeth corn, the people shall curse him:
But blessing shall be upon the head of him that selleth
   it.
                                        —Proverbs 11:25, 26.

He coveteth greedily all the day long:
But the righteous giveth and spareth not.
                                        —Proverbs 21:26.

A poor man that oppresseth the poor
Is like a sweeping rain which leaveth no food.
                                        —Proverbs 28:3.

He that oppresseth the poor to increase his riches,
And he that giveth to the rich, shall surely come to
   want.
                                        —Proverbs 22:16.

Whoso mocketh the poor reproacheth his Maker:
And he that is glad at calamities shall not be unpunished.
                                        —Proverbs 17:5.

He that oppresseth the poor reproacheth his Maker:
But he that honoureth him hath mercy on the poor.
                                        —Proverbs 14:31.

He that by usury and unjust gain increaseth his
   substance,
He shall gather it for him that will pity the poor.
                                        —Proverbs 28:8.

RICHES

The man that wandereth out of the way of under-
   standing
Shall remain in the congregation of the dead.
He that loveth pleasure shall be a poor man:
He that loveth wine and oil shall not be rich.
                                        —Proverbs 21:16, 17.

Better is a dry morsel, and quietness therewith,
Than an house full of feasting with strife.
— Proverbs 17:1.

A faithful man shall abound with blessings:
But he that maketh haste to be rich shall not be
innocent.
— Proverbs 28:20.

The blessing of the LORD, it maketh rich,
And he addeth no sorrow with it.
— Proverbs 10:22.

THE GOOD AND THE EVIL OF RICHES

He becometh poor that dealeth with a slack hand:
But the hand of the diligent maketh rich.
— Proverbs 10:4.

Treasures of wickedness profit nothing:
But righteousness delivereth from death.
— Proverbs 10:2.

Better is the poor that walketh in his uprightness,
Than he that is perverse in his ways, though he be rich.
— Proverbs 28:6.

To have respect of persons is not good:
For for a piece of bread that man will transgress.
—Proverbs 28:21.

Riches profit not in the day of wrath:
But righteousness delivereth from death.
— Proverbs 11:4.

He that trusteth in his riches shall fall:
But the righteous shall flourish as a branch.
— Proverbs 11:28.

Labour not to be rich:
Cease from thine own wisdom.
— Proverbs 23:4.

Wilt thou set thine eyes upon that which is not?
For riches certainly make themselves wings;
They fly away as an eagle toward heaven.

—Proverbs 23:5.

Better is little with the fear of the LORD
Than great treasure and trouble therewith.

—Proverbs 15:16.

BLESSED IS HE WHO CONTROLS HIS ANGER

He that is slow to anger is better than the mighty;
And he that ruleth his spirit than he that taketh a city.

—Proverbs 16:32.

He that is soon angry dealeth foolishly:
And a man of wicked devices is hated.

—Proverbs 14:17.

He that is slow to wrath is of great understanding:
But he that is hasty of spirit exalteth folly.

—Proverbs 14:29.

Go not forth hastily to strive,
Lest thou know not what to do in the end thereof,
When thy neighbour hath put thee to shame.

—Proverbs 25:8.

It is an honour for a man to cease from strife:
But every fool will be meddling.

—Proverbs 20:3.

Say not thou, "I will recompense evil";
But wait on the LORD, and he shall save thee.

—Proverbs 20:22.

Make no friendship with an angry man;
And with a furious man thou shalt not go:
Lest thou learn his ways,
And get a snare to thy soul.

—Proverbs 22:24, 25.

The thoughts of the diligent tend only to plenteousness;
But of every one that is hasty only to want.

—Proverbs 21:5.

The beginning of strife is as when one letteth out water:
Therefore leave off contention, before it be meddled
with.

—Proverbs 17:14.

He loveth transgression that loveth strife:
And he that exalteth his gate seeketh destruction.

—Proverbs 17:19.

An angry man stirreth up strife,
And a furious man aboundeth in transgression.

—Proverbs 29:22.

He that hath no rule over his own spirit
Is like a city that is broken down, and without walls.

—Proverbs 25:28.

The north wind bringeth forth rain:
So doth a backbiting tongue an angry countenance.

—Proverbs 25:23.

Blessed Is He Who Guards His Tongue

Whoso keepeth his mouth and his tongue
Keepeth his soul from troubles.

—Proverbs 21:23.

Even a fool, when he holdeth his peace, is counted wise:
And he that shutteth his lips is esteemed a man of
understanding.

—Proverbs 17:28.

A word fitly spoken
Is like apples of gold in pictures of silver.

—Proverbs 25:11.

A soft answer turneth away wrath:
But grievous words stir up anger.

—Proverbs 15:1.

Pleasant words are as an honeycomb,
Sweet to the soul, and health to the bones.

—Proverbs 16:24.

A talebearer revealeth secrets:
But he that is of a faithful spirit concealeth the matter.

—Proverbs 11:13.

Death and life are in the power of the tongue:
And they that love it shall eat the fruit thereof.

— Proverbs 18:21.

In the lips of him that hath understanding wisdom is
found:
But a rod is for the back of him that is void of understanding.

— Proverbs 10:13.

By long forbearing is a prince persuaded,
And a soft tongue breaketh the bone.

— Proverbs 25:15.

The lips of the wise disperse knowledge:
But the heart of the foolish doeth not so.

— Proverbs 15:7.

The tongue of the wise useth knowledge aright:
But the mouth of fools poureth out foolishness.

— Proverbs 15:2.

A wholesome tongue is a tree of life:
But perverseness therein is a breach in the spirit.

— Proverbs 15:4.

A man hath joy by the answer of his mouth:
And a word spoken in due season, how good is it!

— Proverbs 15:23.

He that blesseth his friend with a loud voice, rising
early in the morning,
It shall be counted a curse to him.

— Proverbs 27:14.

If a ruler hearken to lies,
All his servants are wicked.

—Proverbs 29:12.

A false witness shall not be unpunished,
And he that speaketh lies shall not escape.

— Proverbs 19:5.

An hypocrite with his mouth destroyeth his neighbour:
But through knowledge shall the just be delivered.

— Proverbs 11:9.

Seest thou a man that is hasty in his words?
There is more hope of a fool than of him.
—Proverbs 29:20.

He that hideth hatred with lying lips,
And he that uttereth a slander, is a fool.
In the multitude of words there wanteth not sin:
But he that refraineth his lips is wise.
—Proverbs 10:18, 19.

A man that flattereth his neighbour
Spreadeth a net for his feet.
In the transgression of an evil man there is a snare:
But the righteous doth sing and rejoice.
—Proverbs 29:5, 6.

He that goeth about as a talebearer revealeth secrets:
Therefore meddle not with him that flattereth with
his lips.
—Proverbs 20:19.

The getting of treasures by a lying tongue
Is a vanity tossed to and fro of them that seek death.
—Proverbs 21:6.

"It is naught, it is naught," saith the buyer:
But when he is gone his way, then he boasteth.
—Proverbs 20:14.

The Downfall of Pride

An high look, and a proud heart,
And the plowing of the wicked, is sin.
—Proverbs 21:4.

Seest thou a man wise in his own conceit?
There is more hope of a fool than of him.
—Proverbs 26:12.

Pride goeth before destruction,
And an haughty spirit before a fall.
—Proverbs 16:18.

When pride cometh, then cometh shame:
But with the lowly is wisdom.
—Proverbs 11:2.

Better it is to be of an humble spirit with the lowly,
Than to divide the spoil with the proud.
—Proverbs 16:19.

Who can say, I have made my heart clean,
I am pure from my sin?
—Proverbs 20:9.

If thou hast done foolishly in lifting up thyself, or if
thou hast thought evil,
Lay thine hand upon thy mouth.
—Proverbs 30:32.

Put not forth thyself in the presence of the king,
And stand not in the place of great men:
For better it is that it be said unto thee, "Come up
hither,"
Than that thou shouldest be put lower in the presence of
the prince
Whom thine eyes have seen.
—Proverbs 25:6, 7.

Before destruction the heart of man is haughty,
And before honour is humility.
—Proverbs 18:12.

A man's pride shall bring him low:
But honour shall uphold the humble in spirit.
—Proverbs 29:23.

The Value of Friends

A friend loveth at all times,
And a brother is born for adversity.
—Proverbs 17:17.

Thine own friend, and thy father's friend, forsake not;
Neither go into thy brother's house in the day of thy
calamity:
For better is a neighbour that is near than a brother
far off.
—Proverbs 27:10.

A man that hath friends must shew himself friendly:
And there is a friend that sticketh closer than a
brother.

— Proverbs 18:24.

As in water face answereth to face,
So the heart of man to man.

— Proverbs 27:19.

He that covereth a transgression seeketh love:
But he that repeateth a matter separateth very friends.

— Proverbs 17:9.

A froward man soweth strife:
And a whisperer separateth chief friends.

— Proverbs 16:28.

KINDLINESS

He that despiseth his neighbour sinneth:
But he that hath mercy on the poor, happy is he.

— Proverbs 14:21.

If thine enemy be hungry, give him bread to eat;
And if he be thirsty, give him water to drink.
For thou shalt heap coals of fire upon his head,
And the LORD shall reward thee.

— Proverbs 25:21, 22.

The merciful man doeth good to his own soul:
But he that is cruel troubleth his own flesh.

— Proverbs 11:17.

A righteous man regardeth the life of his beast:
But the tender mercies of the wicked are cruel.

— Proverbs 12:10.

Rejoice not when thine enemy falleth,
And let not thine heart be glad when he stumbleth:
Lest the LORD see it, and it displease him,
And he turn away his wrath from him.

— Proverbs 24:17, 18.

Say not, "I will do so to him as he hath done to me:
I will render to the man according to his work."

— Proverbs 24:29.

The discretion of a man deferreth his anger;
And it is his glory to pass over a transgression.
—Proverbs 19:11.

Hatred stirreth up strifes:
But love covereth all sins. —Proverbs 10:12.

The Cheerful Heart

A merry heart maketh a cheerful countenance:
But by sorrow of the heart the spirit is broken.
—Proverbs 15:13.

A merry heart doeth good like a medicine:
But a broken spirit drieth the bones.
—Proverbs 17:22.

The heart knoweth his own bitterness;
And a stranger doth not intermeddle with his joy.
—Proverbs 14:10.

If thou faint in the day of adversity,
Thy strength is small.
—Proverbs 24:10.

All the days of the afflicted are evil:
But he that is of a merry heart hath a continual feast.
—Proverbs 15:15.

The Value of Wise Reproof

Whoso loveth instruction loveth knowledge:
But he that hateth reproof is brutish.
—Proverbs 12:1.

As an earring of gold, and an ornament of fine gold,
So is a wise reprover upon an obedient ear.
—Proverbs 25:12.

A scorner loveth not one that reproveth him:
Neither will he go unto the wise.
—Proverbs 15:12.

Correction is grievous unto him that forsaketh the
way:
And he that hateth reproof shall die.
—Proverbs 15:10.

A reproof entereth more into a wise man
Than an hundred stripes into a fool.

—Proverbs 17:10.

He that rebuketh a man afterwards shall find more
favour
Than he that flattereth with the tongue.

—Proverbs 28:23.

The ear that heareth the reproof of life
Abideth among the wise.
He that refuseth instruction despiseth his own soul:
But he that heareth reproof getteth understanding.

—Proverbs 15:31, 32.

PARENTS AND CHILDREN

Whoso curseth his father or his mother,
His lamp shall be put out in obscure darkness.

—Proverbs 20:20.

A wise son maketh a glad father:
But a foolish man despiseth his mother.

—Proverbs 15:20.

A foolish son is a grief to his father,
And bitterness to her that bare him.

—Proverbs 17:25.

Children's children are the crown of old men;
And the glory of children are their fathers.

—Proverbs 17:6.

A wise son maketh a glad father:
But a foolish son is the heaviness of his mother.

—Proverbs 10:1.

My son, be wise, and make my heart glad,
That I may answer him that reproacheth me.

—Proverbs 27:11.

Hearken unto thy father that begat thee,
And despise not thy mother when she is old.

—Proverbs 23:22.

Whoso robbeth his father or his mother
And saith, "It is no transgression";
The same is the companion of a destroyer.

—Proverbs 28:24.

He that wasteth his father, and chaseth away his
mother,
Is a son that causeth shame, and bringeth reproach.

—Proverbs 19:26.

Train up a child in the way he should go:
And when he is old, he will not depart from it.

—Proverbs 22:6.

The rod and reproof give wisdom:
But a child left to himself bringeth his mother to shame.

—Proverbs 29:15.

Correct thy son, and he shall give thee rest;
Yea, he shall give delight unto thy soul.

—Proverbs 29:17.

Withhold not correction from the child:
For if thou beatest him with the rod, he shall not die.
Thou shalt beat him with the rod,
And shalt deliver his soul from hell.

—Proverbs 23:13, 14.

A fool despiseth his father's instruction:
But he that regardeth reproof is prudent.

—Proverbs 15:5.

The father of the righteous shall greatly rejoice:
And he that begetteth a wise child shall have joy of
him.

—Proverbs 23:24.

INDUSTRY AND LAZINESS

In all labour there is profit:
But the talk of the lips tendeth only to penury.

—Proverbs 14:23.

He that tilleth his land shall be satisfied with bread:
But he that followeth vain persons is void of understanding.

—Proverbs 12:11.

He that tilleth his land shall have plenty of bread:
But he that followeth after vain persons shall have
    poverty enough.

—Proverbs 28:19.

Slothfulness casteth into a deep sleep;
And an idle soul shall suffer hunger.

—Proverbs 19:15.

The desire of the slothful killeth him;
For his hands refuse to labour.

—Proverbs 21:25.

A slothful man hideth his hand in his bosom,
And will not so much as bring it to his mouth again.

—Proverbs 19:24.

He also that is slothful in his work
Is brother to him that is a great waster.

—Proverbs 18:9.

As vinegar to the teeth, and as smoke to the eyes,
So is the sluggard to them that send him.

—Proverbs 10:26.

Be thou diligent to know the state of thy flocks,
And look well to thy herds.
For riches are not forever:
And doth the crown endure to every generation?
The hay appeareth, and the tender grass sheweth itself,
And herbs of the mountains are gathered.
The lambs are for thy clothing,
And the goats are the price of the field.
And thou shalt have goats' milk enough for thy food,
For the food of thy household,
And for the maintenance for thy maidens.

—Proverbs 27:23–27.

Seest thou a man diligent in his business?
He shall stand before kings;
He shall not stand before mean men.

—Proverbs 22:29.

The slothful man saith, "There is a lion without,
I shall be slain in the streets."

—Proverbs 22:13.

The sluggard will not plow by reason of the cold;
Therefore shall he beg in harvest, and have nothing.

—Proverbs 20:4.

As the door turneth upon his hinges,
So doth the slothful upon his bed.
The slothful hideth his hand in his bosom;
It grieveth him to bring it again to his mouth.
The sluggard is wiser in his own conceit
Than seven men that can render a reason.

—Proverbs 26:14-16.

I went by the field of the slothful,
And by the vineyard of the man void of understanding;
And, lo, it was all grown over with thorns,
And nettles had covered the face thereof,
And the stone wall thereof was broken down.
Then I saw, and considered it well:
I looked upon it, and received instruction.
"Yet a little sleep, a little slumber,
A little folding of the hands to sleep:
So shall thy poverty come as a robber";
And thy want as an armed man.

— Proverbs 24:30-34.

DRUNKENNESS

Hear thou, my son, and be wise,
And guide thine heart in the way.
Be not among winebibbers;
Among riotous eaters of flesh:
For the drunkard and the glutton shall come to
 poverty:
And drowsiness shall clothe a man with rags.

— Proverbs 23:19-21.

Wine is a mocker, strong drink is raging:
And whosoever is deceived thereby is not wise.

— Proverbs 20:1.

Who hath woe? Who hath sorrow?
Who hath wounds without cause?
Who hath redness of eyes?
They that tarry long at the wine;
They that go to seek mixed wine.
Look not thou upon the wine when it is red,
When it giveth his colour in the cup,
When it moveth itself aright.
At the last it biteth like a serpent,
And stingeth like an adder.
Thine eyes shall behold strange things,
And thine heart shall utter perverse things.
Yea, thou shalt be as he that lieth down in the midst
of the sea,
Or as he that lieth upon the top of a mast.
"They have stricken me," shalt thou say,
"And I was not sick; they have beaten me, and I felt
it not:
When shall I awake?
I will seek it yet again."

— Proverbs 23:29–35.

THE YOUNG AND THE OLD

The glory of young men is their strength:
And the beauty of old men is the grey head.

— Proverbs 20:29.

The hoary head is a crown of glory,
If it be found in the way of righteousness.

— Proverbs 16:31.

Proverbs from the Fifth Section

In the proverbs from the fifth section, headed: "These are also proverbs of Solomon, which the men of Hezekiah, King of Judah, copied out," notice that there are often more than two lines. Here also there is no order of subjects treated. Comparison is frequent, and double comparison occasional. These proverbs are often very shrewd observations of life.

AS snow in summer, and as rain in harvest,
So honour is not seemly for a fool.

As the bird by wandering, as the swallow
by flying,
So the curse causeless shall not come.

A whip for the horse, a bridle for the ass,
And a rod for the back of fools.

Answer not a fool according to his folly,
Lest thou also be like unto him.
Answer a fool according to his folly,
Lest he be wise in his own conceit.

He that sendeth a message by the hand of a fool
Cutteth off the feet, and drinketh damage.

The legs of the lame are not equal:
So is a parable in the mouth of fools.

As he that bindeth a stone in a sling,
So is he that giveth honour to a fool.

417

As a thorn goeth up into the hand of a drunkard,
So is a parable in the mouth of fools.

—Proverbs 26:1-9.

He that passeth by, and meddleth with strife belonging
    not to him,
Is like one that taketh a dog by the ears.

As a mad man who casteth fire brands,
Arrows, and death,
So is the man that deceiveth his neighbour,
And saith, "Am not I in sport?"

Where no wood is, there the fire goeth out:
So where there is no talebearer, the strife ceaseth.

As coals are to burning coals, and wood to fire;
So is a contentious man to kindle strife.

The words of a talebearer are as wounds,
And they go down into the innermost parts.

Fervent lips and a wicked heart
Are like a potsherd covered with silver dross.

He that hateth dissembleth with his lips,
And layeth up deceit within him;
When he speaketh fair, believe him not:
For there are seven abominations in his heart.
Though his hatred is covered by deceit,
His wickedness shall be shewed before the whole con-
    gregation.

Whoso diggeth a pit shall fall therein:
And he that rolleth a stone, it will return upon him.

A lying tongue hateth those that are afflicted by it;
And a flattering mouth worketh ruin.   — Proverbs 26:17-28.

Boast not thyself of to-morrow;
For thou knowest not what a day may bring forth.
Let another man praise thee, and not thine own mouth;
A stranger, and not thine own lips.

A stone is heavy, and the sand weighty;
But a fool's wrath is heavier than them both.
Wrath is cruel, and anger is outrageous;
But who is able to stand before envy?

Open rebuke is better
Than love that is hidden.
Faithful are the wounds of a friend;
But the kisses of an enemy are deceitful.

The full soul loatheth an honeycomb;
But to the hungry soul every bitter thing is sweet.
As a bird that wandereth from her nest,
So is a man that wandereth from his place.

Ointment and perfume rejoice the heart:
So doth the sweetness of a man's friend by hearty
    counsel.   — Proverbs 27:1-9.

Withdraw thy foot from thy neighbour's house;
Lest he be weary of thee, and so hate thee.
A man that beareth false witness against his neighbour
Is a maul, and a sword, and a sharp arrow.

Confidence in an unfaithful man in time of trouble
Is like a broken tooth, and a foot out of joint.

As he that taketh away a garment in cold weather,
    And as vinegar upon nitre,
So is he that singeth songs to an heavy heart.
                            — Proverbs 25:17-20.

The Wisdom of Agur

"Where Can I Find God?"

THE WORDS OF AGUR, THE SON OF JAKEH

THE man spake,

"I have wearied myself, O God.
I have wearied myself, O God, and I am
    consumed.
Surely I am more brutish than any man,
And have not the understanding of a man.
I neither learned wisdom,
Nor have the knowledge of the holy.
Who hath ascended up into heaven, or descended?
Who hath gathered the wind in his fists?
Who hath bound the waters in a garment?
Who hath established all the ends of the earth?
What is his name, and what is his son's name, if thou
    canst tell?"

"GOD IS FOUND NOT IN QUESTIONING BUT IN TRUST"

Every word of God is pure:
He is a shield unto them that put their trust in him.
Add thou not unto his words, lest he reprove thee,
And thou be found a liar.

— Proverbs 30:1–6.

"THREE THINGS, YEA, FOUR"

There be three things which are too wonderful for me,
Yea, four which I know not:
    The way of an eagle in the air;
    The way of a serpent upon a rock;

420

The way of a ship in the midst of the sea;
And the way of a man with a maid.

— Proverbs 30:18, 19.

For three things the earth is disquieted,
And for four which it cannot bear:
  For a servant when he reigneth;
  And a fool when he is filled with meat;
  For an odious woman when she is married;
  And an handmaid that is heir to her mistress.

— Proverbs 30:21–23.

There be four things which are little upon the earth,
But they are exceeding wise:
  The ants are a people not strong,
  Yet they prepare their meat in the summer;
  The conies are but a feeble folk,
  Yet make they their houses in the rocks;
  The locusts have no king,
  Yet go they forth all of them by bands;
  The spider taketh hold with her hands,
  And is in kings' palaces.

— Proverbs 30:24–28.

There be three things which go well,
Yea, four are comely in going:
  A lion which is strongest among beasts,
  And turneth not away for any;
  A greyhound; an he goat also;
  And a king, against whom there is no rising up.

— Proverbs 30:29–31.

Praise of a Good Woman

WHO can find a virtuous woman?
For her price is far above rubies.
The heart of her husband doth safely
trust in her,
So that he shall have no need of spoil.
She will do him good and not evil
All the days of her life.

She seeketh wool, and flax,
And worketh willingly with her hands.
She is like the merchants' ships;
She bringeth her food from afar.
She riseth also while it is yet night,
And giveth meat to her household,
And a portion to her maidens.
She considereth a field, and buyeth it:
With the fruit of her hands she planteth a vineyard.
She girdeth her loins with strength,
And strengtheneth her arms.
She perceiveth that her merchandise is good:
Her candle goeth not out by night.

She layeth her hands to the spindle,
And her hands hold the distaff.
She stretcheth out her hand to the poor;
Yea, she reacheth forth her hands to the needy.
She is not afraid of the snow for her household:
For all her household are clothed with scarlet.
She maketh herself coverings of tapestry;
Her clothing is silk and purple.

Her husband is known in the gates,
When he sitteth among the elders of the land.
She maketh fine linen, and selleth it;
And delivereth girdles unto the merchant.
Strength and honour are her clothing;
And she shall rejoice in time to come.

She openeth her mouth with wisdom;
And in her tongue is the law of kindness.
She looketh well to the ways of her household,
And eateth not the bread of idleness.

Her children arise up, and call her blessed;
Her husband also, and he praiseth her.
"Many daughters have done virtuously,
But thou excellest them all."
Favour is deceitful, and beauty is vain:
But a woman that feareth the Lord, she shall be
    praised.
Give her of the fruit of her hands;
And let her own works praise her in the gates.
— Proverbs 31:10–31.

The Book of Ecclesiastes

THERE was a wise man in Israel who asked himself the question, "What is the value of life?" It seemed to him that some people gave the wrong answer. They considered the value of life to be what was "left over" when it was done. They were like some Christian people who answer the question, "Why should a person be good?" by saying, "To get to heaven"; as though a good life were of no value in itself.

It seemed to this wise man that this answer was all wrong for two reasons. In the first place, he did not see that anything was "left over." All man could be sure of was the day as it passed. If he found no value in that, if he threw away what it had to offer, then perhaps he would find that he had lost everything. In the second place, life brought its own value in each day of living. There was joy in living. There was joy in doing work. There was joy in simple pleasures of a simple life; in eating when one is hungry, and resting when one is tired, and enjoying the life of the home; withal remembering to live so that life could be brought to God for his blessing.

So the value of life is not in waiting for pay later, and being miserable while life goes on, but in enjoying the work of each day as it comes; not in dreaming empty dreams about the wonderful things which may come by and by, but in appreciating the little thing we have now; not in refusing to see the hardship and injustice which falls to men, but in seeing that behind it all stands God. Life is "vanity"; that is, it is empty of any later reward; but each day brings its own reward. Life gives board and clothes, but no wages to put in the pocket and carry away. Better enjoy what it does give, he thought, than to worry over what it does not give.

This wise man lived before the days when the hope of a life after death became clear. The New Testament adds that also to the values of life. But even so, this ancient wise man's counsel is still worth attention: So live that each day's life is worth while. That is the value of living.

After the wise man had thought long about it, he wrote a book of little essays on the value of life. The book is not always easy to understand. But the substance is clear. It is always worth remembering: The value of life lies in making every day worth while.

The Problem

The words of the Preacher, the son of David,
King in Jerusalem.

Wherein Lies the Profit of Life

VANITY of vanities, saith the Preacher,
Vanity of vanities; all is vanity.
What profit hath a man of all his labour
Which he taketh under the sun?
— Ecclesiastes 1:1-3.

Introduction: Nature Suggests an Endless Round, With No Profit Left Over

One generation passeth away, and another generation
    cometh:
But the earth abideth forever.
The sun also ariseth, and the sun goeth down,
And hasteth to his place where he arose.
The wind goeth toward the south,
And turneth about unto the north;
It whirleth about continually,
And the wind returneth again according to his circuits.
All the rivers run into the sea;
Yet the sea is not full;
Unto the place from whence the rivers come,
Thither they return again.
All things are full of labour;
Man cannot utter it:
The eye is not satisfied with seeing,
Nor the ear filled with hearing.

The thing that hath been, it is that which shall be;
And that which is done is that which shall be done:
And there is no new thing under the sun.

Is there anything whereof it may be said, "See, this is new"? It hath been already of old time, which was before us. There is no remembrance of former things; neither shall there be any remembrance of things that are to come with those that shall come after.—Ecclesiastes 1:4-11.

An Ideal Biography

THE LIFE OF THE GREATEST KING YIELDS NO PROFIT, BUT SERVES TO SHOW THAT EACH DAY BRINGS ITS OWN REWARD

I, the Preacher, was king over Israel in Jerusalem. And I gave my heart to seek and search out by wisdom concerning all things that are done under heaven: this sore travail hath God given to the sons of man to be exercised therewith. I have seen all the works that are done under the sun; and, behold, all is vanity and vexation of spirit. That which is crooked cannot be made straight: and that which is wanting cannot be numbered.

I communed with mine own heart, saying, "Lo, I am come to great estate, and have gotten more wisdom than all they that have been before me in Jerusalem": yea, my heart had great experience of wisdom and knowledge. And I gave my heart to know wisdom, and to know madness and folly: I perceived that this also is vexation of spirit. For in much wisdom is much grief: and he that increaseth knowledge increaseth sorrow.

I said in mine heart, "Go to now, I will prove thee with mirth, therefore enjoy pleasure: and, behold, this also is vanity." I said of laughter, "It is mad": and of mirth, "What doeth it?" I sought in mine heart to give myself unto wine, yet acquainting mine heart with wisdom; and to lay hold on folly, till I might see what was that good for the sons of men, which they should do under the heaven all the days of their life. I made me great works; I builded me houses; I planted me vineyards: I made me gardens and orchards, and I planted trees in them of all kind of fruits: I made me pools of water, to water therewith the wood that bringeth forth trees: I got me servants and maidens, and had servants born in my house; also I had great possessions of great and small cattle above all that were in Jerusalem before me: I gathered me also silver and gold, and the peculiar treasure of kings and of the provinces: I gat me men singers and women singers, and the delights of the sons of men, as musical instruments, and that of all sorts. So I was great, and increased more than all that were before me in Jerusalem: also my wisdom remained with me. And whatsoever mine eyes desired I kept not from them, I withheld not my heart from any joy; for my heart rejoiced in all my labour: and this was my portion of all my labour.

Then I looked on all the works that my hands had wrought, and on the labour that I had laboured to do: and, behold, all was vanity and vexation of spirit, and there was no profit under the sun.

And I turned myself to behold wisdom, and madness, and folly: for what can the man do that cometh after the king? Even that which hath been already done. Then I saw that wisdom excelleth folly, as far as light excelleth darkness. The wise man's eyes are in his head; but the fool walketh in darkness: and I myself perceived also that one event happeneth to them all. Then said I in my heart, "As it happeneth to the fool, so it happeneth even to me; and why was I then more wise?" Then I said in my heart, that this also is vanity; for there

is no remembrance of the wise more than of the fool forever; seeing that which now is in the days to come shall
all be forgotten. And how dieth the wise man? As the
fool. Therefore I hated life; because the work that is
wrought under the sun is grievous unto me: for all is
vanity and vexation of spirit.

Yea, I hated all my labour which I had taken under
the sun: because I should leave it unto the man that shall
be after me. And who knoweth whether he shall be a
wise man or a fool? Yet shall he have rule over all my
labour wherein I have laboured, and wherein I have
shewed myself wise under the sun. This is also vanity.

Therefore I went about to cause my heart to despair
of all the labour which I took under the sun. For there is
a man whose labour is in wisdom, and in knowledge, and
in equity; yet to a man that hath not laboured therein
shall he leave it for his portion. This also is vanity and
a great evil.

For what hath man of all his labour, and of the vexation of his heart, wherein he hath laboured under the sun?
For all his days are sorrows, and his travail grief; yea, his
heart taketh not rest in the night. This is also vanity.

THE CONCLUSION

There is nothing better for a man, than that he should
eat and drink, and that he should make his soul enjoy
good in his labour. This also I saw, that it was from the
hand of God. — Ecclesiastes 1:12-2:24.

Little Essays on Life

I. MAN CANNOT UNDERSTAND GOD'S TIMES AND SEASONS, BUT HE CAN REJOICE IN HIS WORK

TO every thing there is a season, and a time
     to every purpose under the heaven:
     A time to be born, and a time to die;
     A time to plant, and a time to pluck up
     that which is planted;
A time to kill, and a time to heal;
A time to break down, and a time to build up;
A time to weep, and a time to laugh;
A time to mourn, and a time to dance;
A time to cast away stones, and a time to gather
     stones together;
A time to embrace, and a time to refrain from em-
     bracing;
A time to get, and a time to lose;
A time to keep, and a time to cast away;
A time to rend, and a time to sew;
A time to keep silence, and a time to speak;
A time to love, and a time to hate;
A time of war, and a time of peace.

What profit hath he that worketh in that wherein he laboureth?

I have seen the travail, which God hath given to the sons of men to be exercised in it. He hath made everything beautiful in his time: also he hath set the world in their heart, so that no man can find out the work that God maketh from the beginning to the end. I know that there is no good in them, but for a man to rejoice, and to do good in his life; and also that every man should eat and drink, and enjoy the good of all his labour; it is the gift of God. I know that whatsoever God doeth it shall be forever: nothing can be put to it, nor anything taken from it: and God doeth it, that men should fear before him. — Ecclesiastes 3:1–14.

II. It Is a Crooked World, But Man May Rejoice in His Work

If thou seest the oppression of the poor, and violent perverting of judgment and justice in a province, marvel not at the matter: for he that is higher than the highest regardeth; and there be higher than they.

Moreover the profit of the earth is for all: the king himself is served by the field. He that loveth silver shall not be satisfied with silver; nor he that loveth abundance with increase: this is also vanity.

When goods increase, they are increased that eat them: and what good is there to the owners thereof, saving the beholding of them with their eyes?

The sleep of a labouring man is sweet, whether he eat little or much: but the abundance of the rich will not suffer him to sleep.

There is a sore evil which I have seen under the sun, namely, riches kept for the owners thereof to their hurt. But those riches perish by evil travail: and he begetteth a son, and there is nothing in his hand. As he came forth of his mother's womb, naked shall he return to go as he came, and shall take nothing of his labour, which he may carry away in his hand. And this also is a sore evil, that in all points as he came, so shall he go: and what profit hath he that hath laboured for the wind? All his days also he eateth in darkness, and he hath much sorrow and wrath with his sickness.

THE CONCLUSION

Behold that which I have seen: it is good and comely for one to eat and to drink, and to enjoy the good of all his labour that he taketh under the sun all the days of his life, which God giveth him: for it is his portion. Every man also to whom God hath given riches and wealth, and hath given him power to eat thereof, and to take his portion, and to rejoice in his labour; this is the gift of God. — Ecclesiastes 5:8–19.

III. Some Things Are Better Than Others; and Men May Always Find Joy

A good name is better than precious ointment;
And the day of death than the day of one's birth.

It is better to go to the house of mourning,
Than to go to the house of feasting:
For that is the end of all men;
And the living will lay it to his heart.

Sorrow is better than laughter:
For by the sadness of the countenance the heart is made
better.
The heart of the wise is in the house of mourning;
But the heart of fools is in the house of mirth.

It is better to hear the rebuke of the wise,
Than for a man to hear the song of fools;
For as the crackling of thorns under a pot,
So is the laughter of the fool: this also is vanity.

Surely oppression maketh a wise man mad;
And a gift destroyeth the heart.

Better is the end of a thing than the beginning thereof.
And the patient in spirit is better than the proud in
  spirit.
Be not hasty in thy spirit to be angry:
For anger resteth in the bosom of fools.

Say not thou, "What is the cause that the former days
were better than these?" for thou dost not enquire wisely
concerning this.

Wisdom is good with an inheritance: and by it there
is profit to them that see the sun; for wisdom is a defence,
and money is a defence: but the excellency of knowledge
is that wisdom giveth life to them that have it.

Consider the work of God: for who can make that
straight, which he hath made crooked?

In the day of prosperity be joyful, but in the day of
adversity consider: God also hath set the one over
against the other, to the end that man should find nothing after him.
                                              —Ecclesiastes 7:1–14.

IV. DEATH COMES ALIKE TO ALL, BUT STILL
THERE IS JOY IN LIFE

All things come alike to all: there is one event to the
righteous, and to the wicked; to the good and to the clean,
and to the unclean; to him that sacrificeth, and to him that
sacrificeth not: as is the good, so is the sinner; and he that
sweareth, as he that feareth an oath. This is an evil
among all things that are done under the sun, that there
is one event unto all: yea, also the heart of the sons of
men is full of evil, and madness is in their heart while
they live, and after that they go to the dead. For to
him that is joined to all the living there is hope: for a
living dog is better than a dead lion. For the living know
that they shall die: but the dead know not anything,

neither have they any more a reward; for the memory of
them is forgotten. Also their love, and their hatred, and
their envy, is now perished; neither have they any more
a portion forever in anything that is done under the sun.

> Go thy way, eat thy bread with joy,
> And drink thy wine with a merry heart;
> For God now accepteth thy works.
>
> — Ecclesiastes 9:2-7.

V. Fill Life With Its Full Round of Duties, and Rejoice in Them All

Cast thy bread upon the waters:
For thou shalt find it after many days.
Give a portion to seven, and also to eight;
For thou knowest not what evil shall be upon the earth.
If the clouds be full of rain,
They empty themselves upon the earth:
And if the tree fall toward the south, or toward the
    north,
In the place where the tree falleth, there it shall be.
He that observeth the wind shall not sow;
And he that regardeth the clouds shall not reap.
As thou knowest not what is the way of the spirit,
Nor how the bones do grow in the womb of her that is
    with child:
Even so thou knowest not the works of God who mak-
    eth all.
In the morning sow thy seed,
And in the evening withhold not thine hand:
For thou knowest not whether shall prosper, either
    this or that,
Or whether they both shall be alike good.
Truly the light is sweet,
And a pleasant thing it is for the eyes to behold the sun:

But if a man live many years,
And rejoice in them all;
Yet let him remember the days of darkness;
For they shall be many.
All that cometh is vanity. — Ecclesiastes 11:1–8.

VI. Rejoice in Youth, and Live so That God May
Bless You; for the End Draws on Apace

Rejoice, O young man, in thy youth;
And let thy heart cheer thee in the days of thy youth.
And walk in the ways of thine heart,
And in the sight of thine eyes:
But know thou, that for all these things
God will bring thee into judgment.
Therefore remove sorrow from thy heart,
And put away evil from thy flesh:
For childhood and youth are vanity.
Remember now thy Creator in the days of thy youth,
While the evil days come not,
Nor the years draw nigh, when thou shalt say,
"I have no pleasure in them";
While the sun, or the light, or the moon,
Or the stars, be not darkened,
Nor the clouds return after the rain:
In the day when the keepers of the house shall tremble,
And the strong men shall bow themselves,
And the grinders cease because they are few,
And those that look out of the windows be darkened,
And the doors shall be shut in the streets,
When the sound of the grinding is low,
And he shall rise up at the voice of the bird,
And all the daughters of music
Shall be brought low;
Also when they shall be afraid of that which is high,

And fears shall be in the way,
And the almond tree shall flourish,
And the grasshopper shall be a burden,
And desire shall fail:
Because man goeth to his long home,
And the mourners go about the streets:
Or ever the silver cord be loosed,
Or the golden bowl be broken,
Or the pitcher be broken at the fountain,
Or the wheel broken at the cistern.
Then shall the dust return to the earth as it was:
And the spirit shall return unto God who gave it.
Vanity of vanities, saith the preacher;
All is vanity.   —Ecclesiastes 11:9–12:8.

The Conclusion: Fear God and Keep His Commandments

Let us hear the conclusion of the whole matter:
Fear God, and keep his commandments: for this is
   the whole duty of man.
For God shall bring every work into judgment, with
   every secret thing, whether it be good, or whether
   it be evil.   —Ecclesiastes 12:13, 14.

NOTES ON ECCLESIASTES

Ecclesiastes. The word is the same as that translated "Preacher"
in Verse 1. It is "Koheleth," and that Hebrew word is sometimes used
in English, for no English word very well translates it. "Debater"
is better than "Preacher." It means one who speaks in an assembly.
"Ecclesiastes" is Greek for the same meaning.

Profit. Literally, something left over. When a man has finished life, is anything left over? The writer's reply will be, "No:
therefore let us make each day worth while as it goes."

Vanity is emptiness. The author means that life is like a purse
with nothing in it. This writer uses the word forty times.

"**Eat and drink, and make his soul enjoy good in his labour.**" This is often repeated in substance in the book. The real value of life, the writer believes, consists not in something left over at the end, but in the enjoyment of the day as the day goes on. The simple good things of life and the very labor itself furnish enjoyment which is the real profit of living.

Wisdom, and madness, and folly. He tries both wisdom and wild folly; wisdom is the better, but neither leaves over anything.

"**Rejoice, O young man, in thy youth.**" He wishes the youth to enjoy life to the full, but to live so that he may lay life before God for his judgment.

Evil days. The writer thinks of old age as a time when life has less pleasure than in youth. He uses figures, at least some of which mean the definite disabilities of old age. The "grinders" are the teeth; "those that look out of the windows," the eyes; the "almond-tree," famous for its white bloom in early spring, white hair, and so on. At present, with the aid of glasses and other devices, the disabilities of age are partly removed, and many old people would say that they find old age the happiest part of life.

QUESTIONS ON ECCLESIASTES

Read the ideal biography and see if it shows any service for others, or if its labor is all for self.

What value can you expect of life if it is all for self?

Does this writer think you can enjoy yourself only when work is over, or that you can enjoy your work?

What things are better than others? Why?

How can a young person best enjoy youth?

What is the value of life, according to Ecclesiastes?

Is this a good philosophy of life?

Has the New Testament, with its ideas of service and the future life, anything to add to this estimate of what makes life worth living?

Lamentations

AMONG the books of the Hebrew Bible is a collection of five dirges over the fall of Jerusalem, 586 B.C. It was not for many hundred years that these dirges were ascribed to Jeremiah. When the Greek translation of the Bible, called "The Seventy," was made, the translators called these poems the "Lamentations of Jeremiah," and this title has come down to us. There is no probability that Jeremiah wrote them, but they have helped to give the great prophet the name of the "Weeping Prophet," which he most decidedly does not deserve.

The book has two interesting literary peculiarities: (1) the long stately lines with a pause in the middle; (2) the alphabetic form. The first chapter is composed of verses of three lines each, the first lines of the successive verses beginning with successive letters of the Hebrew alphabet. The following arrangement will illustrate the alphabetic form, using English letters in the place of Hebrew.

A city that sitteth in solitude, she
    that was full of people,
She has become as a widow, she
    that was great among nations;
She has become tributary, she
    that was princess in provinces.

But she weepeth sore in the night,
  and her tears are on her cheeks,
All of her lovers are gone. She
  hath none to comfort her.
All of her friends have turned;
  traitors they are to her.

Chapter 3 is composed of groups of three lines but each line in the group begins with the same letter.

A man that hath seen affliction
  by the rod of his wrath am I;
And he led me to walk in the darkness, and not in the light of day,
Against me he turneth his hand
  again and again all the day.

Broken my bones hath he, my
  flesh and my skin is made old;
Builded against me hath he, and
  surrounded me with affliction,
Brought me to dwell in the darkness, as though I had long been
  dead.

Chapter 4 is like 1 and 2 except that it has two lines to a verse. Chapter 5 is not alphabetically arranged, but it has twenty-two verses, the same number of letters as in the Hebrew alphabet. The lines of the verses are shorter than those of the first four chapters.

The intensity of the emotion shown in most of these poems seems to mark a time not far from the fall of Jerusalem. Chapter 3 may be an exception, and may come from a later date. All represent the prophetic element of the nation. The authors think of the fall of Jerusalem as the result of the sin of the people, and the greatest source of grief is not, after all, the destruction of the nation, but the feeling that their God has turned away from them in anger. Nowhere in literature is there a more stately and dignified expression of profound national sorrow in national disaster than in this group of elegies.

Lamentations

I. The Bitterness of Defeat

HOW doth the city sit solitary, that was full
of people!
How is she become as a widow she that was
great among the nations!
And princess among the provinces and how is
she become tributary!

She weepeth sore in the night, and her tears are on
her cheeks:
Among all her lovers she hath none to comfort her:
All her friends have dealt treacherously with her, they
are become her enemies.

Judah is gone into captivity because of affliction, and
because of great servitude:
She dwelleth among the heathen, she findeth no rest:
All her persecutors overtook her between the straits.

The ways of Zion do mourn, because none come to the
solemn feasts:
All her gates are desolate: her priests sigh,
Her virgins are afflicted, and she is in bitterness.

Her adversaries are the chief, her enemies prosper:
For the LORD hath afflicted her for the multitude of
her transgressions:
Her children are gone into captivity before the enemy.

And from the daughter of Zion all her beauty is departed:
Her princes are become like harts that find no pasture,
And they are gone without strength before the pursuer.

Jerusalem remembered in the days of her affliction
and of her miseries all her pleasant things that
she had in the days of old,
When her people fell into the hand of the enemy, and
none did help her:
The adversaries saw her, and did mock at her Sabbaths.

Jerusalem hath grievously sinned; therefore she is removed:
All that honoured her despise her, because they have
seen her nakedness:
Yea, she sigheth, and turneth backward.

Her filthiness is in her skirts; she remembereth not her
last end;
Therefore she came down wonderfully: she had no comforter.
O Lord, behold my affliction: for the enemy hath
magnified himself.

The adversary hath spread out his hand upon all her
pleasant things:
For she hath seen that the heathen entered into her
sanctuary,

Whom thou didst command that they should not
enter into thy congregation.

All her people sigh, they seek bread;
They have given their pleasant things for meat to relieve the soul:
See, O LORD, and consider; for I am become vile.

Is it nothing to you, all ye that pass by?
Behold, and see if there be any sorrow like unto my sorrow, which is done unto me,
Wherewith the LORD hath afflicted me in the day of his fierce anger.
From above hath he sent fire into my bones, and it prevaileth against them:
He hath spread a net for my feet, he hath turned me back:
He hath made me desolate and faint all the day.

The yoke of my transgressions is bound by his hand:
They are wreathed, and come up upon my neck: he hath made my strength to fall,
The LORD hath delivered me into their hands, from whom I am not able to rise up.

The LORD hath trodden under foot all my mighty men in the midst of me:
He hath called an assembly against me to crush my young men:
The LORD hath trodden the virgin, the daughter of Judah, as in a wine-press.

For these things I weep; mine eye, mine eye runneth down with water,
Because the comforter that should relieve my soul is far from me:
My children are desolate, because the enemy prevailed.

Zion spreadeth forth her hands, and there is none to
   comfort her:
The LORD hath commanded concerning Jacob, that
   his adversaries should be round about him:
Jerusalem is as an unclean thing among them.

The LORD is righteous; for I have rebelled against his
   commandment:
Hear, I pray you, all people, and behold my sorrow:
My virgins and my young men are gone into captivity.

I called for my lovers, but they deceived me:
My priests and mine elders gave up the ghost in the
   city,
While they sought their meat to relieve their souls.

Behold, O LORD; for I am in distress: my bowels are
   troubled;
Mine heart is turned within me; for I have grievously
   rebelled:
Abroad the sword bereaveth, at home there is as
   death.

They have heard that I sigh: there is none to comfort me:
All mine enemies have heard of my trouble; they are
   glad that thou hast done it;
Thou wilt bring the day that thou hast called, and
   they shall be like unto me.

Let all their wickedness come before thee;
And do unto them, as thou hast done unto me for all
   my transgressions:
For my sighs are many, and my heart is faint.

—Lamentations 1.

II. God Has Cast Off His People

How hath the LORD covered the daughter of Zion with
a cloud in his anger,
And cast down from heaven unto the earth the beauty
of Israel,
And remembered not his footstool in the day of his
anger!

The LORD hath swallowed up all the habitations of
Jacob, and hath not pitied:
He hath thrown down in his wrath the strongholds of
the daughter of Judah;
He hath brought them down to the ground: he hath
polluted the kingdom and the princes thereof.

He hath cut off in his fierce anger all the horn of Israel:
He hath drawn back his right hand from before the
enemy,
And he burned against Jacob like a flaming fire, which
devoureth round about.

He hath bent his bow like an enemy: he stood with his
right hand as an adversary,
And slew all that were pleasant to the eye
In the tabernacle of the daughter of Zion: he poured out
his fury like fire.

The LORD was as an enemy, he hath swallowed up Israel;
He hath swallowed up all her palaces, he hath destroyed his strongholds,
And hath increased in the daughter of Judah mourning
and lamentation.

And he hath violently taken away his tabernacle, as if
 it were of a garden: he hath destroyed his places
 of the assembly:
The LORD hath caused the solemn feasts and Sabbaths
 to be forgotten in Zion;
And hath despised in the indignation of his anger the
 king and the priest.

The LORD hath cast off his altar, he hath abhorred his
 sanctuary,
He hath given up into the hand of the enemy the walls
 of her palaces;
They have made a noise in the house of the LORD, as in
 the day of a solemn feast.

The LORD hath purposed to destroy the wall of the
 daughter of Zion:
He hath stretched out a line, he hath not withdrawn his
 hand from destroying:
Therefore he made the rampart and the wall to lament;
 they languished together.

Her gates are sunk into the ground; he hath destroyed
 and broken her bars:
Her king and her princes are among the Gentiles: the
 law is no more;
Her prophets also find no vision from the LORD.

The elders of the daughter of Zion sit upon the ground,
 and keep silence:
They have cast up dust upon their heads; they have
 girded themselves with sackcloth:
The virgins of Jerusalem hang down their heads to the
 ground.

Mine eyes do fail with tears, my bowels are troubled,
My liver is poured upon the earth, for the destruction
    of the daughter of my people;
Because the children and the sucklings swoon in the
    streets of the city.

They say to their mothers, "Where is corn and wine?"
When they swooned as the wounded in the streets of
    the city,
When their soul was poured out into their mothers'
    . bosom.

What thing shall I take to witness for thee? What
    thing shall I liken to thee, O daughter of Jeru-
    salem?
What shall I equal to thee, that I may comfort thee, O
    virgin daughter of Zion?
For thy breach is great like the sea: who can heal thee?

Thy prophets have seen vain and foolish things for thee:
And they have not discovered thine iniquity, to turn
    away thy captivity;
But have seen for thee false burdens and causes of
    banishment.

All that pass by clap their hands at thee;
They hiss and wag their head at the daughter of Jeru-
    salem, saying,
"Is this the city that men call the perfection of beauty,
    the joy of the whole earth?"

All thine enemies have opened their mouth against thee:
They hiss and gnash the teeth: they say, "We have
    swallowed her up:

Certainly this is the day that we looked for; we have
found, we have seen it."

The LORD hath done that which he had devised;
He hath fulfilled his word that he had commanded in
the days of old:
He hath thrown down, and hath not pitied:
And he hath caused thine enemy to rejoice over thee,
he hath set up the horn of thine adversaries.
Their heart cried unto the LORD,
"O wall of the daughter of Zion, let tears run down
like a river day and night:
Give thyself no rest; let not the apple of thine eye cease.

Arise, cry out in the night in the beginning of the
watches:
Pour out thine heart like water before the face of the
LORD:
Lift up thy hands toward him for the life of thy young
children, that faint for hunger in the top of every
street.

Behold, O LORD, and consider to whom thou hast done
this.
Shall the women eat their fruit, and children of a span
long?
Shall the priest and the prophet be slain in the sanctuary of the LORD?

The young and the old lie on the ground in the streets:
My virgins and my young men are fallen by the sword;
Thou hast slain them in the day of thine anger; thou
hast killed, and not pitied.

Thou hast called as in a solemn day my terrors round about,

So that in the day of the LORD's anger none escaped nor remained:

Those that I have swaddled and brought up hath mine enemy consumed."

—Lamentations 2.

III. HOPE STILL IN THE LORD

I am the man that hath seen affliction by the rod of his wrath.

He hath led me, and brought me into darkness, but not into light.

Surely against me is he turned; he turneth his hand against me all the day.

My flesh and my skin hath he made old; he hath broken my bones.

He hath builded against me, and compassed me with gall and travail.

He hath set me in dark places, as they that be dead of old.

He hath hedged me about, that I cannot get out: he hath made my chain heavy.

Also when I cry and shout, he shutteth out my prayer.

He hath inclosed my ways with hewn stone, he hath made my paths crooked.

He was unto me as a bear lying in wait, and as a lion in secret places.

He hath turned aside my ways, and pulled me in pieces: he hath made me desolate.

He hath bent his bow, and set me as a mark for the arrow.

He hath caused the arrows of his quiver to enter into my reins.

I was a derision to all my people; and their song all the day.

He hath filled me with bitterness, he hath made me drunken with wormwood.

He hath also broken my teeth with gravel stones, he hath covered me with ashes.

And thou hast removed my soul far off from peace: I forgat prosperity.

And I said, "My strength and my hope is perished from the LORD":

Remembering mine affliction and my misery, the wormwood and the gall.

My soul hath them still in remembrance, and is humbled in me.

This I recall to my mind, therefore have I hope.

It is of the LORD's mercies that we are not consumed, because his compassions fail not.

They are new every morning: great is thy faithfulness.

The LORD is my portion, saith my soul; therefore will I hope in him.

The LORD is good unto them that wait for him, to the soul that seeketh him.

It is good that a man should both hope and quietly wait for the salvation of the LORD.

It is good for a man that he bear the yoke in his youth.

He sitteth alone and keepeth silence, because he hath borne it upon him.

He putteth his mouth in the dust; if so be there may be hope.

He giveth his cheek to him that smiteth him: he is filled full with reproach.

For the LORD will not cast off forever:

But though he cause grief, yet will he have compassion according to the multitude of his mercies.

For he doth not afflict willingly nor grieve the children of men.

To crush under his feet all the prisoners of the earth,

To turn aside the right of a man before the face of the most High,

To subvert a man in his cause, the LORD approveth not.

Who is he that saith, and it cometh to pass, when the LORD commandeth it not?

Out of the mouth of the most High proceedeth not evil and good?

Wherefore doth a living man complain, a man for the punishment of his sins?

Let us search and try our ways, and turn again to the LORD.

Let us lift up our heart with our hands unto God in the heavens.

We have transgressed and have rebelled: thou hast not pardoned.

Thou hast covered with anger, and persecuted us: thou hast slain, thou hast not pitied.

Thou hast covered thyself with a cloud, that our prayer should not pass through.

Thou hast made us as the offscouring and refuse in the midst of the people.

All our enemies have opened their mouths against us.
Fear and a snare is come upon us, desolation and destruction.
Mine eye runneth down with rivers of water for the destruction of the daughter of my people.

Mine eye trickleth down, and ceaseth not, without any intermission,
Till the Lord look down, and behold from heaven.
Mine eye affecteth mine heart because of all the daughters of my city.

Mine enemies chased me sore, like a bird, without cause.
They have cut off my life in the dungeon, and cast a stone upon me.
Waters flowed over mine head; then I said, "I am cut off."

I called upon thy name, O Lord, out of the low dungeon.
Thou hast heard my voice: hide not thine ear at my breathing, at my cry.
Thou drewest near in the day that I called upon thee: thou saidst, "Fear not."

O Lord, thou hast pleaded the causes of my soul; thou hast redeemed my life.
O Lord, thou hast seen my wrong: judge thou my cause.
Thou hast seen all their vengeance and all their imaginations against me.

Thou hast heard their reproach, O LORD, and all their
imaginations against me;

The lips of those that rose up against me, and their device against me all the day.

Behold their sitting down, and their rising up; I am
their music.

Render unto them a recompence, O LORD, according to
the work of their hands.

Give them sorrow of heart, thy curse unto them.

Persecute and destroy them in anger from under the
heavens of the LORD.   —Lamentations 3.

IV. THE DISTRESS OF THE SIEGE OF JERUSALEM

How is the gold become dim! How is the most fine gold
changed!

The stones of the sanctuary are poured out in the top of
every street.

The precious sons of Zion, comparable to fine gold,

How are they esteemed as earthen pitchers, the work of
the hands of the potter!

Even the sea-monsters draw out the breast, they give
suck to their young ones:

The daughter of my people is become cruel, like the
ostriches in the wilderness.

The tongue of the sucking child cleaveth to the roof of
his mouth for thirst:

The young children ask bread, and no man breaketh it
unto them.

They that did feed delicately are desolate in the streets:

They that were brought up in scarlet embrace dunghills.

For the punishment of the iniquity of the daughter of
my people is greater than the punishment of the
sin of Sodom,
That was overthrown as in a moment, and no hands
stayed on her.

Her Nazarites were purer than snow, they were whiter
than milk,
They were more ruddy in body than rubies, their polish-
ing was of sapphire:

Their visage is blacker than a coal; they are not known
in the streets:
Their skin cleaveth to their bones; it is withered, it is
become like a stick.

They that be slain with the sword are better than they
that be slain with hunger:
For these pine away, stricken through for want of the
fruits of the field.

The hands of the pitiful women have sodden their own
children:
They were their meat in the destruction of the daughter
of my people.

The Lord hath accomplished his fury; he hath poured
out his fierce anger,
And hath kindled a fire in Zion, and it hath devoured the foundations thereof.

The kings of the earth, and all the inhabitants of the
world, would not have believed

That the adversary and the enemy should have entered into the gates of Jerusalem.

For the sins of her prophets, and the iniquities of her priests,
That have shed the blood of the just in the midst of her,

They have wandered as blind men in the streets, they have polluted themselves with blood,
So that men could not touch their garments.

They cried unto them, "Depart ye; it is unclean; depart, depart, touch not!"
When they fled away and wandered, they said among the heathen, "They shall no more sojourn there."

The anger of the LORD hath divided them; he will no more regard them:
They respected not the persons of the priests, they favoured not the elders.

As for us, our eyes as yet failed for our vain help:
In our watching we have watched for a nation that could not save us.

They hunt our steps, that we cannot go in our streets:
Our end is near, our days are fulfilled; for our end is come.

Our persecutors are swifter than the eagles of the heaven:
They pursued us upon the mountains, they laid wait for us in the wilderness.

The breath of our nostrils, the anointed of the LORD, was taken in their pits,
Of whom we said, "Under his shadow we shall live among the heathen."

Rejoice and be glad, O daughter of Edom, that dwellest
    in the land of Uz;
The cup also shall pass through unto thee: thou shalt
    be drunken, and shalt make thyself naked.

The punishment of thine iniquity is accomplished, O
    daughter of Zion; he will no more carry thee away
    into captivity:
He will visit thine iniquity, O daughter of Edom; he
    will discover thy sins.   —Lamentations 4.

V. "Turn Thou Us Unto Thee, O Lord"

Remember, O Lord, what is come upon us:
Consider, and behold our reproach.
Our inheritance is turned to strangers,
Our houses to aliens.
We are orphans and fatherless,
Our mothers are as widows.
We have drunken our water for money;
Our wood is sold unto us.
Our necks are under persecution:
We labour, and have no rest.
We have given the hand to the Egyptians,
And to the Assyrians, to be satisfied with bread.
Our fathers have sinned, and are not;
And we have borne their iniquities.
Servants have ruled over us:
There is none that doth deliver us out of their hand.
We gat our bread with the peril of our lives
Because of the sword of the wilderness.
Our skin was black like an oven
Because of the terrible famine.
They ravished the women in Zion,
And the maids in the cities of Judah.

Princes are hanged up by their hand:
The faces of elders were not honoured.
They took the young men to grind,
And the children fell under the wood.
The elders have ceased from the gate,
The young men from their music.
The joy of our heart is ceased;
Our dance is turned into mourning.
The crown is fallen from our head:
Woe unto us, that we have sinned!
For this our heart is faint;
For these things our eyes are dim.
Because of the mountain of Zion, which is desolate,
The foxes walk upon it.
Thou, O LORD, remainest forever;
Thy throne from generation to generation.
Wherefore dost thou forget us forever,
And forsake us so long time?
Turn thou us unto thee, O LORD, and we shall be
　　turned;
Renew our days as of old.
But thou hast utterly rejected us;
Thou art very wroth against us.　　　　—Lamentations 5.

QUESTIONS

For what purpose was Lamentations written? What literary peculiarities has it? Compare it with Tennyson's "In Memoriam," Milton's "Lycidas," Cowper's "Mother's Picture." These are all dirges for individuals. Is Lamentations a nobler group of poems? Compare also with Whitman's "When Lilacs Last in the Doorway Bloomed," and Lowell's "Commemoration Ode." These are nationalistic. Are they equal in thought or expression to the Hebrew poems?

The
Book of Ecclesiasticus

ECCLESIASTICUS is a book of moral teachings for right living. It was much used in the early church for instruction of the young, so that it became an ecclesiastical book, which probably accounts for its name "Ecclesiasticus." The original name was "The Wisdom of the Son of Sirach."

The book was written in Hebrew by a wise man living in Jerusalem. It was translated into Greek in Egypt by his grandson, as is told in the Prologue. The date of writing was approximately 190–180 B.C. The writer's purpose of instruction, his years of study, his familiarity with the Scriptures, his fine and sincere character, are detailed in his grandson's interesting Prologue. The contents of the book show his deep piety and his practical common sense. His reverent trust in God is profound, his demand that all serve God sincerely is insistent, and at the same time his comments on life are very shrewd and often witty. He advises the talkative person, if he has been told a secret, to let it die with him: "Be of good courage; it will not burst you." "When I want to read some worldly wisdom," said one man, "I go to the book of Ecclesiasticus." It is worldly wisdom, but it is that wisdom built upon the strong foundation of Divine Wisdom. The writer drank deep of the wells of Scripture before he wrote, especially of Proverbs and Job.

The form of the book, although not made up of proverbs, is like the first nine chapters of Proverbs, consisting of short poems, little essays in verse on life and how to live it. Toward the end, Chapters 44–50, is a section describing the heroes of the Bible, beginning with Enoch and Noah, and extended to include a glowing tribute to Simeon, a high priest of his own time. The beginning of this section, The Praise of Famous Men, is perhaps the most familiar passage in the book. It is included among the selections here given.

In time the Hebrew original of the book was lost, and only the Greek translation was known. The recovery of a part of the Hebrew text is one of the romances of scholarship in our day. Scholars began to work over the old manuscripts in the store-room of a Jewish synagogue in Cairo. Such a store-room is attached to many old synagogues. When rolls used in the synagogue became torn or soiled they were not destroyed, but put away in this genizah, or store-room. These scholars found much of interest in the old Cairo genizah. Among other things, they found fragments of four different manuscripts of The Wisdom of the Son of Sirach in Hebrew. These fragments were published between 1896 and 1900. Together they cover nearly two-thirds of the book. Sometimes they differ from the text known before. The passage about Famous Men has a special title: "Praise of the

Fathers of Old." On the whole, however, the changes are no more than might be expected, and do not affect the essential teaching of the book.

The text here used is the Authorized Version, with certain changes which conform to the better texts now known.

The story of Ecclesiasticus is taken from the Apocrypha, an explanation of which is found in Volume 8.

What follows is not the entire book, which contains fifty-one chapters, but is a selection of classified passages.

The Wisdom of Jesus, the Son of Sirach, or Ecclesiasticus

A Prologue Made by an Uncertain Author

THIS Jesus was the son of Sirach, and grandchild to Jesus of the same name with him: this man therefore lived in the latter times, after the people had been led away captive, and called home again, and almost after all the prophets. Now his grandfather Jesus, as he himself witnesseth, was a man of great diligence and wisdom among the Hebrews, who did not only gather the grave and short sentences of wise men, that had been before him, but himself also uttered some of his own, full of much understanding and wisdom. When as therefore the first Jesus died, leaving this book almost perfected, Sirach, his son, receiving it after him, left it to his own son Jesus, who, having gotten it into his hands, compiled it all orderly into one volume, and called it Wisdom, entitling it both by his own name, his father's name, and his grandfather's; alluring the hearer by the very name of Wisdom to have a greater love to the study of this book. It containeth therefore wise sayings, dark sentences, and parables, and certain particular ancient godly stories of men that pleased God; also his prayer and song; moreover, what benefits God had vouchsafed his people, and what plagues he had heaped upon their enemies. This Jesus did imitate Solomon, and was no less famous for wisdom and learning, both being indeed a man of great learning, and so reputed also.

The Prologue of the Wisdom of Jesus the Son of Sirach
(written by the grandson of the author)

Whereas many and great things have been delivered unto us by the law and the prophets, and by others that have followed their steps, for the which things Israel ought to be commended for learning and wisdom; and whereof not only the readers must needs become skilful themselves, but also they that desire to learn be able to profit them which are without, both by speaking and writing: my grandfather Jesus, when he had much given himself to the reading of the law, and the prophets, and other books of our fathers, and had gotten therein good judgment, was drawn on also himself to write something pertaining to learning and wisdom; to the intent that those which are desirous to learn, and are addicted to these things, might profit much more in living according to the law.

Wherefore let me intreat you to read it with favour and attention, and to pardon us, wherein we may seem to come short of some words, which we have laboured to interpret. For the same things uttered in Hebrew, and translated into another tongue, have not the same force in them: and not only these things, but the law itself, and the prophets, and the rest of the books, have no small difference, when they are spoken in their own language.

For in the eight and thirtieth year coming into Egypt, when Euergetes was king, and continuing there some time, I found a book of no small learning: therefore I thought it most necessary for me to bestow some diligence and travail to interpret it; using great watchfulness and skill in that space to bring the book to an end, and set it forth for them also, which in a strange country are willing to learn, being prepared before in manners to live after the law.

The Praise of Wisdom

All wisdom cometh from the Lord,
And is with him forever.
Who can number the sand of the sea,
And the drops of rain,
And the days of eternity?
Who can find out the height of heaven, and the breadth of the earth,
And the deep, and wisdom?
Wisdom hath been created before all things,
And the understanding of prudence from everlasting.
The word of God most high is the fountain of wisdom;
And her ways are everlasting commandments.
To whom hath the root of wisdom been revealed?
Or who hath known her wise counsels? There is one wise and greatly to be feared,
The Lord sitting upon his throne. He created her, and saw her, and numbered her,
And poured her out upon all his works. She is with all flesh according to his gift,
And he hath given her to them that love him.

— Ecclesiasticus 1:1–10.

The parables of knowledge are in the treasures of wisdom:
But godliness is an abomination to a sinner.
If thou desire wisdom, keep the commandments
And the Lord shall give her unto thee.
For the fear of the Lord is wisdom and instruction:
And faith and meekness are his delight.

— Ecclesiasticus 1:25–27.

Wisdom exalteth her children,
And layeth hold of them that seek her.
He that loveth her loveth life;

And they that seek to her early shall be filled with joy.
He that holdeth her fast shall inherit glory;
And wheresoever she entereth, the LORD will bless.
They that serve her shall minister to the Holy One:
And them that love her the LORD doth love.
Whoso giveth ear unto her shall judge the nations:
And he that attendeth unto her shall dwell securely.
If a man commit himself unto her, he shall inherit
    her;
And his generation shall hold her in possession.
For at the first she will walk with him by crooked ways,
And bring fear and dread upon him,
And torment him with her discipline,
Until she may trust his soul,
And try him by her laws.
Then will she return the straight way unto him, and
    comfort him
And shew him her secrets.
But if he go wrong, she will forsake him,
And give him over to his own ruin.
                              —Ecclesiasticus 4:11–19.

THE FEAR OF THE LORD

The fear of the LORD is honour, and glory, and glad-
    ness,
And a crown of rejoicing.
The fear of the LORD maketh a merry heart
And giveth joy, and gladness, and a long life.
Whoso feareth the LORD, it shall go well with him at
    the last,
And he shall find favour in the day of his death.
To fear the LORD is the beginning of wisdom:
And it was created with the faithful in the womb.
She hath built an everlasting foundation with men,
And she shall continue with their seed.

To fear the LORD is fulness of wisdom,
And filleth men with her fruits.
She filleth all their house with things desirable,
And the garners with her increase.
The fear of the LORD is a crown of wisdom,
Making peace and perfect health to flourish;
Both which are the gifts of God:
And it enlargeth their rejoicing that love him.
Wisdom raineth down skill and knowledge of understanding,
And exalteth them to honour that hold her fast.
The root of wisdom is to fear the LORD,
And the branches thereof are long life.
The fear of the LORD driveth away sins:
And where it is present, it turneth away wrath.

—Ecclesiasticus 1:11–21.

Ye that fear the LORD, wait for his mercy;
And go not aside, lest ye fall.
Ye that fear the LORD, believe him;
And your reward shall not fail.
Ye that fear the LORD, hope for good,
And for everlasting joy and mercy.
Look at the generations of old, and see;
Did ever any trust in the LORD, and was confounded?
Or did any abide in his fear, and was forsaken?
Or whom did he ever despise, that called upon him?
For the LORD is full of compassion and mercy,
Long-suffering, and very pitiful,
And forgiveth sins, and saveth in time of affliction.

Woe be to fearful hearts, and faint hands,
And the sinner that goeth two ways!
Woe unto him that is fainthearted! for he believeth not;
Therefore shall he not be defended.

Woe unto you that have lost patience!
And what will ye do when the LORD shall visit you?

They that fear the LORD will not disobey his word;
And they that love him will keep his ways.
They that fear the LORD will seek that which is well-
  pleasing unto him;
And they that love him shall be filled with the law.
They that fear the LORD will prepare their hearts,
And humble their souls in his sight,
Saying, "We will fall into the hands of the LORD, and
  not into the hands of men:
For as his majesty is, so is his mercy."
                                    — Ecclesiasticus 2:7–18.

For the wisdom of the LORD is great,
And he is mighty in power, and beholdeth all things:
                                    — Ecclesiasticus 15:8.

SERVING THE LORD: ITS COST AND ITS PAY

My son, if thou come to serve the LORD,
Prepare thy soul for temptation.
Set thy heart aright, and constantly endure,
And make not haste in time of trouble.
Cleave unto him, and depart not away,
That thou mayest be increased at thy last end.
Whatsoever is brought upon thee take cheerfully,
And be patient when thou art changed to a low estate.
For gold is tried in the fire,
And acceptable men in the furnace of adversity.
Believe in him, and he will help thee;
Order thy way aright, and trust in him.
                                    — Ecclesiasticus 2:1–6.

"HUMBLE THYSELF, AND THOU SHALT BE EXALTED"

Exalt not thyself, lest thou fall,
And bring dishonour upon thy soul,

And so God discover thy secrets,
And cast thee down in the midst of the congregation,
Because thou camest not in truth to the fear of the
    Lord,
But thy heart is full of deceit.   —Ecclesiasticus 1:30.

My son, go on with thy business in meekness;
So shalt thou be beloved of him that is approved.
The greater thou art, the more humble thyself,
And thou shalt find favour before the Lord.
Many are in high place, and of renown.
But mysteries are revealed unto the meek.
For the power of the Lord is great,
And he is honoured of the lowly.
Seek not out the things that are too hard for thee,
Neither search the things that are above thy strength.
But what is commanded thee, think thereupon;
For thou hast no need of the things that are in secret.
Be not curious in unnecessary matters:
For more things are shewed unto thee than men
    understand.
For many are deceived by their own vain opinion;
And an evil suspicion hath overthrown their judgment.
Without eyes thou shalt want light:
Profess not the knowledge therefore that thou hast
    not.   —Ecclesiasticus 3:17–25.

Do no evil, so shall no harm come unto thee.
Depart from the unjust,
And iniquity shall turn away from thee.
My son, sow not upon the furrows of unrighteousness,
And thou shalt not reap them sevenfold.
Seek not of the Lord preeminence,
Neither of the king the seat of honour.

Justify not thyself before the LORD;
And boast not of thy wisdom before the king.
Seek not to be judge, being not able to take away
　　iniquity;
Lest at any time thou fear the person of the mighty,
And lay a stumbling block in the way of thy up-
　　rightness.
Offend not against the multitude of a city,
And then thou shalt not cast thyself down among
　　the people.　　　　　　　　　— Ecclesiasticus 7:1-7.

BEFRIEND THE POOR

My son, defraud not the poor of his living,
And make not the needy eyes to wait long.
Make not an hungry soul sorrowful;
Neither provoke a man in his distress.
Add not more trouble to an heart that is vexed;
And defer not to give to him that is in need.
Reject not the supplication of the afflicted;
Neither turn away thy face from a poor man.
Turn not away thine eye from the needy,
And give him none occasion to curse thee:
For if he curse thee in the bitterness of his soul,
His prayer shall be heard of him that made him.

Get thyself the love of the congregation,
And bow thy head to a great man.
Let it not grieve thee to bow down thine ear to the
　　poor,
And give him a friendly answer with meekness.
Deliver him that suffereth wrong from the hand of the
　　oppressor;
And be not fainthearted when thou sittest in judg-
　　ment.

Be as a father unto the fatherless,
And instead of an husband unto their mother:
So shalt thou be as the son of the most High,
And he shall love thee more than thy mother doth.

— Ecclesiasticus 4:1-10.

WEALTH AND POVERTY

Set not thy heart upon thy goods;
And say not, "I have enough for my life."
Follow not thine own mind and thy strength,
To walk in the ways of thy heart:
And say not, "Who shall control me for my works?"
For the LORD will surely revenge thy pride.

— Ecclesiasticus 5:1-3.

The poor man is honoured for his skill,
And the rich man is honoured for his riches.
He that is honoured in poverty, how much more in
riches?
And he that is dishonourable in riches, how much
more in poverty?

— Ecclesiasticus 10:30, 31.

Wisdom lifteth up the head of him that is of low
degree,
And maketh him to sit among great men.

— Ecclesiasticus 11:1.

A rich man beginning to fall is held up of his friends:
But a poor man being down is thrust also away by
his friends.
When a rich man is fallen, he hath many helpers:
He speaketh things not to be spoken, and yet men
justify him:
The poor man slipped, and yet they rebuked him too;
He spake wisely, and could have no place.
When a rich man speaketh, every man holdeth his
tongue,

And, look, what he saith, they extol it to the clouds:
But if the poor man speak, they say, "What fellow
    is this?"
And if he stumble, they will help to overthrow him.

Riches are good unto him that hath no sin,
And poverty is evil in the mouth of the ungodly.
               — Ecclesiasticus 13:21–24.

Watching for riches consumeth the flesh,
And the care thereof driveth away sleep.
Watching care will not let a man slumber,
As a sore disease breaketh sleep.
The rich hath great labour in gathering riches to-
    gether;
And when he resteth, he is filled with his delicates.
The poor laboureth in his poor estate;
And when he leaveth off, he is still needy.
He that loveth gold shall not be justified,
And he that followeth corruption shall have enough
    thereof.
Gold hath been the ruin of many,
And their destruction was present.
It is a stumbling-block unto them that sacrifice unto it,
And every fool shall be taken therewith.
Blessed is the rich that is found without blemish,
And hath not gone after gold.
Who is he? and we will call him blessed:
For wonderful things hath he done among his people.
Who hath been tried thereby, and found perfect?
Then let him glory.
Who had the power to offend, and hath not offended?
Or to do evil, and hath not done it?
His goods shall be established,
And the congregation shall declare his alms.
               — Ecclesiasticus 31:1–11.

Set not thine heart upon goods unjustly gotten;
For they shall not profit thee in the day of calamity.

— Ecclesiasticus 5:8.

THE DAMAGE DONE BY FOOLISH TALK

Winnow not with every wind, and go not into every
  way:
For so doth the sinner that hath a double tongue.
Be stedfast in thy understanding;
And let thy word be the same.
Be swift to hear; and let thy life be sincere;
And with patience give answer.
If thou hast understanding, answer thy neighbour;
If not, lay thy hand upon thy mouth.
Honour and shame is in talk:
And the tongue of man is his fall.
Be not called a whisperer,
And lie not in wait with thy tongue:
For a foul shame is upon the thief,
And an evil condemnation upon the double tongue.
Be not ignorant of anything in a great matter or a
  small.

— Ecclesiasticus 5:9–15.

Instead of a friend become not an enemy;
For thereby thou shalt inherit an ill name, shame, and
  reproach:
Even so shall a sinner that hath a double tongue.

— Ecclesiasticus 6:1.

He that is hasty to trust is light-minded;
And he that sinneth shall offend against his own soul.
Whoso taketh pleasure in wickedness shall be con-
  demned:
But he that resisteth pleasures crowneth his life.
He that can rule his tongue shall live without strife;

And he that hateth babbling shall have less evil.
Rehearse not unto another that which is told unto thee,
And thou shalt fare never the worse.
Whether it be to friend or foe, talk not of other men's
    lives;
And if thou canst without offence, reveal them not.
For he heard and observed thee,
And when time cometh he will hate thee.
If thou hast heard a word, let it die with thee;
Be of good courage, it will not burst thee.

—Ecclesiasticus 19:4–10.

There is a reproof that is not comely:
Again, some man holdeth his tongue, and he is wise.
It is much better to reprove, than to be angry secretly:
And he that confesseth his fault shall be preserved from
    hurt.
How good is it, when thou art reproved, to shew re-
    pentance!
For so shalt thou escape wilful sin.
There is one that keepeth silence, and is found wise:
And another by much babbling becometh hateful.
Some man holdeth his tongue, because he hath not to
    answer:
And some keepeth silence, knowing his time.
A wise man will hold his tongue till he see opportunity:
But a babbler and a fool will regard no time.
He that useth many words shall be abhorred;
And he that taketh to himself authority therein shall
    be hated.

—Ecclesiasticus 20:1–8.

To slip upon a pavement is better than to slip with the
    tongue:
So the fall of the wicked shall come speedily.
A man without grace is as a tale out of season;

It will be continually in the mouth of the unwise.
A wise sentence shall be rejected when it cometh
    out of a fool's mouth;
For he will not speak it in due season.
                                    — Ecclesiasticus 20:18–20.

A lie is a foul blot in a man,
Yet it is continually in the mouth of the untaught.
A thief is better than a man that is accustomed to lie:
But they both shall inherit destruction.
The disposition of a liar is dishonourable,
And his shame is ever with him.   — Ecclesiasticus 20:24–26.

Who shall set a watch before my mouth,
And a seal of wisdom upon my lips,
That I fall not suddenly by them,
And that my tongue destroy me not?
                                    — Ecclesiasticus 22:27.

The stroke of the whip maketh marks in the flesh:
But the stroke of the tongue breaketh the bones.
Many have fallen by the edge of the sword:
But not so many as have fallen by the tongue.
Well is he that is defended from it,
And hath not passed through the venom thereof;
Who hath not drawn the yoke thereof,
Nor hath been bound in her bands.
For the yoke thereof is a yoke of iron,
And the bands thereof are bands of brass.
The death thereof is an evil death,
The grave were better than it.
It shall not have rule over them that fear God,
Neither shall they be burned with the flame thereof.
Such as forsake the Lord shall fall into it;
And it shall burn in them, and not be quenched;
It shall be sent upon them as a lion,

And devour them as a leopard.
Look that thou hedge thy possession about with thorns,
And bind up thy silver and gold,
And weigh thy words in a balance,
And make a door and bar for thy mouth.
Beware thou slide not by it,
Lest thou fall before him that lieth in wait.
— Ecclesiasticus 28:17–26.

MAKING FRIENDS AND KEEPING THEM

Sweet language will multiply friends:
And a fair-speaking tongue will increase kind greetings.
Be in peace with many:
Nevertheless have but one counsellor of a thousand.
If thou wouldest get a friend, prove him first,
And be not hasty to credit him.
For some man is a friend for his own occasion,
And will not abide in the day of thy trouble.
And there is a friend that turneth to enmity
And he will discover strife to thy reproach.
Again, some friend is a companion at the table,
And will not continue in the day of thy affliction.
But in thy prosperity he will be as thyself,
And will be bold over thy servants.
If thou be brought low, he will be against thee,
And will hide himself from thy face.
Separate thyself from thine enemies,
And take heed of thy friends.
A faithful friend is a strong defence:
And he that hath found such an one hath found a
    treasure.
Nothing doth countervail a faithful friend,
And his excellency is invaluable.
A faithful friend is the medicine of life;
And they that fear the LORD shall find him.

Whoso feareth the LORD shall direct his friendship
  aright:
For as he is, so shall his neighbour be also.

—Ecclesiasticus 6:5-17.

Admonish a friend, it may be he hath not done it;
And if he have done it, that he do it no more.
Admonish thy friend, it may be he hath not said it:
And if he have, that he speak it not again.
Admonish a friend: for many times it is a slander,
And believe not every tale.
There is one that slippeth in his speech, but not from
  his heart;
And who is he that hath not offended with his tongue?
Admonish thy neighbour before thou threaten him;
And not being angry, give place to the law of the most
  High.

—Ecclesiasticus 19:13-17.

Whoso discovereth secrets loseth his credit;
And shall never find friend to his mind.
Love thy friend, and be faithful unto him:
But if thou betrayest his secrets, follow no more after
  him.
For as a man hath destroyed his enemy;
So hast thou lost the love of thy neighbour.
As one that letteth a bird go out of his hand,
So hast thou let thy neighbour go, and shalt not get
  him again.
Follow after him no more, for he is too far off;
He is as a gazelle escaped out of the snare.
As for a wound, it may be bound up;
And after reviling there may be reconcilement:
But he that betrayeth secrets is without hope.

—Ecclesiasticus 27:16-21.

"Thou God Seest Me"

Say not thou, "I will hide myself from the LORD:
Shall any remember me from above?
I shall not be remembered among so many people:
For what is my soul among such an infinite number of
    creatures?"
Behold, the heaven, and the heaven of heavens,
The deep, and the earth, and all that therein is,
Shall be moved when he shall visit.
The mountains also and foundations of the earth shall
    be shaken with trembling,
When the LORD looketh upon them.
No heart can think upon these things worthily:
And who is able to conceive his ways?
There is a tempest which no man can see:
For the most part of his works are hid.
Who can declare the works of his justice?
Or who can endure them?
For his covenant is afar off,
And the trial of all things is in the end.
He that wanteth understanding will think upon vain
    things:
And a foolish man erring imagineth follies.

                   — Ecclesiasticus 16:17–23.

The Value of Foresight

Learn before thou speak,
And have a care for thy health or ever thou be sick.
Before judgment examine thyself,
And in the day of visitation thou shalt find mercy.
Humble thyself before thou be sick,
And in the time of sins shew repentance.
Let nothing hinder thee to pay thy vow in due time,
And defer not until death to be justified.

Before thou prayest, prepare thyself;
And be not as one that tempteth the Lord.
Think upon the wrath that shall be at the end,
And the time of vengeance, when he shall turn away
　　his face.
When thou hast enough, remember the time of hunger:
And when thou art rich, think upon poverty and need.
From the morning until the evening the time is changed,
And all things are speedily before the Lord.
A wise man will fear in every thing,
And in the day of sinning he will beware of offence:
But a fool will not observe time.
Every man of understanding knoweth wisdom,
And will give praise unto him that found her.
They that were of understanding in sayings became
　　also wise themselves,
And poured forth exquisite parables.

—Ecclesiasticus 18:19–29.

The Fool

Whoso teacheth a fool is as one that glueth a potsherd
　　together,
And as he that waketh a sleeper from a sound sleep.
He that telleth a tale to a fool speaketh to one in a
　　slumber:
When he hath told his tale, he will say, "What is the
　　matter?"
Weep for the dead, for he hath lost the light:
And weep for the fool, for he wanteth understanding:
Make little weeping for the dead, for he is at rest:
But the life of the fool is worse than death.
Seven days do men mourn for him that is dead;
But for a fool and an ungodly man all the days of his life.
Talk not much with a fool,
And go not to him that hath no understanding:

Beware of him, lest thou have trouble,
And thou shalt never be defiled with his fooleries:
Depart from him, and thou shalt find rest,
And never be disquieted with madness.
What is heavier than lead?
And what is the name thereof, but a fool?
Sand, and salt, and a mass of iron, is easier to bear,
Than a man without understanding.
As timber girt and bound together in a building cannot
    be loosed with shaking:
So the heart that is stablished by advised counsel shall
    fear at no time.
A heart settled upon a thought of understanding
Is as an ornament of plaster on the wall of a gallery.
Pales set on an high place will never stand against the
    wind:
So a fearful heart in the imagination of a fool cannot
    stand against any fear.   — Ecclesiasticus 22:7–18.

THE GRACE OF FORGIVENESS

Malice and wrath, even these are abominations;
And the sinful man shall have them both.
He that revengeth shall find vengeance from the LORD,
And he will surely keep his sins in remembrance.
Forgive thy neighbour the hurt that he hath done unto
    thee,
So shall thy sins also be forgiven when thou prayest.
One man beareth hatred against another,
And doth he seek pardon from the LORD?
He sheweth no mercy to a man, which is like himself:
And doth he ask forgiveness of his own sins?
If he that is but flesh nourish hatred,
Who will intreat for pardon of his sins?
Remember thy end, and let enmity cease;

Remember corruption and death, and abide in the
  commandments.
Remember the commandments, and bear no malice
  to thy neighbour:
Remember the covenant of the Highest, and wink at
  ignorance. — Ecclesiasticus 27:30—28:7.

CONTENTMENT

The chief thing for life is water, and bread,
And clothing, and an house to cover shame.
Better is the life of a poor man in a mean cottage,
Than delicate fare in another man's house.
Be it little or much, hold thee contented,
That thou hear not the reproach of thy house.
For it is a miserable life to go from house to house:
For where thou art a stranger, thou darest not open thy
  mouth.
Thou shalt entertain, and feast, and have no thanks:
Moreover thou shalt hear bitter words:
"Come, thou stranger, and furnish a table,
And feed me of that thou hast ready."
"Give place, thou stranger, to an honourable man;
My brother cometh to be lodged, and I have need of
  mine house."
These things are grievous to a man of understanding;
The upbraiding of houseroom, and reproaching of the
  lender. — Ecclesiasticus 29:21-28.

WHEN DEATH IS BITTER AND WHEN SWEET

O Death, how bitter is the remembrance of thee to a
  man that liveth at rest in his possessions,
Unto the man that hath nothing to vex him, and that
  hath prosperity in all things:
Yea, unto him that is yet able to receive meat!

O death, acceptable is thy sentence unto the needy,
and unto him whose strength faileth,
That is now in the last age, and is vexed with all things,
And to him that despaireth, and hath lost patience!
Fear not the sentence of death,
Remember them that have been before thee, and that
come after;
For this is the sentence of the LORD over all flesh.
And why art thou against the pleasure of the most
High?
There is no inquisition in the grave,
Whether thou have lived ten, or an hundred, or a
thousand years. — Ecclesiasticus 41:1–4.

THE PRAISE OF GOOD WORKMEN

The wisdom of a learned man cometh by oppor-
tunity of leisure:
And he that hath little business shall become wise.
How can he get wisdom that holdeth the plough,
And that glorieth in the goad,
That driveth oxen, and is occupied in their labours,
And whose talk is of bullocks?
He giveth his mind to make furrows;
And is diligent to give the kine fodder.
So every carpenter and workmaster, that laboureth
night and day:
And they that cut and grave seals,
And are diligent to make great variety,
And give themselves to counterfeit imagery,
And watch to finish a work:
The smith also sitting by the anvil, and considering
the iron work,
The vapour of the fire wasteth his flesh,
And he fighteth with the heat of the furnace:

The noise of the hammer and the anvil is ever in
  his ears,
And his eyes look still upon the pattern of the
  thing that he maketh;
He setteth his mind to finish his work,
And watcheth to polish it perfectly:
So doth the potter sitting at his work,
And turning the wheel about with his feet,
Who is alway carefully set at his work,
And maketh all his work by number;
He fashioneth the clay with his arm,
And boweth down his strength before his feet;
He applieth himself to finish the glazing;
And he is diligent to make clean the furnace:

All these trust to their hands:
And every one is wise in his work.
Without these cannot a city be inhabited:
And men shall not sojourn, nor walk up and down
  therein.
They shall not be sought for in public counsel,
Nor sit high in the congregation:
They shall not sit on the judges' seat,
Nor understand the sentence of judgment: they
  cannot declare justice and judgment;
And they shall not be found where parables are
  spoken.
But they will maintain the state of the world,
And their prayer is in the work of their craft.

— Ecclesiasticus 38:24–34.

Hate not laborious work, neither husbandry,
Which the most High hath ordained.

— Ecclesiasticus 7:15.

The High Privilege of the Scholar

He that giveth his mind to the law of the most
    High,
And is occupied in the meditation thereof,
Will seek out the wisdom of all the ancients,
And be occupied in prophecies.
He will keep the sayings of the renowned men:
And where subtile parables are,
He will be there also.
He will seek out the secrets of grave sentences,
And be conversant in dark parables.
He shall serve among great men,
And appear before princes:
He will travel through strange countries;
For he hath tried the good and the evil among men.
He will give his heart to resort early to the Lord
    that made him,
And will pray before the most High,
And will open his mouth in prayer,
And make supplication for his sins.
If the great Lord will,
He shall be filled with the spirit of understanding:
He shall pour out wise sentences,
And give thanks unto the Lord in his prayer.
He shall direct his counsel and knowledge,
And in his secrets shall he meditate.
He shall shew forth that which he hath learned,
And shall glory in the law of the covenant of the
    Lord.
Many shall commend his understanding;
And so long as the world endureth, it shall not be
    blotted out;
His memorial shall not depart away,

And his name shall live from generation to genera-
tion.
Nations shall shew forth his wisdom,
And the congregation shall declare his praise.
If he die, he shall leave a greater name than a
thousand:
And if he live, he shall increase it.

— Ecclesiasticus 39:1–11.

GOD OF ALL NATURE

I will now remember the works of the LORD,
And declare the things that I have seen:
In the words of the LORD are his works.

The sun that giveth light looketh upon all things,
And the work thereof is full of the glory of the LORD.
The LORD hath not given power to the saints to declare
all his marvellous works,
Which the Almighty LORD firmly settled,
That whatsoever is might be established for his glory.
He seeketh out the deep, and the heart,
And considereth their crafty devices:
For the LORD knoweth all that may be known,
And he beholdeth the signs of the world.
He declareth the things that are past, and to come,
And revealeth the steps of hidden things.
No thought escapeth him,
Neither any word is hidden from him.
He hath ordered the excellent works of his wisdom,
And he is from everlasting to everlasting:
Unto him may nothing be added,
Neither can he be diminished,
And he hath no need of any counsellor.

Oh, how desirable are all his works!
And a man may see this even to a spark.

All these things live and remain forever for all uses,
And they are all obedient.
All things are double one against another:
And he hath made nothing imperfect.
One thing establisheth the good of another:
And who shall be filled with beholding his glory?

The pride of the height, the clear firmament,
The beauty of heaven, with his glorious shew;
The sun when it appeareth, bringing tidings at his rising,
Is a marvellous instrument, the work of the most High:
At noon it parcheth the country,
And who can abide the burning heat thereof?
A man blowing a furnace is in works of heat,
But the sun burneth the mountains three times more
Breathing out fiery vapours,
And sending forth bright beams, it dimmeth the eyes.
Great is the LORD that made it;
And at his commandment it runneth hastily.

He made the moon also to serve in her season
For a declaration of times, and a sign of the world.
From the moon is the sign of feasts,
A light that decreaseth in her perfection.
The month is called after her name,
Increasing wonderfully in her changing,
Being an instrument of the armies above,
Shining in the firmament of heaven;
The beauty of heaven, the glory of the stars,
An ornament giving light in the highest places of the
    LORD.
At the commandment of the Holy One they will stand
    in their order,
And never faint in their watches.

Look upon the rainbow, and praise him that made it;
Very beautiful it is in the brightness thereof.
It compasseth the heaven about with a glorious circle,
And the hands of the most High have bended it.

By his commandment he maketh the snow to fall
    apace,
And sendeth swiftly the lightnings of his judgment.
Through this the treasures are opened:
And clouds fly forth as fowls.
By his great power he maketh the clouds firm,
And the hailstones are broken small.
At his sight the mountains are shaken,
And at his will the south wind bloweth.
The noise of the thunder maketh the earth to tremble:
So doth the northern storm and the whirlwind:
As birds flying he scattereth the snow,
And the falling down thereof is as the lighting of grass-
    hoppers:
The eye marvelleth at the beauty of the whiteness
    thereof,
And the heart is astonished at the raining of it.
The hoarfrost also as salt he poureth on the earth,
And being congealed, it is as the points of thorns.

When the cold north wind bloweth,
And the water is congealed into ice,
It abideth upon every gathering together of water,
And clotheth the water as with a breastplate.
It devoureth the mountains, and burneth the wilderness,
And consumeth the grass as fire.
A mist coming speedily is the healing of all things.
A dew coming after heat refresheth.
By his counsel he hath stilled the deep,

And planteth islands therein.
They that sail on the sea tell of the danger thereof;
And when we hear it with our ears, we marvel thereat.
For therein be strange and wondrous works,
Variety of all kinds of beasts and whales created.
By him the end of them hath prosperous success,
And by his word all things consist.

We may speak much, and yet come short:
Wherefore the sum of our words is, "He is all."
How shall we be able to magnify him?
For he is great above all his works.
The LORD is terrible and very great,
And marvellous is his power.
When ye glorify the LORD, exalt him as much as ye can;
For even yet will he far exceed:
And when ye exalt him, put forth all your strength, and
    be not weary;
For ye can never go far enough.
Who hath seen him, that he might tell us?
And who can magnify him as he is?
There are yet hid greater things than these be,
For we have seen but a few of his works.
For the LORD hath made all things;
And to the godly hath he given wisdom.
— Ecclesiasticus 42:15–43:33.

PRAISE OF THE FATHERS OF OLD

Let us now praise famous men,
And our fathers that begat us.
The LORD hath wrought great glory by them,
Even his great power from the beginning.
Such as did bear rule in their kingdoms,
Men renowned for their power, giving counsel by
    their understanding,

And declaring prophecies:
Leaders of the people by their counsels,
And by their knowledge men of learning for the
　　people,
Wise and eloquent in their instructions:
Such as found out musical tunes,
And recited verses in writing:
Rich men furnished with ability,
Living peaceably in their habitations:
All these were honoured in their generations,
And were the glory of their times.
There be of them, that have left a name behind
　　them,
That their praises might be reported.
And some there be, which have no memorial;
Who are perished, as though they had never been;
And are become as though they had never been
　　born;
And their children after them.
But these were merciful men,
Whose righteousness hath not been forgotten.
With their seed shall continually remain a good
　　inheritance,
And their children are within the covenant.
Their seed standeth fast,
And their children for their sakes.
Their seed shall remain forever,
And their glory shall not be blotted out.
Their bodies are buried in peace;
But their name liveth forevermore.
The people will tell of their wisdom,
And the congregation will shew forth their praise.

— Ecclesiasticus 44:1–15.

The Search for Wisdom

Blessed is the man that doth meditate good things in
    wisdom,
And that reasoneth of holy things by his understanding.
He that considereth her ways in his heart
Shall also have understanding in her secrets.
Go after her as one that tracketh,
And lie in wait in her ways.
He that prieth in at her windows
Shall also hearken at her doors.
He that doth lodge near her house
Shall also fasten a pin in her walls.
He shall pitch his tent nigh unto her,
And shall lodge in a lodging where good things are.
He shall set his children under her shelter,
And shall lodge under her branches.
By her he shall be covered from heat,
And in her glory shall he dwell.   Ecclesiasticus 14:20-27.

He that feareth the Lord will do good;
And he that hath the knowledge of the law shall obtain
    her.
And as a mother shall she meet him,
And receive him as a wife married in her virginity.
With the bread of understanding shall she feed him
And give him the water of wisdom to drink.
He shall be stayed upon her, and shall not be moved;
And shall rely upon her, and shall not be confounded.
She shall exalt him above his neighbours,
And in the midst of the congregation shall she open his
    mouth.
He shall find joy and a crown of gladness,
And she shall cause him to inherit an everlasting name.
But foolish men shall not attain unto her,

And sinners shall not see her.
For she is far from pride,
And men that are liars cannot remember her.
Praise is not seemly in the mouth of a sinner,
For it was not sent him of the LORD.
For praise shall be uttered in wisdom,
And the LORD will prosper it. —Ecclesiasticus 15:1–10.

"I SOUGHT FOR WISDOM, AND GOD GAVE IT TO ME"

When I was yet young, or ever I went abroad,
I desired wisdom openly in my prayer.
I prayed for her before the temple,
And will seek her out even to the end.
Even from the flower till the grape was ripe hath my
    heart delighted in her:
My foot went the right way, from my youth up sought
    I after her.
I bowed down mine ear a little, and received her,
And gat much learning.
I profited therein,
Therefore will I ascribe the glory unto him that giveth
    me wisdom.
For I purposed to do after her,
And earnestly I followed that which is good;
So shall I not be confounded.
My soul hath wrestled with her,
And in my doings I was exact:
I stretched forth my hands to the heaven above,
And bewailed my ignorances of her.
I directed my soul unto her,
And I found her in pureness:
I have had my heart joined with her from the be-
    ginning,
Therefore shall I not be forsaken.

My heart was troubled in seeking her:
Therefore have I gotten a good possession.
The LORD hath given me a tongue for my reward,
And I will praise him therewith.
Draw near unto me, ye unlearned,
And dwell in the house of learning.
Wherefore are ye slow, and what say ye of these things,
Seeing your souls are very thirsty?
I opened my mouth, and said,
"Buy her for yourselves without money.
Put your neck under the yoke,
And let your soul receive instruction:
She is hard at hand to find.
Behold with your eyes,
How that I have had but little labour,
And have gotten unto me much rest.
Get learning with a great sum of money,
And get much gold by her.
Let your soul rejoice in his mercy,
And be not ashamed of his praise.
Work your work betimes,
And in his time he will give you your reward."

— Ecclesiasticus 51:13–30.

The Song of Solomon

THIS little book is like nothing else in the Bible. It is a collection of love songs; vivid, passionate, marvelously rich with oriental imagery. It may be their origin was in a cycle of wedding songs sung by professional singers during the long festivities of the eastern wedding, when the village groom and bride were transformed by poetic license into King Solomon and his queen. Whatever their origin, their content is clear. They are love poems, frank and unabashed. In them sentiments are exchanged which are, from the eastern point of view, idealizations; but with a poetry so full of touches of nature and of human emotion that poetic spirits have always reveled in them. It is impossible to say how many songs there are, or where some of them begin or end. Some seem to be very short; though they may have been sung with others as question and answer.

It is fitting that there should be songs of love in the Bible, for love makes much of the joy and the sorrow of life. But the early Jewish rabbis questioned very seriously whether poems of this nature should be included in Scripture. They tried to justify their inclusion by allegorizing them. The songs became an allegory of the love of God to Israel. When the Christian church took over the Old Testament, it acknowledged the allegory of the book as expressing the love of Christ and the church. This allegorizing is still found in the chapter headings of the Authorized Version; but we must remember that this meaning is an interpretation put upon the book, and is not a part of the book itself. Bearing this in mind, these poems may serve as figures of the love of Christ for the Church, even though the writers of them had no thought of any such meaning.

The songs here printed are from the Authorized Version, with occasional changes for clearness to the words of the Revised Version. In general the Revised is in this book distinctly preferable to the Authorized Version.

The Song of the Modest Maiden

I AM black, but comely,
O ye daughters of Jerusalem,
As the tents of Kedar,
As the curtains of Solomon.
Look not upon me, because I am black,
Because the sun hath looked upon me:
My mother's sons were angry with me;
They made me the keeper of the vineyards;
But mine own vineyard have I not kept.

Tell me, O thou whom my soul loveth,
Where thou feedest, where thou makest thy flock to
    rest at noon:
For why should I be as one that turneth aside
By the flocks of thy companions?   —Song of Solomon 1:5-7.

Love in Springtime

The voice of my beloved! behold, he cometh
Leaping upon the mountains, skipping upon the hills.
My beloved is like a roe or a young hart:
Behold, he standeth behind our wall,
He looketh in at the windows,
Glanceth through the lattice.
My beloved spake, and said unto me,
"Rise up, my love, my fair one, and come away.
For, lo, the winter is past,
The rain is over and gone;
The flowers appear on the earth;
The time of the singing of birds is come,
And the voice of the turtle dove is heard in our land;
The fig-tree ripeneth her green figs,
And the vines are in blossom;
They give forth their fragrance.
Arise, my love, my fair one, and come away."
O my dove, that art in the clefts of the rock, in the
　　covert of the steep place
Let me see thy countenance, let me hear thy voice;
For sweet is thy voice, and thy countenance is comely.
"Take us the foxes, the little foxes, that spoil the
　　vineyards,
For our vineyards are in blossom."
My beloved is mine, and I am his:
He feedeth his flock among the lilies.
Until the day break, and the shadows flee away,
Turn, my beloved, and be thou like a roe or a young
　　hart
Upon the mountains of Bether.　　　—Song of Solomon 2:8-17

THE BRIDAL PROCESSION

Who is this that cometh out of the wilderness like
    pillars of smoke,
Perfumed with myrrh and frankincense,
With all powders of the merchant?
Behold it is the litter of Solomon;
Threescore valiant men are about it, of the valiant of
    Israel.
They all hold swords, and are expert in war:
Every man hath his sword upon his thigh
Because of fear in the night.
King Solomon made himself a chariot
Of the wood of Lebanon.
He made the pillars thereof of silver,
The bottom thereof of gold, the covering of it of
    purple,
The midst thereof being paved with love,
From the daughters of Jerusalem.

Go forth, O ye daughters of Zion, and behold King
    Solomon
With the crown wherewith his mother crowned him in
    the day of his espousals,
And in the day of the gladness of his heart.

—Song of Solomon 3:6-11.

The Garden of Love

Come with me from Lebanon, my bride,
With me from Lebanon:
Look from the top of Amana,
From the top of Shenir and Hermon,
From the lions' dens,
From the mountains of the leopards.

Thou hast ravished my heart, my sister, my bride;
Thou hast ravished my heart with one of thine eyes,
With one chain of thy neck.
How fair is thy love, my sister, my bride!
How much better is thy love than wine!
And the fragrance of thine ointments than all spices!
Thy lips, O my bride, drop as the honeycomb:
Honey and milk are under thy tongue;
And the smell of thy garments is like the smell of
    Lebanon.

A garden inclosed is my sister, my bride;
A spring shut up, a fountain sealed.
Thy plants are an orchard of pomegranates, with
    precious fruits;
Henna, with spikenard,
Spikenard and saffron;
Calamus and cinnamon, with all trees of frankin-
    cense;
Myrrh and aloes, with all the chief spices:
Thou art a fountain of gardens,
A well of living waters,
And flowing streams from Lebanon.

Awake, O north wind; and come, thou south;
Blow upon my garden, that the spices thereof may
    flow out.

Let my beloved come into his garden,
And eat his pleasant fruits.

"I am come into my garden, my sister, my bride:
I have gathered my myrrh with my spice;
I have eaten my honeycomb with my honey;
I have drunk my wine with my milk:
Eat, O friends;
Drink, yea, drink abundantly, O beloved."

—Song of Solomon 4:8–5:1.

THE SUMMIT OF MOUNT HERMON

Photograph by Underwood & Underwood

The long, snow covered ridge of Mount Hermon rises 9,200 feet above the Mediterranean, the loftiest of all the mountains of Palestine. This was probably the "Mount of Transfiguration," the glorious summit on which that great scene was enacted. The picture must have been taken in summer for the slopes are nearly bare of snow.

The Dream of a Fruitless Search

I sleep, but my heart waketh:
It is the voice of my beloved that knocketh, saying,
"Open to me, my sister, my love, my dove, my undefiled:
For my head is filled with dew,
And my locks with the drops of the night."

"I have put off my coat; how shall I put it on?
I have washed my feet; how shall I defile them?"

My beloved put in his hand by the hold of the door,
And my heart was moved for him.
I rose up to open to my beloved;
And my hands dropped with myrrh,
And my fingers with sweet smelling myrrh,
Upon the handles of the lock.
I opened to my beloved;
But my beloved had withdrawn himself, and was
     gone:
My soul failed when he spake:
I sought him, but I could not find him;
I called him, but he gave me no answer.

The watchmen that went about the city found me,
They smote me, they wounded me;
The keepers of the walls took away my veil from me.

I charge you, O daughters of Jerusalem, if ye find my
     beloved,
That ye tell him, that I am sick from love.

—Song of Solomon 5:2-8.

THE PRICELESS GIFT OF LOVE

Set me as a seal upon thine heart, as a seal upon thine
 arm:
For love is strong as death;
Jealousy is cruel as the grave:
The flashes thereof are flashes of fire,
A very vehement flame.
Many waters cannot quench love,
Neither can floods drown it:
If a man would give all the substance of his house
 for love,
He would utterly be contemned. —Song of Solomon 8:6, 7.

NOTES ON THE SONG OF SOLOMON

Kedar. A Bedouin Arab tribe. The tents of the Bedouin Arabs are woven of camel's hair and are a dark brown, appearing black against the gray desert background.

Curtain of Solomon. The poet links the poor Arab tents with royal draperies, so suggesting the rich value of this maiden who keeps the vineyards.

Mine own vineyard. She has had no time to attend to her own adornment.

Tell me. The part of the selection beginning here may be another song.

The voice of my beloved. Behold he cometh. Or, "Hark! My love is coming." The poem represents him as coming to call his loved one to the vineyards.

The fig-tree ripeneth. The fig-tree bears fruit before the leaves appear, and that the fruit is beginning to ripen shows that the warmth of spring has come.

Take us the foxes. This couplet is a snatch of song, sung by the lover in the joy of his heart.

My beloved is mine. The maiden's response to her lover's wooing.

Bether. There was a place called Bether on a high ridge not far from Jerusalem; but this may mean "mountains of ravines" rather than any particular place.

Chariot. More properly as Revised Version, "palanquin." This accords with the "litter" mentioned above.

Pillars. Columns supporting the covering.

Crown. The groom and bride were crowned in wedding festivities.

Amana, a peak near Hermon.

Shenir. Deut. 3:9 gives this as the Amorite name for Hermon.

Spring shut up. Where water was precious the owner of a well often kept it sealed up for his own use. Compare Gen. 29:1-8.

I sleep, but my heart waketh. The bride narrates a dream. Her beloved comes, but she teasingly calls to him that it is too late. To her dismay he takes her at her word and goes. She follows after, only to be beaten by the city watchmen. The little song ends with an expression of the longing of love.

Set me as a seal. This song has been called by a scholar of English literature the best example known to him of absolutely perfect English.

Jealousy. Rather, "passionate love."

Be contemned. Literally, "they would surely despise him." Love is priceless.